TWO SAMS

SHARON ROBART-JOHNSON

Two Sams
© 2024 Sharon Robart-Johnson

Cover design: Rebekah Wetmore, from a 1788 watercolour by Captain
    William Booth.
Editor: Andrew Wetmore

ISBN: 978-1-998149-29-2
First edition March, 2024

MOOSE HOUSE
PUBLICATIONS

2475 Perotte Road
Annapolis County, NS
B0S 1A0
moosehousepress.com
info@moosehousepress.com

We live and work in Mi'kma'ki, the ancestral and unceded territory of the
Mi'kmaw people. This territory is covered by the "Treaties of Peace and
Friendship" which Mi'kmaw and Wolastoqiyik (Maliseet) people first
signed with the British Crown in 1725. The treaties did not deal with
surrender of lands and resources but in fact recognized Mi'kmaq and
Wolastoqiyik (Maliseet) title and established the rules for what was to be
an ongoing relationship between nations. We are all Treaty people.

Also by Sharon Robart-Johnson

Africa's Children: a History of Blacks in Yarmouth, Nova Scotia

Jude and Diana

Dedicated to my husband, Arthur Johnson,
who tolerated the many hours I spent researching and writing this story.
Love you, Arthur.

This is a work of fiction, built around what we know of the real people who lived the events in this story. The author has created conversations, interactions, and events, drawing on contemporary narratives and records, and on recent scholarly works; and any resemblance of any character to any person now living is coincidental.

To learn more about the times these people lived through, consult the author's notes and the "Sources" page at the end of the book.

Two Sams

Prologue

I covered my ears so I wouldn't hear my boy screamin' when the whip was tearin' in his back. He was tied to the old wooden post that Henry made from a tree trunk that was used for whippin' the slaves. My boy was just holdin' on, his chest leanin' 'gainst it.

Henry kep' whippin' and whippin' and my boy kep' screamin' and screamin'. Blood was comin' from his lips. *When is Henry gonna stop? My boy has had 'nough.*

Henry brought that whip down again. Punishin' my boy for what. He didn't do nothin' wrong, but Henry, he don't need no 'scuse. Sometimes he made up the 'scuses for usin' that whip on Master's slaves.

Tears was runnin' down my face every time my boy screamed. I has gotta stop Henry b'fore my boy is dead. I don't care if Henry puts the whip to me. I do anythin' to take the pain my boy is gettin'.

But then he stopped whippin' and looked to where the big house was. I looked to see what he was lookin' at and seen Master Bulloc comin' on a run.

Trouble for Henry? I wondered. *No*, I said to myself. *Cause Henry would lie and say my boy was doin' somethin' he wasn't doin'.* Henry always lied on the other slaves to save his own black skin. Today ain't gonna be no different.

I runned to my boy as he dropped to the ground after Henry untied him.

Master looked down at my boy layin' there bleedin'. "What's going on here, Henry? What did I tell you about whipping the slaves without my say-so? I can't afford to have my workers laid up because you beat them half to death. What did he do?"

"Massa," said Henry, "he was stealin' from the cellar."

I wasn't gonna stand there and listen to Henry lie. "My boy never stole nothin', Henry. You is lyin'. You is lyin' on my boy cause it was prob'ly you what stole from the cellar," I said as I held my boy tighter to my chest.

Master looked at Henry. "Is that so?"

It was the first time I seen fear in Henry's eyes, when Master asked him if he stole. You could hear the fear in his voice.

"No, suh," said Henry and the sweat was runnin' down his forehead. "I got no reason to steal from you, I gits plenty without stealin'."

Master looked from Henry to me. He wasn't sure who was lyin', but I knew, and it wasn't me.

I think he was believin' me cause, when he turned to go, he looked over at Henry and said, "Henry, you whip one more worker without my say-so and you will find yourself standing on the box at the slave market." Then he turned and went back to the house.

I knew that wasn't gonna stop Henry, and when he said the nex' words I knew he was gonna come after me. I wasn't gonna 'llow that black bastard to put no whip to me.

He looked at me and he said, "You turn is comin' Sam. You turn is comin'."

I stared that poor 'scuse for a man in his eyes. "You think you is gonna whip me, does you, Henry? How can you do that to 'nother slave? You should be shamed of you self. You is a slave just like me and you heard what Master said. You won't be here no more, you'll be sold to the highest bidder and I shore wish I could see that."

Henry smiled through his rotten teeth. "I gits more food than you does, don't I? And I gits paid money. I wouldn't care if *you* was my papa, I'd do the same." Then he walked away.

Bastard, I said to myself.

I picked my boy up in my arms and took him home to his Mam for doctorin'.

Sam the Father

Sharon Robart-Johnson

1

Sam the father says:

We had 'nough of Master Bulloc and Henry. We was gonna run away. We been plannin' on runnin' away for a long time, almos' three years. It was almos' time.

But don't you know, the day before we was to go, Henry, come down on my boy again. Sam didn't do nothin' for Henry to beat him for, just that he was the closest to Henry when he took it in his head he wanted to whip somebody.

Now, my boy can't go when we does and I shore ain't gonna leave without him.

"We'll wait till you is well 'nough to go. We all goes tagether or none of us goes," I said to my boy.

"No, Pap, You has to go. I'll find you. Somehow, I'll find you."

"How's you gonna find us, Sam? How?"

"Don't worry 'bout me, Pap."

"Sam," said his Mam. "We can't leave you here. We can't. The next time Henry takes it in his head to beat you, he might kill you. If we go, who'll tend to you if he beats you again, if you don't die? I didn't think I was gonna stop the bleedin' on your back this time. It was bad, Sam. It was bad."

Sam Jr very carefully sat up on his cot. Pain and fire shot through his back that his mother had so painstakingly doctored the day before. He knew just how bad this beating had been. His mother had tended to his wounds from all the beatings he'd had.

He had to somehow reassure his family that he would be okay. They had to leave now or they might never have another chance.

"I know it was bad, Mam, but I'll be okay. You has to go. Don't worry 'bout me. I'll find you. I promise," he said as he hugged his mother, father, and sister. "But you has to go now while it's dark."

I was thinkin' to myself 'bout what my boy said and I knew he would never find us again. *We won't see our boy again.* But I made up my mind that we wasn't gonna leave tonight like we planned. We was gonna wait a few days so his Mam can tend to his cuts. It don't make no matter what he says, me and the wife will have a story to tell him 'bout why we ain't leavin' tonight. But my boy is right, we has to leave soon as we can. And we will, but not tonight.

Well, we never got to go.

I guess we was worryin' 'bout Henry for nothin', cause after my boy's last whippin' by Henry, Master sold us to Master Stoffle Van Nostrant.

I was s'prised he did that. He should'a just sold Henry. But there was talk 'mong the slaves that Master needed some money. I don't know if that's true, but least we is away from Henry.

2

We been with Master Stoffle awhile and he ain't got no overseer. He don't b'lieve in whippin' his slaves. He ain't too bad to us, but we is still slaves and he might sell us to 'nother master who might like whippin' us down.

I still been thinkin' 'bout runnin' away. We is the only four slaves Master got and if we runned away, he won't have none.

I said to my Sarrahs and boy, "I is thinkin' 'bout runnin' away again. Is you with me?"

They just stared at me like I was crazy.

"Sam," said wife, Sarrah, "what you on 'bout? Runnin' away? Where is we gonna go and how does you plan to do it? Why you want to run away now? We was gonna run away when we was at Master Bulloc's and we didn't go."

"You got a lotta questions, wife. You know we didn't go cause Henry put that beatin' on our boy and we wasn't goin' without him. Then we was sold. Didn't I say we all goes together? I is tired of bein' a slave. I is tired of bein' told we can't do what we wants to do. I wants to be free."

"Sam, you is always gonna be a slave, it don't make no matter what you wants. Master Stoffle, he ain't gonna set none of us free. What you been thinkin' in that head of yours?"

I looked at daughter, Sarrah, and my boy, Sam. They wasn't sayin' nothin', just starin' at me.

"Well, what you two think, does you think I is crazy like your Mam says?"

They still never said nothin' for a minute, then daughter said, "I don't want to be no slave no more, Pap, but I has to ask the same as Mam. How is we s'pposed to do it and does you know where we is gonna go? You know if we gets caught we'll be sent back here and you don't know what Master will do. He ain't got no Henry, and he might'a been good to us so far, but he got white workers he might tell to take the whip to us or maybe he'll take it in his head to do the whippin' his self. Or maybe he'll put us in the stocks and leave us there with no food or water. He'll make us suffer for runnin' away for shore."

I looked at my boy. "Sam, boy, what does you think?"

"Pap, I think we should do it, but we has to do some plannin' so we know where we is gonna go to be safe. We has to make better plans than we had the last time. We can't stay in New Jersey cause everybody knows Master and for shore they is gonna send us back. Wherever we goes, we gotta make people b'lieve we is free. I don't know how we is gonna do that, but I is willin' to try."

"Boy, you must'a been thinkin' on that for some time."

"I been thinkin' on that since we was at Master Bulloc's. I don't wanna be a slave no more either."

I looked at wife and daughter again. "What you think? Like our boy said, we is gonna have to do us a lotta plannin'. We ain't gonna do it to-morrow. Maybe nex' year cause winter is comin' on us now."

Wife never said nothin' for a minute, but I could tell she was thinkin' on it. Daughter too.

"I is just askin' you and daughter to think on it and maybe you all can have a plan for what to do."

"We'll think on it, Sam. We'll think on it."

My boy, he's willin' to try cause he's tired of bein' a slave, too. That's all we know how to do, but it ain't nice and ain't nobody gonna think it is. My two Sarrahs, they'll think on it, but they'll go where I goes. All slaves thinks 'bout runnin' away and some does and some doesn't. Daughter, she was right. If we runned away and got our selfs caught and brought back to Master, he would have a mad on for a long time.

My two Sarrahs, they didn't take a long time to think on it. We is gonna run away, but we don't know when or where we is goin'.

I has to laugh sometimes 'cause wife, she always says I never listens to what people is sayin' and I misses the 'portant news that's bein' said. Most'a the time I doesn't listen, but when I told her 'bout the black sol-diers workin' with the Patriots she said, "Where you hear that, Sam? You never hears nothin' most'a the time."

"Some of Master's white workers was talkin' and they was sayin' 'bout the Blacks workin' for the Patriots and how come they 'llowed those Nig-gers to work for them. They wasn't payin' no 'ttention to me bein' close by cause they think I is stupid and wouldn't know what they was talkin' 'bout anyway. But I listened and I never forgot nothin' they said cause we is gonna be runnin' away and we has to know where we is gonna go and who we is gonna trust, don't we? We don't want to go where black soldiers is gonna take us prisoner, does we? I don't know how a black man can work with the Patriots after all they done to us. They must not be gettin' whipped or hanged or have the dogs set on them or starved, so they has to do what they is told. Maybe that's why they is turnin' on they own."

"Sam, black folks will do what they has to do to keep alive. Maybe they gots no choice."

"They gots a choice, wife, they can run away like we is gonna do. I think we should go to New York, that's where the British is. That's where we gotta go."

"How you know they is in New York?"

"Cause I heard the talkin'! None of the folks on Master's farm likes the British. They says they should all be killed then there won't be no war. They said America is gonna win and the British is gonna be sent runnin' back to where they come from. I hope the British wins, cause if they do, then we'll be free like they promised. So we gotta get our selfs to New York."

"How is we gonna get there, Sam? How is we gonna get 'cross the river?"

"If we can't get 'cross the river then we'll walk 'round. We'll find us a way, wife. We ain't done plannin', is we? We gotta be real careful we don't get caught, cause I heard when they ketch a runaway they torture them or sometimes they just shoot them. I don't want to be tortured, we is tortured 'nough here. And I ain't gonna get my self shot."

"Sam, you been hearin' a lot. You be shore to listen to all the things that is bein' said and don't you forget nothin'."

"I ain't gonna forget nothin, Sarrah."

3

I don't remember what my last name was, if I even had one, so me an' my fam'ly has to use Master's name for our own. I think I was born a slave somewhere in Alabama or Mississippi and was owned by a man named Caldwell. He only called me Sam, and when I was older he sold me to Master Bulloch. That's where I met my Sarrah and we had our boy and girl. When we was sold to Master Stoffle, he made us take his name, Van Nostrant. I s'ppose so everybody knows that we is his.

I guess we should be glad we has us a last name. I know we is glad we ain't with Master Bulloch no more cause we don't have to worry 'bout Henry comin' at us. We has some stories we can tell 'bout Henry.

It was a hard decision. Who does we trust? We heard 'bout a Lord Dunmore promisin' freedom to all the indentured servants and black folks who was gonna fight for the British in the war. But is they only words to get us to fight? Will he sell us back to our masters after the war is over? I have my fam'ly to think 'bout.

I wonder what they wants to do. Does they still want to go? They'll tell me yes like they always does, but sometimes makin' a decision, 'portant as this one is, can be a bad one.

Far as I is concerned you can't trust the British or the Patriots. They both lie to the black folks, but promisin' slaves they is gonna be free when we has always been slaves, what else can we do? We gotta go now.

It's gonna be a long hard time we is gonna have to travel. I is scared and I ain't 'fraid to say so. I got me so many questions. I guess I'll have to keep listenin' to what Master's other workers is sayin'.

~

On a warm day in the spring, in the middle of the night, me, wife, Sarrah, and daughter, Sarrah, packed what little bit of belongin's we had and what food we was able to sneak. The last time we was plannin' on runnin' away, Henry come down on my boy and we couldn't go nowheres. This time, we made our plans and our boy is goin' with us.

But, my boy, he up and said he wasn't goin'.

"Boy, what you mean you ain't goin' with us? You ain't been whipped half to death like you was the last time and you ain't sick. Why ain't you goin'?

"I ain't goin' cause I don't wanna go. You go and I'll find you like I said last time. If you don't go now, you ain't never gonna go, just like last time."

I stared at my boy. I wondered what he was on 'bout.

His Mam she said, "Sam, why don't you wanna go? You tell me the truth, now."

"I ain't goin', Mam. No point to you stayin' cause I don't wanna go. We is the only slaves Master's got, and if we all runs away, he'll shorely hunt us down and make us suffer for runnin'. Now, you know I is right. Long as he still got his self one slave, he'll be mad, but he might not be killin' mad. Now, you all, you gotta go. I ain't argerrin' with you, but I ain't goin'. I'll find you."

Seems he had his mind made up. I looked at my Sarrahs. "We is goin'. Our boy will find us, if he can."

"Sam?"

"We is goin', Sarrah."

~

It was black night when we runned down to the river. The water was freezin' cold when we jumped in. It was up to our chests, but we got 'cross the river without bein' caught. We hid in the marsh for a long time, hopin' the chill that was deep in our bones from the cold water would be gone soon.

We crawled 'long through the grasses, in and out of the river again and again to hide our smell from Master's dogs. Master Stoffle, he wouldn'a set his dogs on a man, but we didn't know for shore. We had to be careful.

I looked back at wife and daughter. I knew they was alright, but I had to be shore. "Wife, is you and daughter alright?"

Wife was holdin' daughter's hand. "We is fine, Sam. We has to keep goin' or we'll be caught. We has come too far to get caught."

I was always s'prised at the strength wife always has. Sometimes she's stronger than me.

"Yes, Pap," said daughter, "we is fine. Just get us where we has to go.

Where is we goin' anyway?" She said, sounding s'prised that we come this far and she didn't know. If her Pap said we was goin', then she was goin'.

I laughed. "I don't know, daughter, I don't know. First, we gotta find us a way to get 'cross the big river. And when we gets b'hind British lines, all kinds of good things will come to us."

"What kind of good things, Sam?" asked wife.

"I heard we can work and make money and live in a house and we can go to church if we wants, and I heard that slaves is even 'llowed to get legal married."

"Sam, we don't need to get legal married. We been tagether more'n twenty years and we got us a son and daughter. I don't need no piece a paper that says you is my husband. Far as I is concerned, you *is* my husband. What big river you talkin' 'bout, Sam?"

"The North River, wife."

"Why is we crossin' the North River? We ain't goin' to New York, is we?"

"Well," said Sam. "Ain't that where I said the British is?"

"But, Sam, I heard Master's white workers sayin' that the British is in New Jersey, too."

"They is? I never heard that, but I ain't always where those white folks is when they is talkin' 'bout the British. I is glad you heard what they was sayin'. We has to find where the British is in New Jersey. I would'a went to New York if we had to, but it's better to stay where we knows the land. And remember, everybody knows Master in New Jersey, so we has to be careful we don't get our selfs caught."

Wife, Sarrah, didn't say nothin' cause she was thinkin' the same thing. I knew we would have to do whatever come our way if we was gonna survive.

4

We got us to a spot we figgered was safe, but we knew we would be runnin' outta food soon and we was gonna have to steal some food so we don't starve. Our clothes was gettin' kind of raggedy, too, but we couldn't come outta hidin' just yet. We didn't want the Patriots to see us cause we would'a been took prisoner and maybe sent back to Master Stoffle and we wasn't goin' back there no matter what we had to do. We had to be real careful.

We come to this farm and we seen it had a cellar and we knew it had food in it cause it looked like the cellar Master had. We got us some food that day.

One time at 'nother place we took us some britches for me cause mine got kind'a tore up when we was runnin' through the woods. We didn't think nobody was home so we took them right offa the line outside where they was dryin' and nobody seen us. My Sarrahs they took some britches for them selfs cause it pertected their legs and kep' them warm.

I never seen my Sarrahs in britches b'fore and I told them, "You shore looks funny in britches."

"Maybe we does, but it's better goin' through the woods with britches on."

We kep' goin' through the woods cause we figgered it was safe, but we was always listenin' for soldiers comin our way and we had to make shore it was gonna be safe to 'cross the river. We had to be careful cause we heard that black folks what was caught was put in a fort that was seen over by black soldiers. I was hopin' they was British soldiers, but they was Patriots.

I heard that some of the blacks that was kep' there, they took some of the logs that was there for the Patriot army and they tied them tagether and made a raft that they went 'cross the river on to 'scape to the British. They was smart to do that, far as I can see, but they was lucky they didn't get shot cause I heard that fort had cannons in it. Now, they is free.

Seems like we gets more news bein' slaves than the white man gets. I guess that's cause we is always lookin' for a way to get free.

We kep' lookin for a way 'cross the river, but we seen it wasn't safe so we kep' walkin', stealin' food 'long the way.

One day we seen three black men hangin' from a tree in the swamp and it seemed like they been hangin' there for a time, cause of the smell comin' offa them.

Daughter, Sarrah, she got sick in the bushes, but, wife, she knew why they was left hangin'.

"They was left hangin'," she said, "so they souls they can't go back to Africa."

"How you know this, wife? And why would they souls go back to Africa, they is here, ain't they?"

"They must'a been brought here from Africa, they wasn't borned here."

"Well, my soul ain't goin' back to Africa, cause I was borned right here."

"How does you know, Sam? You don't remember where you come from, cause all you remember is your masters and where they is. You might'a been a baby when you come over here. B'sides, them Patriots don't know who was born in Africa. They'll take any Blacks and hang them in the tree."

I couldn't say nothin' to that cause she might'a been right.

"Wife, should we take them down and give them a proper buryin' b'fore they rots right offa the rope and falls to the ground and the anim-als gets to them?"

"No, Sam. It's gonna be hard to leave them, but it will take too long and the Patriots might come 'long and cetch us, then we be hangin' there with them. We has to go."

We was walkin' away, but we turned 'round to look at them one more time. I wish I could'a buried them.

~

Two years went by and we was still in New Jersey. We couldn't get 'cross the river without bein' caught, but mostly we was still in New Jersey cause we met people who would help us when we couldn't find 'nough work to get us through the tough times.

The first winter wasn't a bad one, but the nex' one we didn't know how we was gonna get through. The people who helped us b'fore was havin' it hard as us. We all had to steal to survive.

I knew we was takin' a big chance every time we stole somethin', cause if we was caught we could be sent back to Master or killed cause we was criminals. Thinkin' 'bout dyin' if we got caught was worse than bein' sent back to Master cause we didn't know what he would'a done to us, but he prob'ly wouldn'a killed us cause he would'a had to buy his self more slaves.

We was in the same perdicament as the other slaves was. We all wants to be free. Is we all dreamin 'bout bein' free? Is we gonna die slaves?

Nobody wants to hire us no more. It seems like they is 'fraid of us or somethin'. I don't know why cause we never hurt nobody. We did our work when we had it. But the white folks they wasn't payin' us much as they was b'fore. And some of the things the Blacks who was helpin' the British was promised, we still ain't 'llowed to do.

Maybe if we was livin' in New York it be different, but we is still in New Jersey and I guess the British they never heard of all that was s'pposed to be promised to the black people if they was behind their lines.

Would Master put a reward on us? I didn't think he would'a, even losin' three of his slaves, but I knew we had to get far b'hind British lines as we could so we'd be pertected from bein' sent back. I was 'termined that we wasn't gonna go back.

The first coupl'a winters we stole food and clothes when we couldn't find work, but we only stole from the rich white folks who wasted more food than they ate. Them times, we had our selfs a mighty feast.

One fam'ly even throwed clothes away. One time after we raided their garbage box, I held up treasure. To us it was treasure.

"Wife, daughter," I said when I hold up three coats. "We be warm this winter."

We runned back to our one-room cabin. It wasn't much and the owner made us pay one shillin' a week, which was like chargin' us a hunderd shillin's. It was just as hard to get one as it was a hunderd, but I was 'termined we wasn't gonna have to sleep outdoor, and I always found the money one way or 'nother.

We got in our cabin and I give coats to my Satrahs. I kep' the biggest one for my self. Wife, Sarrah, put her coat on and danced 'round the room like she just got her self a new coat 'stead of one outta a garbage box

"Sam, it's beautiful and it's so soft," she said as she run her hands up and down the sides of the coat. "It has some holes in it and it's tore under the arm, but I can fix it. I seen holes in the other coats that I can fix too."

Daughter, Sarrah, put hers on. It was a little big, but she didn't mind, cause she could wear one of her old sweaters under it when it was really cold.

"I love my coat, Pap. We was lucky to go there today or we might not a' found them."

It was my turn to try mine on. I turned to show it off and they both had their hands over their mouths tryin' not to laugh.

"What's the matter? Why is you laughin' at my coat?" I asked.

Then I seen. I looked from my coat to theirs.

"This is a woman's coat," I said. "Oh, well. It don't matter if it's a woman's coat, I got me a fine coat to keep me warm this winter."

We danced 'round the cabin, laughin' like we was havin' a party.

5

I didn't think the winter was ever gonna end. Even though we had us some warm coats and we was able to steal us 'nough food when we couldn't find us a job, I was still worried. What was we gonna do? We gotta find us some work.

I didn't like stealin' all the time. It made me feel like I wasn't man 'nough to take care of my fam'ly. Sometimes I wondered why I took it in my head to run away.

One day I heard 'bout a group of Black fightin' men, women, and even young'uns. They was called the Black Brigade and they took any blacks who was willin' to help the British, cause the British, they wanted to win the war bad. I can fight long as I wasn't gonna be separated from my fam'ly. Maybe my two Sarrahs can join up too. If we got with this brigade, we'd have food and clothes and I heard they paid money and they was gettin' paid purty good. I had to find out what it was all 'bout. I started askin' 'round.

Wife, Sarrah always knew when there was somethin' on my mind, cause I couldn't keep nothin' from her. When I come home from one of my food huntin' trips she seen that I was excited 'bout somethin'.

"What is it, Sam? You is excited 'bout somethin'. Did you find us some more warm clothes? Boots maybe?"

"I shore is excited, wife. I shore is. But it ain't warm clothes I found. I met a man today who told me 'bout a group of black men, women and young'uns who is fighters."

"Fighters," said Sarrah. "What kinda fighters and why does you want to fight and who is you gonna fight?"

"Let me tell you, wife," I said, gettin' frustrated cause she was askin' so many questions and not 'llowin' me to talk.. "They is a group of slaves fightin' for the British cause the British needs them to pertect New York City that they is holdin' cause it is a 'portant place for them. Sarrah, there must be close on a hunderd of them Blacks and some of them is from

New Jersey. The fighters is called the Black Brigade. That's what I is hearin'."

"Why is they so 'portant to the British here, Sam? What does they do?"

"The Blacks from New Jersey is 'portant cause they know where the Patriots live and they can raid their houses without no trouble."

"Raid their houses for what, Sam? We only steals when we needs food and clothes for us. Is you shore 'bout this, Sam?"

"I is shore. Don't you worry, Sarrah."

"I does worry. What kinda trouble is we gonna get our selfs in?"

I looked from wife to daughter and for the first time in two years I seen real fear in their eyes. When we was almost caught a lotta times when we was stealin' for our selfs, we wasn't as 'fraid as my two Sarrahs looked now. Why was my Sarrahs 'fraid?

I asked her, "What is you 'fraid of, wife?"

"I don't know, Sam. What is I 'fraid of? What if we get caught? What does you think is gonna happen? I'll tell you what's gonna happen," she said. "We'll be shot, that's what. Who did you talk to 'bout this? Sam, you be shore 'bout this b'fore you take us some place that ain't safe. How does you know 'bout this?"

Now I was beginnin' to doubt if I should'a said my fam'ly would join these fightin' Blacks without talkin' to my Sarrahs first. Wife, Sarrah, she was right. This ain't the same as stealin' cause we need food and clothes. What we took b'fore was stuff that was throwed away, so it wasn't really stealin'. Sometimes we took clothes offa the line outdoors, but we didn't go in nobody's house.

I looked at wife and knew I better tell her everythin'. If I don't and she finds out, cause she would, somehow, I'd rather come face to face with the enemy than my Sarrah when she gets mad.

I took a deep breath and I started tellin' her what I knew. "I was 'pproached by a man named Titus, but he calls himself Tye. He's a run-away slave and he's the Colonel of these fightin' Blacks."

"What did he tell you, Sam? You tell me everythin' and don't you lie to me, cause I'll know. And why didn't you say that when you first started talkin' 'stead of sayin' you was hearin'?"

I had no answers to that. 'Stead, I said, "Sarrah, we'll be paid money and we can buy food and clothes 'stead of stealin' them. Tye said we is gonna have to steal cattle, food and firewood and he'll give it to the British."

"We has to steal all a' that? Why is he givin' it to the British?"

"He said cause they needs it for their soldiers and the Loyalist people in New York."

"Why don't they steal it them selfs?"

"I don't know, wife. We is gettin' paid to do it, ain't that 'nough to know? B'sides, we is gonna be helpin' other slaves to 'scape to the British lines, too."

"We helps other slaves?"

"We does."

"And that is all we has to do? We don't has to kill nobody?"

"Tye didn't say we had to."

I wasn't gonna tell her we might have to. She asked me the question I knew I could give her a answer to.

"Sam, what if he says we has to kill people?"

"Well, I ain't killin' nobody, wife, less me and my fam'ly is in danger. I is gonna tell him that. If he says we has to, then we ain't joinin' his people."

"Okay, Sam, but you do the right thing. Don't you get us in nothin' that's gonna be bad for us."

I was worried now, too, cause I was beginnin' to think Tye didn' tell me everythin' and he was just tryin' to get folks to join up to help the British. I don't mind helpin' the British, if they gives us what they promised. Us bein' set free.

Wife was quiet for a bit and I figgerred I better say somethin'. "I only talked to Tye for a bit, but I seen some of his men an' they was laughin' an' carryin' on like there was nothin' wrong, so maybe everythin' will be okay. Sarrah, we is only raidin' places that b'longs to the slave owners. Look what they took from us. And did they give us anythin' 'cept stripes 'cross our backs? We'll only be takin' what should'a been give to us in the first place, but we is givin' it to the British and gettin' paid money for doin' it."

At least that's what I hoped. I had a bad feelin' in my belly.

"Sam, you know you ain't never been whipped, not once, but what if you get caught and sold to 'nother Master. He might whip you till you is dead. And if you ain't captured and sold, you might get killed anyway."

"I ain't gonna get captured and I might get hurt sometimes, but I shore is gonna try not to. And I ain't gonna get my self killed. I don't know what the women will be doin', but what if you gets hurt? Does you think I won't be hurtin' cause I took you and daughter into this?"

Sarrah sat quietly thinking for several minutes. "Alright, Sam. We'll go with you, but if we don't like what we has to do, we is leavin' whether you comes with me and daughter or not. Just remember that."

I nodded. There was nothin' I could say. When wife said she was gonna do somethin', she did it.

6

I convinced my Sarrahs that everythin' was gonna be okay, but it was hard to convince my self.

After we joined the Black Brigade we did what we was told. Me and my Sarrahs, we didn't like the raidin' part of it. Tye told me we had to move outta our cabin cause he said the brigade had to stay together. We was gonna have to live in a place called Refugeetown, close by a British base where sailors and other runaway slaves was livin'.

I told Tye we wasn't goin', we'd go 'nother time.

He didn't like nobody questionin' his orders, but I told him we was stayin' in our cabin, or we was gonna leave the brigade and find us some work some place else. I was hopin' he would say it was okay cause we didn't want to live nowheres with a whole lotta other folks.

B'fore the first raid Titus come to me. "Sam, we is goin' on a raid to-morrow. You up to it?"

"Where is we goin'? I never done nothin' like this b'fore. What is I s'posed to do?"

"Jes do what you sees the other slaves a doin'."

I wasn't sure 'bout that, but I would do what I was told. For now.

One thing he said and it could be a good thing, was that all the raids was gonna be done at night when the slave owners was sleepin'. We would cetch them off guard and maybe nobody would see us comin' and cetch *us* off guard.

We stole horses and broke in the houses, takin' what the British could use or sell. I seen some of the men put stuff in the pockets of their baggy pants when they thought nobody was lookin'.

But I was lookin'.

The people what owned some of the houses must'a been rich, cause the women had fancy bracelets for their arms and hair. I wonder what my Sarrahs would think if I brought them home a bracelet. I wonder if Tye knew that his fighters was keepin' some of the stuff for their self.

A big raid was comin' up and we was told to hunt down a Patriot man name of Joseph Murray. The British said he killed the British people who was took prisoner. Hunt him down and kill him, we was told.

And some of the Brigade did. I watched everythin', but I didn't fight that time.

I knew there was gonna be more killin's, I heard Tye talkin' 'bout it. What was I gonna do if he ordered me to kill? I wasn't killin' nobody. I said that soon as I joined Tye's people and I meaned it.

Maybe I should take my fam'ly and run away like we did from Master Stoffle, b'fore Tye tells me I has to kill.

Maybe I is worried for nothin' cause he never said I had to do no killin'. Tye trained some of his other men to do the killin's.

I looked the other way when some things was done that I didn't like, 'cept when I couldn't 'void them, but I was proud of me and my fam'ly when we was leadin' 'scapin' slaves to freedom inside the British lines.

"Come on, hurry up. We gotta get outta here b'fore the Patriots sees us," I said to the slaves me and my Sarrahs let out of the pen they was kep' in like dogs.

They falled all over each other tryin' to 'scape, but one old man stopped and took my hand and said, "Tank you, young fella. Tank you."

I seen he was draggin' his left leg. He was only a little man and I knew if I didn't help him, he would never 'scape. I put my arms 'round his back and under his legs and I picked him up and runned fast as I could to where it was safe.

When I put him down, he looked in my face and he wiped a tear from his eyes and he said again, "Tank you, young fella. Tank you."

I don't think nobody ever done this for this crippled man b'fore. I was s'prised he was still livin' cause most slave owners don't want no cripples. They can't do no hard work no more.

~

People didn't like us cause we was black and some white folk heard that the black slaves was gonna kill all the white folk in a place called Elizabethtown. The black slaves was always bein' blamed for somethin' when usu'lly it was the Patriots what done the killin'. Maybe it was the Blacks who fight with the Patriots what done the killin' and they is blamin' all us Blacks.

I remember one raid when Tye and some of his other Blacks and a white Loyalist man named Mr. John Moody raided a place and stole horned cattle, horses, and clothes and furniture from the people of 'nother place called Shrewsbury. Nobody got killed that time. They was lucky, to my way of thinkin'.

I said to my Sarrah one time, "Most'a the time when stuff gets stole, they blames it on us angry blacks. That's how they sees us, angry all the time. As if we ain't got no reason to be angry. I thinks we was borned angry."

Tye told us we had to pertect New York for the British.

"Why?" I asked him.

"Cause we has to watch everybody what is comin' in and we gotta help pertect the soldiers. We has to pertect them White Loyalists too so they can keep a hold on New York. We has to fight 'longside a them so the Patriots don't win. Them Patriots, they fears us cause we is masters of guerrilla warfare and we is black men and black men is gonna fight hard to be free."

Now, ain't that somethin', I said to myself. Them Patriots is more 'fraid of us brigade troops than they is the whole Bitish army. It shore feels good when somebody is 'fraid of me 'stead of me bein' 'fraid of them.

They b'lieved that us Negroes was barbarians and we didn't have no human feelin's. But the British, they needed us cause we knew all the places of the county. Least they calls us Negroes, 'stead of that other word.

Tye, he said we was masters of guerrilla warfare. Guerrilla?

I told Tye, "I ain't no gorilla, I is a man!"

He laughed at me. Well, I ain't.

We ain't no barbarians either. They is, for keepin' us like animals. But we is gettin' it back on them.

'Nother day, we had to go on 'nother raid. I didn't much like goin' in people's houses after them, but Tye said sometimes we has to. Too much chance for us to get hurt or killed them times.

From what Tye said, this was 'nother 'portant Patriot soldier, name of Barnes Smock. What a funny name. I never heard that name b'fore, but if Tye said he was 'portant, then he must be.

We was s'pposed to capture him and anybody who was there and we had to distroy all his weapons.

There was more soldiers there than we was told there was gonna be, but we got them all and we distroyed his cannon. Other Patriots what lived 'round there, I know they was 'fraid cause if Smock could get caught then, one of them days, they would too.

Well, they don't know just how good we is at fightin'. If we has to cetch somebody, we will.

I was thinkin' strong again 'bout takin' my fam'ly and runnin' cause I really didn't like what we was doin' no more and I knew my Sarrahs didn't either, but where was we gonna go? I been doin' what Tye said I has to do for so long, I was doin' anythin' he told me to do. 'Cept kill. I still ain't gonna kill nobody less they is threatenin' me or my fam'ly.

I was almost caught a few times when we was out on a mission stealin', two of them times when my Sarrahs was with me. When we was altagether, white Patriots seen only a black fam'ly out lookin' for whatever they could find.

It was the middle of summer, just after dark. We waited and watched for the white fam'ly Tye said lived there to leave their house. We didn't think they was ever gonna leave and one time we was 'pproached by two Patriots who looked at us 'spiciously.

"What are you doing here?" they asked.

I had to think fast, but before I could say anythin', wife, Sarrah, put that look on her face that she knew how to do to fool people.

"We is sorry," she said. "We isn't doin' nothin'. I has a bad leg."

She lifted her skirt to show them her torn up leg, bit up by a dog that got hold of her on Master Bulloc's farm.

The soldiers looked at her leg. I could tell they thought she was in pain by the 'spression on her face, but I knew she wasn't and I wanted to laugh at the look they had on their faces, but I didn't cause I think it might'a been on my face, too. I don't think they ever seen anythin' like that. She had them fooled.

"Who is your owner?" they asked.

"We be free, Suh," she said. "We worked hard and we buyed ar freedom, it be four years ago now."

"Where are your papers?"

Sarrah put her hand in the pocket she made in her skirt to show them the fake papers she always kep' there, but he said, "Never mind. You be on your way and don't be out after dark again if you don't want to be arrested."

I figgered they didn't want to be 'round us any longer than they had to. Lookin' at my Sarrah's leg must'a made them feel pity for her, I could tell by how they looked at it.

"Yes, Suh. Thank you, Suh," Sarrah said, bobbin' her head and puttin' her skirt down.

I walked to my Sarrah's side and put my arm 'round her shoulders. "Is you okay, Sarrah? Does you leg hurt?" I asked, all concerned like.

"It pains some, Sam, but I is alright."

The soldiers was watchin' us, I could see out of the corner of my eye. They kep' watchin' as we hurried down the street. Sarrah was still limpin' so they would think she was in pain.

Her leg was bad lookin', real bad lookin', but she wasn't in no pain, and she didn't have no limp.

I always admar'd her strength, cause when that dog got a hold of her leg we thought she was gonna lose it, but she doctored it like she did our boy's back and she worked and worked to get the strength back in it and now she can walk like she didn't have no bad leg. She only pretended she did when she had to, like today, to fool them soldiers.

They watched till we was outta sight, but I heard one of them say b'fore they was too far away, "I don't like Niggers, but that woman, she gotta be in pain. Looks like a dog got hold of her."

The other man didn't say nothin'.

The soldiers didn't know they was bein' watched. Me and my Sarrahs, we got the all-clear sign from two of Tye's men who always went on these house breaks in case soldiers come by, like they did tonight.

We went back a diff'rent way to the same house. When we got close we was laughin' and jokin', like most fam'lies do, with our arms 'round each other, cause if somebody was comin' they wouldn't think we was gonna be up to no good.

We only had to wait a little while b'fore the owners fin'lly left their house. They didn't know that this happy black fam'ly, me and my Sarrahs. was 'bout to go in their house and come away with some of their eatables and whatever else we seen that the British needed.

Me and my Sarrahs waited ten minutes to be shore they didn't come right back, then we was through the door.

Wife, Sarrah, she always went lookin' for the food. She knew that these people was rich, she could tell by how they was dressed, so she knew they would have a pantry to store their supplies. Folks like these people throwed away a lotta food in one day, sometimes we seen other Blacks goin' and pickin' in the garbage boxes and gettin' all kinds of stuff. Them white folks, they wastes their food when other folks goes hungry. They should be hungry and see what it's like.

We was lucky we didn't have to steal our food no more. Cause we could buy some food with the money we made workin' for Tye. But sometimes we does it for fun. We don't take us a lot, just somethin' we never had b'fore, or some of them jams some of them women makes.

I got me a taste for some sweet stuff, but we can't always get none.

Some of them white folks' women, they know how to make stuff like that, and when I can get me some, I takes it. I think 'bout what they took from us and it don't bother me none.

I heard wife, Sarrah, talkin' to herself and I knew she found somethin' good. I walked to the door of the pantry and she was standin' there with her hands on her hips and grinnin' so wide I wanted to laugh. She was lookin' at bins of taters, carrots, squash, and bags she couldn't see through, but she knew it had to be some kind a food. She started to fill up the big sack she found in there, leavin' them 'nough so they'd know somebody been there.

I went to the kitchen to wait for wife and a few minutes after, she come in draggin' the sack.

"Got a lotta good stuff tonight, Sam," she said. "A lotta good stuff."

I looked in her sack. "You didn't take it all, did you, wife? There looks like a awful lotta stuff in there."

"Now, Sam, you is askin' me that. You knows I ain't gonna do that. We'd be no better'n them if we did that, now would we? But this sack is heavy, you is gonna have to carry it for me."

I picked up the sack. "What you got in there, rocks?"

"I got us some squash and taters and carrots and a coupl'a them bags we couldn't see in."

"Did you get me some of that jam?"

"A big jar, Sam," she said as she reached in the sack and took it out..

"That's my Sarrah."

I turned to my daughter with a smile still on my face. "And what did you find, Sarrah?"

My young, Sarrah, liked lookin' at people's clothes and jewelry. She showed us a pretty red sweater made outta yarn.

She asked. "Can I keep this, Pap?"

"Yes, daughter. You can keep it. Just don't let nobody see it till after the summer is over an' winter comes. We can say we got it somewhere else. We deserves to have somethin' for our selfs sometimes. And what is one sweater with all the other things they got? And the missus of the house probably ain't gonna miss it what with all the clothes she got hangin in that closet."

"Pap," daughter said. "The missus what lives here, she had fifteen sweaters. Now, how can a body wear fifteen sweaters and most all of them is red," she said, holdin' the sweater tight. "I won't tell nobody."

"Wife, we is gonna keep some of them taters and a coupl'a them squash and carrots for our selfs. Them British ain't gonna miss them."

34

We found out later the sacks we couldn't see in was rice.

7

One day, Tye called some of his people to the big room he used for meetins. He told us 'bout a man named Captain Josiah Huddy. He said he was a bad man who captured and killed Loyalists just 'cause they was Loyalists. Tye told us he was puttin' tagether a army of his Blacks and some refugees to fight 'long side 'nother group of men called Queen's Rangers.

I ain't never heard of them b'fore, but Tye, he said they was good fightin' men. I guess he must'a knew what he was talkin' 'bout. I know Tye and he would'a killed the rebels 'stead of capturin' them, but if he was told to capture somebody, killin' him was more'n he dared do.

Wife stared at me and I could see she was worried. I squeezed her hand when I thought she was gonna say somethin' to Tye. She was 'gainst killin' like I was, but, like me, she would kill if me and daughter was in danger. I seen her in battle b'fore and she wasn't lettin' nobody get the better of her. I thought, "Don't mess with my Sarrah." I is so proud of her.

I knew this raid was gonna be diff'rent. I let him know right off that I wanted no part of it if we had to do killin'.

He looked at me and said, "You has no choice."

"You don't need me and my fam'ly," I said. "You has 'nough men without us there."

Tye didn't say nothin' at first. He started to walk away then he turned and said, "You is a coward, Sam." Then he kep' walkin'.

"I ain't no coward and I ain't no fool. I got me a bad feelin' 'bout this."

Wife, Sarrah, she didn't like Tye callin' me a coward. "I got me a bad feelin' bout this. I got me a bad feelin'," she said. "When does you think we is s'pose to do it?"

"He only said soon. But you know Tye's soon, it can be nex' week or nex' year. It'll be alright, Sarrah," I said, hopin' that was so.

We kep' on raidin' till the day to go after Huddy come. Then Tye come to us and said, "Today's the day, men. I got all the men tagether. Some of the women is gonna be goin' too. We might need us some extra hands in the fightin'. Is you and you fam'ly with us, Sam?"

I looked at wife and she was starin' at me. I could tell by the look in her eyes that she still had that bad feelin'. I had a bad feelin' too. Somethin' bad was gonna happen. I could feel in in the bottom of my belly.

I 'tempted to smile at her to make her feel better, but she knew we was gonna go. I wasn't lettin' Tye call me no coward.

We got to Huddy's and Tye didn't 'spect Huddy to fight back so strong. He was hopin' we would capture him and be on our way back home with our prisoner. But it didn't go the way he planned. Huddy was gonna fight to the end. Him and his lady friend, they fooled us by runnin' from one room to the nex', firin' their muskets at us, makin' us think the house was full of Patriot soldiers.

Tye ain't a patient man and he was gettin' tired of the fight that wasn't goin' nowheres. He ordered us to set the house to fire to make Huddy run out, but Huddy kep' fightin' till he had to get outta the burnin' house.

When he run outta the house we captured him for a bit, but my bad feelin' was gettin' worse when Patriot soldiers come outta the woods to help Huddy and he 'scaped. Guns was a blazin'.

One of the Patriots shot Tye in the wrist with a musket ball.

"I'se ben shot, I'se ben shot!" he cried.

What a big baby, I thought. You'd think he was dyin' or somethin'. He only got shot in the wrist.

He was took back to Refugeetown where he was doctored good, but he got a 'fection called tetnus or somethin' like that and his hand started to turn black, well, blacker than it was. Somebody said 'nother 'fection called gangarene set in the wound. It didn't look good for him.

He kep' gettin' worse and some days later he died from what the doc said was lockjaw.

I ain't never heard of so many things for a body to get. I hope I never gets any of them, cause Tye, he was sufferin some at the end.

Our leader was gone, what was we gonna do now?

I turned to wife. "Wife, who does you think will take over for Tye? None of our men can do it."

"I don't know, Sam. I hope whoever it is, they ain't like him."

"What you mean?"

"You know well as I do that he liked killin'. Seems like he injoyed it too much an' I didn't like him."

"How come you is just sayin' that now, Sarrah?"

"I ain't just sayin' it now. I been sayin' it all 'long, you ain't been listenin'. You must'a liked him cause' you called him your friend. I don't think he was nobody's friend. He called you a coward, didn't he? A friend ain't gonna call his friend no coward."

I sighed. "I didn't like him, Sarrah. I let him think I did so's I could get away not doin' some of the things he wanted me to do."

"Sam, how come you is sayin' that now? Why didn't you tell me b'fore?"

"Cause I didn't want nobody to hear me say that and tell him. There is other Blacks 'round us all the time and if one of them had'a heard me say I didn't like Tye, they would'a went right to him and told him."

"You is a cagey one, Sam. It's a good thing you kep' it to you self, but what is we gonna do now? Is we gonna stay?"

"We'll stay till we sees who is gonna take Tye's place."

We didn't have to wait a long time. Colonel Stephen Blucke, he become our new leader. but a lot of the men didn't like him.

Sarrah didn't and she said right off. "Sam, that new Colonel, he's a crook."

"Sarrah, how you know that? He only been here a week. Did you see him stealin' somethin'?"

"I don't needs to see him stealin' to know he's a crook. He got shifty eyes."

I would'a laughed, but wife always seemed to know when somebody ain't of good char'cter. She ain't been wrong yet. I is gonna have to keep my eyes on Blucke.

8

When we had us a few minutes to our selfs, we would sit and talk 'bout what was goin' on or how we felt 'bout somethin'. Today it was wife, Sarrah's, time to say her 'pinions 'bout what we was doin'.

"Does you want to keep fightin' for the British, Sam?"

"Yes, I does, wife. If we fight for the British, we'll be free after the war is over and the British wins."

"And what if the Patriots win, Sam? We won't never be free, we'll be took back to Master Stoffle and he might have one of his workers whip us an' he won't stop till he kills us. An' if we ain't dead, we'll be so crippled we won't be no good for nothin' anyway, so we might as well be dead."

"Sarrah, you shore knows how to say words to make a man feel bad. But I says the British is gonna win, and we is gonna be free. I just know it. And b'sides, if Master tells his man to whip us, he ain't gonna tell him to whip us till we is dead or crippled, cause we won't be no good to him. He needs workers for his farm, not slaves who is no good for nothin'."

"You best be right, Sam. You best be right. But I'll say to you now, the next soldier what calls me Nigger he's gonna be dead cause I is tired of the names we is called all the time."

"Sarrah, does you think we does what the British tells us to do all the time?"

We might be fightin' for them, but we is really fightin' for us. We know the British can't be trusted all the time."

"What if one of the soldiers tries to sell us back to our master?"

"Nobody knows who our master is, Sarrah. I told Tye we bought our freedom a long time ago and I don't remember our master's name."

Sarrah hugged me. "You is a smart man, Sam, most'a the time, but no slave don't know his master's name. Tye would'a know'd it too cause he was a runaway and he knew his master's name. I is s'prised he didn't say somethin' to you."

"He never said nothin'. Maybe he thought it best I didn't tell nobody our master's name, that way they couldn't hunt for him and try to sell us back."

Sarrah thought a minute. "Maybe you is right, Sam. But I still wonders why he never said nothin' to you. Does you remember the day we went after that man Huddy an' Tye got himself shot and you was wounded, too? My heart near dropped outta my chest, it hurt that bad."

"Remember? How can I forget when you sewed me up like a old rag. I remember like it was yesterday."

I got quiet cause I was rememberin'. That was the day we had to do our first killin's and we was still livin' in our cabin. We didn't move to Refugeetown till after Colonel Blucke come.

That day we was fightin', it was kill or we would'a been killed when them Patriots come outta the woods and I shore wasn't gonna be killed.

When the Patriots come to help Huddy, the battle got bad. Me and my Sarrahs was in the thick of it. I looked to my right and watched as wife runned right to the Patriot soldiers, knockin' some of them down as she runned. She had a sword over her head and she was yellin', swingin' it left and right when she was chargin' at the soldiers. They was s'prised to see a woman racin' at them and before they knew it, four of them was down, two was dead and two was bad hurt.

"They didn't see that one a comin'," I said to myself. I shouldn'a been s'prised to see wife fightin' like a man soldier, but it s'prised me every time.

I did what I seen wife do. I held my sword high and I runned in the middle of the soldiers.

This black man ain't gonna die today. I thought.

The Patriots had muskets and swords and some of our brigade, they had muskets too, but we only had us swords cause I told Tye we didn't want no muskets. But we was 'termined that if we was goin' down, we was goin' down fightin'.

I swinged my sword at one of the soldiers. I missed him, but my sword caught 'nother one and he falled to the ground with a cut on his side so big I almost emptied my belly on the ground in the blood that was comin' outta it.

I was goin' after 'nother one when I felt a burnin' in my leg. All the times I said I wasn't never gonna kill nobody less me or my fam'ly was in danger, today I thought I was gonna die.

I killed the next soldier what come at me. I put my hand to my leg and when I looked it was bleedin' bad. I thought I was shot with a musket ball. The top part of my pants was red with the blood that was comin' outta my wound.

I remember fallin' to the ground and I don't remember no more till wife was to my side.

"Sam, where is you hurt? Where is you hurt?"

When she seen the blood coverin' my pants, she said. "Get up, Sam. We has to get to a safe place."

"I think I been shot." I thought I was talkin' loud, but wife told me later she had to put her ear to my mouth to hear me.

"I can't get up, wife. I is bleedin' bad. Leave me be here and you and daughter get your selfs to where it's safe."

"We ain't leavin' you, Sam. Don't talk fool talk."

I seen, outta the corner of my eye, daughter, runnin' over.

She looked at my leg and said. "You hasn't been shot, Pap, you been cut. It's bleedin' bad, but I can fix it till we get you home."

The pain was bad when daughter pressed the rag she tore from her skirt to the cut. Then she tied 'nother piece 'round it. I almost shouted out, but I didn't want them Patriot soldiers to hear me and come runnin' to finish killin' me and they might'a killed my Sarrahs.

"Where you learn to do that, daughter?" I asked just above a whisper.

"Hush now, Pap. Mam, help me get him up so we can take him away from here. We gotta try to get him home."

We had a ways to go, and by the time we got home they was almost carryin' me. The cut, it was deep and it hurt somethin' fierce. I lost a lotta blood, but I knowed I was gonna be alright, cause my Sarrahs was tendin to me.

"I ain't gonna die. God, he ain't ready for me yet. B'sides, I gotta see my boy again."

Wife, Sarrah, she told me later that I was talkin' outta my head. I don't remember doin' that, but if wife said I did, then I must'a.

I remember hearin' daughter say, "Mam, we gotta clean the cut. You got any of that ointment you made when I cut my hand last year? You is gonna have to sew it closed first."

I might'a been almost unconscious, but I heard that and my eyes popped wide open. I was almos' yellin'. "You is gonna have to sew it closed first? No you ain't."

Weak as I was, I jumped up on one foot and I almos' falled over. I was gonna try to run to the door. Nobody was gonna put a needle to my skin.

"Sarrah, you keep that needle 'way from me."

I remembered when daughter cut her hand and her Mam fixed it. She was sewin' it like she sewed her quilts. She ain't doin' that to me.

"Don't be a baby, Sam. If I don't close the cut you is gonna bleed to death."

"Then let me bleed to death," I said eyin' the needle in wife's hand. It looked bigger than the sword what cut me. If I'd seen the sword, that is.

"Don't whine, Sam. Sit down and close your eyes. Sit down," she said again when it looked like I was gonna run.

I would'a runned if I could'a, but I know I would'a falled down on my face. I was gettin' weaker and weaker and I was ready to fall down cause I didn't feel good.

Daughter, my own precious baby, was standin' in front of me so I couldn't get outta the door. The traitor.

"You ain't goin' nowhere, Pap. Now, do what Mam said."

Before daughter finished talkin', I could feel my eyes rollin' back in my head and I knew I was done for. They had me where they wanted me when I falled like a rock to the floor.

When I waked up it was almos' two days later. The cut was sewed up and it had a cloth wrapped 'round it. And I was hungry as a bear comin' outta hibernation.

"Wife, I is hungry. Can't a man get somethin' to eat?" I said.

When I tried to get out of bed the pain in my leg stabbed me somethin' fierce. I reached down and touched the bandage on my leg.

"Good mornin', Sam. You is awake."

When she said. "Now, don't you get up, you'll tear open all my neat sewin'," I falled back on my cot.

I stared up in her face. "You sewed me when I said leave me bleed to death?" I knew I sounded like a baby, but I didn't care. She put that needle to my leg when I told her no. A man can't even trust his own wife.

"Don't be silly. I wasn't gonna let you bleed to death just cause you is a scared of a needle. Remember when Tye was hurt and they told us he was cryin' like a baby when he was dyin' cause he didn't want nobody to tend to his wound cause it hurt? They said he hit one of the soldiers an' knocked him to the ground when he tried to clean the 'fection out of the wound. Well, Sam, he's dead ain't he? Does you want to be dead? Now, eat your soup," she said, puttin' a big bowl on the chair b'side my cot.

She patted me on the shoulder when I sat up on the side of the cot again. "You needs to get you strength back."

I had me a big bowl of chicken soup made with a chicken daughter stole from a farm close by. She was gettin' as good at stealin' as we was.

Just then daughter come in with her arms filled with clothes and food. She said, "I wasn't gonna take it back to Refugeetown so Colonel Blucke could give it to the British soldiers. It's time we kep' a little somethin' for our selfs, Pap. You need good food to help you get strong again. Colonel Blucke, what he don't know 'bout, he can't come on us for. And I bet he keeps stuff for his self. Look what I found."

"Where you find that?" I said when apples falled from her arms.

"I was hidin' in the bushes, tryin' to get home b'fore somebody seen me, and some British soldiers was goin' past with a wagon full of clothes and food. Then outta the bushes come some Patriot soldiers and they 'ttacked them. They killed the two British soldiers, but when they heard somebody comin' they runned in the woods leavin' b'hind the supplies. I heard somebody comin' too, but I runned to the wagon an' grabbed what I could carry and runned fast as I could home. I did good, didn't I, Pap?"

"You did better'n good, daughter." I said, so proud of her.

Wife started pickin' through the stuff she had wrapped in the clothes.

I put my soup down and made my way to sit on the foot of the cot. My leg was burnin' up, it felt like, but I wasn't gonna say nothin' to wife to give her no 'scuse to come at me with that needle again.

"Sam", she said. "Is your leg hurtin' you?"

"No wife, my leg is fine." I kep' smilin' so she wouldn't know I was hurtin'.

But who does I think I was foolin', wife knew everythin'. I couldn't keep nothin' from her. I had to get her thinkin' 'bout somethin' else.

I picked up a sweater and a big bunch of carrots falled outta it and landed on my bare feet like a bag of rocks. I rubbed my achin' toes.

Daughter laughed. "Pap, I had to wrap the food in the clothes cause how else was I gonna carry all this stuff?"

I ruffled her hair like I did when she was a young'un. "You must be smart like your Mam says your Pap is."

I looked over at wife and she rolled her eyes at me, makin' us laugh.

There was even pig's feet wrapped up in a jacket. We never had us pig's feet b'fore, but we sure had them that night.

I rubbed my finger on the meat and tasted it. "It's salty, Sarrah."

She smiled at me. "They has to be boiled to cook them," she said. "That's s'pposed to take some of the salt out."

"They is gonna be good, wife, but how do you know 'bout cookin' them that way?"

"I seen Master Stoffle's wife cookin' some one day when I was in the house scrubbin' the floors."

"Oh," was all I said. What do I know, I is no cook. I would'a put them on a stick and put them over a fire.

9

We fin'lly had us a day that we didn't have to go out stealin' from people or tryin' to capture somebody. We was sittin' 'round our table starin' through our one little window and watchin' the sun settin' for the night. It felt good that we didn't have to fight and steal every day.

Wife said to me, "Sam, is you havin' any more pain in your leg?"

"No, Sarrah, it healed real good."

"Even if I sewed you up like a quilt?" she said, laughin'.

"Yup, even that."

She got quiet for a time, then she said, "Sam, how you feel 'bout movin' over to New York City?"

I was s'prised to hear her say that. "Why you want to do that, wife?"

She didn't answer right away. I looked deep in her eyes and she looked sad and I knew it was cause of the way we was livin'.

"Cause, Sam, we can get us some real work and get paid for doin' it without havin' to worry we is gonna get caught and killed. And maybe we can get us a nice place to live in and a table that don't wobble cause one leg is shorter than the others. And maybe we can go to church. And maybe we can learn to read."

"That's a lotta maybes, wife. How long has you been feelin' that way? How come you never said nothin' b'fore? We get all we want, things that we take from the slave owners. They owes us, Sarrah, for all they took from us."

"Does we, Sam? Does we get all we want? Doesn't you want more than stealin' from other folks and havin' to give it all to the British? Sometimes what we steals ain't no good. Sometimes we kep' some stuff for our selfs, like the other Blacks do, but most'a the time we give it all to the British. We don't have to steal nothin' for us no more cause we can buy what we need cause we gets paid for what we is doin'. It was better when we didn't have no money and we stealed cause we needed it for our selfs. You remember them britches? You needed new ones cause yours was full of holes. You stole them britches and they had more holes than yours. Sometimes we get good stuff an' sometimes it should'a stayed in the garbage box we took it from. Sam, the money we is makin' it's blood money, not honest workin' money. That's what I mean. But I think you got to like stealin' too much and that ain't good, Sam. That ain't good. You think 'bout it."

I didn't know what to say. Deep down I knew she was right, but we didn't know nothin' else. "Sarrah, what else can I do? I don't know no trade."

"You don't know no trade! Sam, what did you do on Master Stoffle's farm? That's a trade and you can get work doin' that. Master ain't got the only farm."

"What trade does I have? All I did on Master's farm was..." I stopped when I re'lized what I was gonna say. "Was fix his farm 'quipment. That's a trade, ain't it?"

"That's a trade, Sam. That's a trade. And don't you get tired of fightin' all the time?"

I sighed. She was right, like she us'ally is. It shouldn'a s'prised me that wife *and* daughter was thinkin' the same way. Daughter, she said the same thing to me one day when her Mam was out doin' her job of gettin' rich folks to trust her by lettin' her in their houses to clean for them when they wasn't there. When she left them houses, their supplies was a little lighter. And them folks they never seen her again and didn't know where to look for her. She never told them where she come from.

I looked over at wife again. "Yes, wife, I does get tired of it sometimes, but I liked what we was takin' for our selfs when Tye didn't know 'bout it. And we still got paid money. And like you said, now that Colonel Blucke's in charge, he prob'ly keeps some of the stuff for his self too, like Tye did."

10

It took almos' a month b'fore my leg got all better. I did a lotta thinkin' durin' that time 'bout what wife said 'bout movin' to New York and tryin' to find a honest job. Get away from the fightin', killin' and stealin'. Become s'pectable citizens.

Wife never said nothin' 'bout bein' s'pectable citizens, but I shore liked the sound of that. It would be nice if nobody was huntin' us down like criminals. B'sides, I don't like Colonel Blucke cause there is somethin' 'bout him I don't trust. Maybe wife is right 'bout him bein' a crook. Maybe if we can get away from him and the Black Brigade, it might be better. But it wasn't gonna be easy as I thought.

Me and wife was 'lone in the cabin one afternoon. Daughter, Sarrah, said that one of Blucke's soldiers was 'talkin' her up' and she wanted to see if he was a good man or just liked to hear his self talk, 'cause he was always braggin'.

"Sarah," I said to wife. "Do you think our Sam got away from Master Stoffle?" Sometimes when our daughter ain't here, I calls wife, Sarrah, but most times I calls her wife.

"Yes, Sam, I think he did. He told us he'd find us when he got away, didn't he? Then he'll find us. I ain't worried 'bout him and you shouldn't be either." But she was worried.

"But, Sarrah, it's been six years since we left Master's. When do you think he got away? If he did."

"He got away. I don't know why he didn't come with us, but he's gone. Master prob'ly had some of his other men keep a watch on him after we runned away. The boy said he would find us, don't you remember, and I gotta b'lieve he will."

"Yes, I remember, but it ain't gonna be easy for him gettin' away like it was for us."

Sarrah shuddered. "I is glad Master don't b'lieve in settin' his dogs on a body. I know what that's like." She reached down and rubbed her leg.

I is glad she didn't see the look on my face when she was rubbin' her leg. I knew what dogs could do to a body if they was set out to kill, and that dog would'a killed her that day if Master Bulloc hadn'a come runnin' and shot his dog. That was the time he wondered how come his dog went wild.

"Sam, not much point to worryin' 'bout somethin' we can't do nothin' 'bout," she said.

"You is right, Sarrah. You is right."

Don't mean I ain't gonna worry 'bout my boy just the same.

~

I always wondered if we was ever gonna be free. One day Colonel Blucke, he come to us and said the British was losin' the war and we was gonna have to leave New York. Where was we gonna go? we asked him.

"There is a New Land across the water called Nova Scotia and there is talk that come spring ships will be leaving New York to take the white and black Loyalists there."

I listened to him talkin' like the white man. Maybe that's why I don't trust him. If he was a slave one time, where he learn to talk like the white man? He shore wasn't teached by them. Least wise, I don't know none who is.

"When is we gonna go?" I asked him.

"Because we are soldiers and the British will need us to protect what they still own, we will be some of the last to go. Maybe in the fall, but it will be before winter."

"Will we still be raidin' and stealin' supplies?"

He didn't answer, he just stared at me. I don't think he knew what we was s'pposed to do.

~

One night me and wife we was sittin' at the table. Wife was awful quiet for a long time. I could tell she was worried 'bout somethin'. Maybe she was worried 'bout our girl bein' gone so long, but I wasn't cause she knew what to do to keep safe. Long as we been here she ain't never got in no trouble yet. She's a smart girl.

"What's the matter, wife? Is you worried "bout our girl cause she ain't back yet?"

"I ain't worried 'bout our girl. Sam, ain't you heard what's bein' said?"

"What's bein' said?"

"There's talk that all Blacks was gonna be gived back to their masters. You know what that means? We ain't never gonna be free."

"They can't give us back. All us Blacks was promised we was gonna be free if we was fightin' for the British."

"But Sam, the British is losin' the war and there is talk that the treaty that was gonna be signed says that when the Britsh leaves they can't take nothin' that b'longs to the Americans. That's us, Sam. That's us."

"I don't care what that paper says, wife. We ain't a goin' back to Master."

"Sam, folks is also sayin' there was a big argerrment b'tween a General in the British Army and General Washington, who said cause the Blacks was free when the treaty was signed, they gotta be left free. General Washington, he called us stolen property and we has to go back to our masters."

"Stolen property?" I yelled. "Nobody stole us from nobody. We runned away on our own."

When I yelled, I think I scared wife. She never heard me yell like that b'fore.

"Calm down, Sam. Some of the Blacks say that certificates sayin' we is free is gonna be gived to all Blacks who want to go to the New Land. And, Sam, nobody can stop them."

"Where did you hear all that?" I asked. "I heard some of what you is sayin', but I didn't hear nothin' 'bout them certificates. Is you shore 'bout that?"

""Yes, Sam, I is shore. I also heard that b'fore we can get on any ship our names has to be put in a book with the names of all the Negroes who is goin' to the New Land."

"Sarrah, how do we get us these certificates?"

"We has to prove we was fightin' for the British."

"We can shore prove that! Tye, he kept records of all the men, women and young'uns who was under his command, and Colonel Blucke, he has them books with all our names in them."

I put my arms 'round wife. "Sarrah, if the British loses the war, I guess we'll be goin' to the New Land."

I settled some after hearin' that news. "We might be leavin' and goin' to a new place," I almos' sang. Maybe I was hopin' the British didn't win cause we would be goin' away from here. We ain't gonna have to go back to Master's or maybe sold to 'nother slave owner. We'll be free for shore in a New Land.

Months went by and nothin' happened. The war was still goin' on and I was gettin' worried when we seen Blacks bein' kidnapped right offa the streets. We had to keep a close watch for Master. Maybe he would send some of his white workers. We wouldn't know who they was so we had to be real careful.

We heard that some Blacks was took right outta their beds by people wantin' to make money by sellin' them as slaves. A woman named Betsy was 'llowed to be took by her master even though she was s'pposed to be free cause she was b'hind British lines. They said her master gived one of the soldiers a lotta money to give her to him. I don't know if it's true, but that's what I heard.

Nobody was takin' me and my fam'ly. But word was spreadin' fast like a burnin' fire that the black folk was bein' took and it didn't matter if they had one of them certificates or not. I had to keep my fam'ly safe.

All 'round us it was gettin' crazy. There was so many people all over. I didn't know how many there was, but some of the brigade soldiers said there was thousands of black slaves lookin' to be free. They was packed like fish in a barl in the British forts. I don't know how there could be thousands, but I can't say there ain't either.

The war was over and the British they lost. We had to see 'bout how we was goin' to this New Land called Nova Scotia. If all them Blacks was goin' they shore would need a lotta ships.

Colonel Blucke, he told us we didn't have to worry, there was gonna be 'nough ships to take everybody, but like he said b'fore, we was gonna be the last to leave after the British gived New York back to the Americans.

It was gettin' close to the time when we was to leave New York for the New land. They was evacuatin' Black and White Loyalists all spring and summer. Bein' Black Brigade members, we knew our duties as soldiers wasn't done. We would be leavin' New York, but we didn't know when.

Fin'lly it was our turn. We boarded the last ship and we was gettin' ready to leave. All us Black Brigade members was gived them Certificates to make sure we would be safe and not be took offa the ship and sent back to our masters.

But black folk was still bein' took. I was 'fraid every livin' day that would be us, so I was always makin' plans on where we was gonna run to if they come after us.

It was almost time for us to go. I don't know why it was takin' so long. The ship we was goin' on, the 'bondance or somethin' like that, was just sittin' in the harbour and it been there for three days now. The British, they lost the war and we had to get outta there fast.

We was fin'lly on the ship and me and my Sarrahs, we was watchin' the Patriots on the other side of the water tryin' to take the last British flag down. We was laughin' so hard our bellies was achin' cause some of us brigade members we greased the pole so it was slippery and them poor fellas kep' slidin' back down.

I tapped wife on the arm and said, "Look, Sarrah. That one, he ain't stupid. He put dirt all over his body so he won't slide down. Does he think it's gonna work? Well, I'll be, there he goes and he ain't slidin' back down. There goes our flag and I ain't sorry to see it go cause it means we is gonna be leavin."

"Sam, you ain't sorry that we has to leave the only place we ever know'd to go to a strange land? What is we gonna do when we gets there?"

"No, wife, I ain't sorry cause we has been promised land and shelter and we don't have to fight for it."

I put my arm 'round her shoulders as the ship slowly sailed on outta the harbour. We was goin' to freedom in the New Land called Nova Scotia. I gived a big sigh of relief, cause I thought all the bad things that went on where we lived all our life, was gonna be gone.

11

I don't know how long we was sailin'. Somebody said we was on that ship for nine days, but they wasn't shore.

We fin'lly seen land. My legs they was like rubber and I was sick most'a the time. I shore won't be sorry to see the back end of that ship.

My Sarrahs, they wasn't sick, not once, and I thought they was gonna laugh at me cause I was, but wife, she just held my head on her legs till I was feelin' better. And I didn't think I was ever gonna feel better.

I was lookin' all 'round when the ship was gettin' close to land. I was kinda disappointed at what I was seein'. Most I seen was a lotta sand and trees and not much farmin' land. The sand, it seemed like it went a long ways.

Wife, she looked at me. "Sam, is this where they 'spects us to live? It's only woods and sand. Where's the farmin' land? What is we s'posed to do?"

"This can't be where we is gonna live, wife. There has to be 'nother place. Colonel Blucke, he said he was gonna meet us. Now, we hasn't landed yet, Sarrah. Wait till we has then we'll see."

Well, we landed and the land it didn't look no better up close than it did from the ship. It looked worse. I was startin' to wonder what we was gonna do.

And it was cold. It was December now, and the wind it was comin' right offa the water and eatin' right through our old coats. I was glad there was no snow on the ground. What would we'da done then?

Where's we gonna go and how's we gonna live? Some of the other men and women they was gettin' restless. Blucke better come soon or there be trouble.

I heard one man, Dublin, say, "Iffen Colonel Blucke don't come soon and find us a place to live, when I sees him I is gonna kill him with my barr hands."

And I know he would'a cause Dublin, he was a hot-headed cuss. Tye had problems with him and Blucke did too.

The Colonel better watch his self cause none of the other men will help him cause nobody liked him. Most of them thought the same as wife, Sarrah. He was a crook.

I was thinkin', I hope I can find work on some of the white folks' farms fixin their tools and such', but what is I gonna do if none of the white folks wants to hire me? If they's like some of the white folks back in New Jersey, they's afraid of black folk. I don't know why. Maybe the black folk what's here gived them trouble.

But we ain't at war like we was where we come from, we ain't gonna cause no trouble, less they gives us cause to.

Maybe they got their own man to fix their tools.

I know my Sarrahs. They's worried they might not be able to find work cleanin' people's houses and, from what I can see, there ain't too much rich people livin' here. There ain't even no houses. Maybe away from the water there is, but there shore ain't none 'here. All I see is huts and tents and they ain't big.

Is that all there is? What's we s'pposed to live in? These folks look poor as us.

Maybe when the Colonel comes and takes us to where there is some houses, we'll find us some jobs, I have to think that. Can't think no other way.

Wife looked 'round. "Sam, is this where we is gonna be livin'?" she asked.

"I don't know." I said when I looked where she was lookin'. "The Colonel, he didn't tell us what we was s'pposed to do when we got here."

"Well, when is he gonna?"

"Sarrah, I don't know. But I is gonna find out."

"How is you gonna find out, Sam? Blucke didn't come when we come; he come in the spring to get things ready for his people. Did you see him come to meet the ship when it come in? Did he come here? Where is he? And what did he do all the time he was here? I don't see nothin' ready for us. And, Sam, I ain't callin' no crook, Colonel."

I was wonderin' the same thing, but I never said nothin' to my Sarrahs. "He gotta be 'round here somewhere, Sarrah?"

"Where is we, Sam? I see some white folk comin' this way, but, Blucke, he ain't with them."

"Wife, the Colonel, he ain't no white man. If he was with them you would see him right off."

"I know he ain't no white man. You think I is stupid," she said, gettin' angry.

Wife was gettin' upset cause she didn't know what was gonna happen. Some of the other Blacks was too.

"I didn't mean nothin' by what I said. I was jokin'. I know you know he ain't no white man. Wife, you might be gettin' worried for nothin'. We'll be alright, you wait and see."

"I hope you is right, Sam. I hope you is right. But that don't tell us where we is."

"I'll go ask somebody."

I didn't go far when I seen the captain from the ship we come on. I didn't know his name, but that didn't matter, I was gonna ask him anyway.

"Suh, where is we and has you seen Colonel Blucke?" I asked when I got to where he was.

"We have landed at Port Mouton and we will be staying here until spring. There is no need to worry, you will have provisions and a place to stay. I can't say about this Colonel Blucke, as I haven't seen him," he said with a smile on his face.

"He was s'pposed to meet us when the ship landed," I said.

"Is he a black man?"

"He's 'bout the colour of my Sarrah," I said, pointin' to wife.

"I'm sorry, but there wasn't anyone like that here when we landed."

"Thank you, Suh."

He turned and walked away.

I went back to where my Sarrahs was. "We is in a place called Port Mutton and we'll be here till spring. He said we was gonna get provisions and a place to stay and we got nothin' to worry 'bout. He was a nice fella and he even smiled at me."

"Where's we gonna go after that, Sam, and how is we gonna get there? Is we gonna walk? Did he tell you that?"

"No, wife, he didn't say nothin' 'bout that. But wherever we is goin' in the spring, we ain't gonna be walkin' cause there ain't no roads. We must be gonna get back on the ship again."

I didn't know what I was talkin' 'bout, but I had to say somethin' cause wife would'a been askin' questions all day. And I ain't got the answers she wants to hear.

"We best be gettin' to lookin' for a shelter, cause the white man, he ain't gonna do it."

"Does we have to build it our selfs? What is we gonna build it with? I see some tents over there that was made outta the sails from the ships, but I bet they ain't gonna give us one of them. What's that over there?" she asked, pointin' to a place to the edge of the woods.

"I don't know, but it looks like a hut that ain't done. If you is makin' a hut, you makes the roof after the hut is made."

A man was comin' our way and he stopped .

"Suh, what's that over there?" I said pointin' to the roof.

He looked to where I was pointin'. "That is a roof over a pit in the ground. It is for shelter. You might need one of those to live in for the winter."

"We has to live in a hole in the ground with a roof over it? How is we s'pposed to dig the hole? We ain't got no tools."

"I will see that you get what you need. You will have to dig the hole deep enough so that it is below the frost. And for the sod roof, use wet sand mixed with brushwood. You can look at how that one over there is made."

I didn't know what to say and my Sarrahs, they was just lookin' at that roof sittin' on the ground same as I was.

"Thank you, Suh," I said, never takin' my eyes offa the roof.

Wife, she looked at me. I could tell she was mad and I didn't blame her. We was livin' in a cabin with four walls and a roof made outta wood, now we is told we has to live in a hole in the ground with a roof over us made outta sand and brushwood.

Wife, she was quiet a long time starin' at that roof and I was waitin' for her to say somethiin' mad, but she put a shock on me. "Well, Sam, we best be gettin' busy gettin' our shelter built b'fore the ground freezes so hard we ain't gonna be able to dig no dirt."

That man, he come back like he said he would and he brought us some tools and he said we could keep them. But b'fore we started diggin', the captain come back and told us we could live in the shelter we was lookin' at, cause he said nobody was gonna live in it. There must be other ones built for the rest of our folks, but if they is, I ain't seen none. Maybe they has to dig they own. Well, we got us one and we wasn't long pickin' up what little bits of stuff we had and goin' to our shelter.

Comin' outta the roof, I seen what I didn't see b'fore, there was a chim-ley. That meaned we could have us a fire. I wondered what kind'a stove was in there.

When we went inside, it was only a open pit made of rocks, but that was okay, least we would be able to have us a fire to keep warm and to cook.

It was a good thing we still had our coats we got outta the rich fam'ly's garbage box. Raggedy as they was, we was gonna need them. We settled in to wait for the winter to come.

It was a long winter and we had us some bad storms. We had to stay inside most all the time. It was kind'a hard, cause when we runned outta wood, we had to go out in the snow, that was sometimes up over our knees, to find us more wood.

I told my Sarrahs to stay inside, but wife, she said, "We worked tagether in New Jersey, Sam, and we is gonna work together here."

"Okay, wife." No point to argerrin' with wife, cause I never wins.

The white folks, they wasn't pr'pared for the bad storms we had cause they didn't have them selfs 'nough clothes. And they wasn't used to livin' close together. They was argerrin' and they was gettin' in fights. I seen them fightin' with their fists and a coupl'a other men they used sticks. I thought for shore they was gonna kill each other.

Then the captain, one day he comed out with a long knife. It looked almost like a sword, but it wasn't long as one.

Wife, she seen that and she said, "I wish I had'a got one of them in New Jersey. They's sharper than a sword."

"They might'a been sharper, but they ain't long and you would'a had to get awful close to stick one in somebody. Then you prob'ly would'a got your self hurt," I said.

"Maybe, but I would'a hurt them first."

"Maybe you would'a and maybe you wouldn'a."

I think I must'a won that time cause she never said no more.

It was easy for us bein' close together in one room all the time cause we was used to it. But it wasn't only the argerin' mongst the white folks. There wasn't a whole lotta food and there was no fresh meat or veg'tables that the white folks was used to b'fore they come here and they was eatin the same food we was eatin', salt pork, and them hard biscuits.

Them biscuits was fillin', but they was hard for me to eat, cause I ain't got much teeth in my head. I had to soak mine in the coffee we was gived. They give us some salt cod fish too. Sometimes the white folks caught them selfs some rabbits in the snares they set. But some of them, they got sick and some of them died.

We was lucky we didn't get sick, but we was used to eatin' almos' nothin' sometimes anyway.

Spring was fin'lly comin' and we was glad the winter was almos' over. We was cold most'a the time, but we was used to that too cause we been cold b'fore. We was used to a lotta things the white man wouldn'a been used to.

We was still wonderin' what we was gonna do, where we was gonna go cause the captain, he said we was only gonna be here till spring. And we still ain't seen the Colonel.

We watched them bury the ones what died cause they couldn't bury them in the winter. There was some sad folks watchin' their folks bein' put in the ground. They didn't have no buryin' ground and they buried them in what they called water-lots. I guess they called them that, cause they was b'tween a road and a crik. I never asked nobody, so I don't know for shore.

One day wife was cleanin' up 'round the hut. We called it a hut even though it was a hole in the ground and it didn't have no walls. She heard somebody shoutin' 'fire'.

She called to me and sent me runnin' to her.

"What is it, wife?"

She pointed to the wood houses that got built over the winter and they was burnin' somethin' fierce. It didn't take that fire long to burn everythin' right to the ground. I guess we was lucky we was livin' in the ground.

But what was everybody gonna do?

After all the excitement was over the captain, he come to us and told us we was gonna be goin' to 'nother place far away from here. He said, "The government is going to remove everyone and take them further up the river to build a new town."

"Why can't they build one here? Is there 'nother town close by we can go to?" I asked.

"The only other place close by is Liverpool and that is going that way."

Well, that was the same way as the place the gove'ment was gonna send us.

Dublin, he stepped up and asked, "Where is you takin' us, some place we don't wants to go?"

"What if we don't want to go where you want to send us?" I asked.

"Where else would you go?" asked the captain.

"What 'bout this Birchtown place we been hearin' 'bout?. We heard some of the white folks say this Birchtown is just for the black folks. Why can't we go there?"

Everybody was talkin' tagether now. Some was gettin' mad cause we was bein' told we had to go where we don't want to go. I had to step up and try to calm them, but they wasn't listenin' to me.

Then, wife, she got in front of us and when wife talks they listen.

"Everybody, hush now," she said. "If we don't want to go where they want to take us, we don't have to. We is free ain't we?"

"We's free," shouted Dublin. "You cain't make us go where we don't wants to go. We ain't a goin'."

Dublin was gettin' right up in the captain's face. I put my hand on his arm.

"Dublin, hush," said wife. "No point gettin' all mad, it ain't the captain's fault. We has to make a plan for what we want to do."

She looked over at the captain, who was standin' there starin' at us. Prob'ly thinkin' if we went our own way, he wouldn't have to bother with us. That's fine by me, long as he helps us get to where we want to be and that's this Birchtown place.

"Well, Captain," said wife, "how's we gonna get to this Birchtown? Cause it seems that's where we all want to go."

"If Birchtown is where you want to go, it is in the other direction from where the rest of us are going. We are going by ship to the new town we are going to build and you will have to walk to Birchtown, which is that way," he said, pointin' over my head.

That didn't tell me nothin'. How was I s'pposed to know where that way was. I might'a been a slave b'fore, but I ain't stupid. If you gives me good d'rection, I can find where you want me to go. Where he was pointin' looked to be woods.

"How's we gonna get there?" I asked. "All I see is woods."

Some of the other folks was shoutin', "How we gonna get there? That's where we wants to go."

"Hush!" shouted wife. "Let the captain talk."

"You can follow the shore line for a way, then you will have to go though the woods because there are no roads. I don't know how far Birchtown is, but they say that Shelburne is about thirty-one miles from here. Birchtown is further than that. It would be better for you to go to Liverpool, it is only about twelve miles."

I know we has to walk anyway and tellin' us how far it is don't mean nothin' to us. I looked over at my Sarrahs.

"Sam, we'll go where you go," said wife. "If we has to go through the woods, we'll go through the woods."

After lookin' at the rest of the folks standin' by shakin their heads yes, I said, "Thank you, Suh, but we want to go to Birchtown."

"You will be on your own, but if that is what you want then I will try to get you some supplies to last you a few days."

"Thank you, Suh. Thank you," I said to him again.

We had to make plans for when we was goin'. It was gonna be a long walk cause we had to go through the woods that ain't been cut. We was lucky that the little bit of b'longin's we all had didn't get burned by the fire.

12

We didn't go for some time, almos' the end of the summer, cause the captain asked us to help the white folks what lost all their b'longin's. Why
should we help them, cause they wouldn'a helped us if we lost all ours?
They would'a looked the other way. Well, I can't say all of them, cause
there was a coupl'a folks who talked nice to us, but would they a' helped
us?

Wife said we should help them, even if they wouldn'a helped us, cause
God would'a wanted us to. I guess God don't talk to the white folks when
they goes to church and tells them they gotta help us cause they shore
don't help us no way.

I only 'greed to help cause the captain asked us and he was always
nice to us. He said he was gonna get us supplies when we was ready to
leave and I has to b'lieve he will.

We had to do a lotta convincin' of the other Blacks, cause they said
they wasn't gonna help no white man do nothin'. And, Dublin, he was
goin' if he had to go by his self. It took wife to convince him that we all
has to go together.

I don't know why they listens to wife, but they seems to think she
knows everythin'. Maybe that's good, cause we is all goin' together.

When we was gettin' ready to go, it only took us a coupla days, but we
fin'lly had what we needed. You wouldn'a thought it would'a took us that
long, cause most everybody else only had the rags on their backs, but
Dublin, when we was tryin' to dicide the best way to go, he only wanted
to go by the water all the way. But the captain, he told us we can only go
that way for a bit then we had to go through the woods.

It was gonna be hard for them. I think, it was gonna be hard for all of
us.

The captain, he didn't lie to us, he got us some supplies to take with
us. We tied what he give us in old sacks. We figgered it would be hard
goin', but we knew where we wanted to go, and we was goin'. We know

hard and it can't be no worse than the hard of bein' a slave.

Deep in my heart I knew that we was gonna meet up with our boy. He might not be in this Birchtown, but we'll find him. I had to hope that he got his self on one of the other ships that come to this New Land.

I looked over at my Sarrahs. "Wife, you and daughter ready?"

"Yes, Sam, we is ready."

"Ready as we is gonna be, Pap."

I looked over at the other folks. "Is you all ready?"

'We is ready. Let's get a goin'!" they shouted.

"Okay, let's get a goin'."

The people what was left, they waved to us till we was outta sight. Prob'ly thought we was crazy people.

Well, we was on our own now.

Good thing it was summer, cause it was warm out. We started walkin' 'long the shore cause the sand it went right up to the woods and it was easier walkin'. We didn't know how far we could go 'long the water, but we hoped it was a long way. We had to go in the woods for a time, and one time the woods was so thick a branch hit me square in the face. I can't say it put a red mark on my face cause, even if it did, you wouldn'a seen it on my black face.

We couldn't make no fire cause we didn't have nothin' to make a fire with. We caught us some fish and we ate them raw. Wasn't the first time we done that and prob'ly wasn't gonna be the last. We had us a good feed b'fore settlin' in for the night.

We went in the woods when we had to, 'specially when the wind was blowin', the trees pertected us from it some. We couldn't walk in the woods in the dark cause we couldn't see where we was goin', so we had to get our selfs settled till mornin'.

Some days when we stopped to rest and eat, we stayed right where we was for the night. The supplies the captain give us would'a last 'bout three days, but that was alright cause with the fish we caught, we was makin' them last longer.

It took us better'n a week to get to this place called Shelburne, not sure just how long it was, but we wasn't in no hurry. We knew we was gonna get there sometime. And we had young'uns with us so we couldn't do no rushin'.

We was standin' there lookin' all 'round. Where was we goin' now?

"Well, Sam, we're here, but where is we gonna go?" Dublin said. He got purty quiet on that long walk. I don't think he re'lized how far we was gonna have to walk. Or how hard it was gonna be. The ones what had young'uns had to carry them a ways on their backs sometimes.

Wife, she come beside me. "I see houses, but I don't think they is for us. And where is Blucke. He's prob'ly hidin' so he don't have to do nothin' for us," she said. "He was s'pposed to meet us when the ship landed, wasn't he?"

Just then we seen him comin'. Somebody must'a told him there was more Black folks comin'. He looked 'round at all of us. There must'a been twenty-five or thirty of us. I don't think he 'spected to see so many of us as he was seein'. Well, that was too bad, he had to do his job and find us a place to live and get us some supplies.

"Well, I see you made it safely." he said with a big smile on his face. "Do you have all your supplies with you?"

"What supplies you talkin' 'bout?" said wife. "We ain't got no supplies."

"Weren't you given any supplies when you got off the ship?"

"You think we is just gettin' here?" I said. "We been in Port Mutton all the winter."

"You didn't land in Shelburne?" he said.

"Didn't my Sam just say we was in Port Mutton? How come you don't know where your people is gonna be?"

Blucke didn't say nothin' to that. He looked 'round at all of us and he said. "I will try to get you supplies. We have a little walk to get to your new homes. They're not mansions," he said with a funny little laugh, "but they will get you through the winter until you can build better ones in the spring. Are you ready to go?"

Wife, I know she was sayin' to her self, "I'd like to smack that smile right offa his face with my fist connectin' with his jaw."

13

The Colonel, he 'splained what he been doin' while he was here and why we didn't see him b'fore today.

"I went with the surveyor to plot out land for our own community. It required some clearing. We got some done, but there is still more to do. We are settled mostly in the woods because some of the land is swampy, but you will be okay."

"Blucke, how is we gonna live? Where is we gonna get food? Can we get us a job so we can make us some money to get us what we need?" Wife was firin' questions at him faster then the fire that burned down the houses in Port Mutton.

It seemed like he didn't want to answer her. Maybe he didn't have no answers or maybe we wouldn'a liked the answers he give.

Wife, she wasn't leavin' till he answered her, if it took all day. "You didn't tell us 'bout the houses. What is they like? How big is they?"

Colonel, he knew better'n not answerin' cause he knew she wasn't gonna move till he told her and if she didn't move, no one else would'a. It was like they all waited on what she was gonna do.

"Well, Mrs. Sarrah. The houses is in a little village called Birchtown. They isn't big, but there is some huts and I will make sure you get what you need to build your shelter."

"Shelter? You mean we is goin' there and there ain't gonna be no place for us to live?"

The rest of the Blacks waitin' to go to Birchtown started talkin' all at once. "Where is we all gonna live?" "We come all this way and they ain't no houses for us to live in?"

"What you been doin' here all this time. You been here almos' a year, ain't it?" Dublin said.

Wife, Sarrah, she didn't like his answers and I could tell by the narrowin' of her eyes that she was gonna tear somethin' offa the Colonel. He might not have no eyes left time she gets done with him. "What kinda shelter is you talkin' 'bout?"

"Well, Mrs. Sarrah," He said lookin' round at the rest of us. He could see none of us liked what he already been sayin' and I knew he thought we was gonna riot and he knew he had to calm us down. But this time he was gonna have his self a hard time doin' it.

I could see it in his eyes, he wasn't gonna answer wife's questions. Prob'ly thought that was for the best. 'Stead he said, "We better be going before it gets dark."

Then he started walkin' real fast down a small dirt path.

I was standin' next to wife and I wondered. What did I get my fam'ly into? We'll go to this Birchtown and see what the Colonel has for us. We is here now, what else can we do.

I rubbed wife's arm. "We might as well go see what's there, Sarrah, an' do what we can. If we has to build a shelter we best get to this Birchtown and get to it."

Colonel didn't tell us we had to walk six miles.

We asked him why we couldn't rest for the night in Shelburne and he said we best get to Birchtown cause the white folk didn't like the free Blacks hangin' 'round the streets. We picked up our belongin's and followed him off down the path that was worn down by people walkin'.

When we got close to Birchtown, I was wonderin' how many other Blacks was gonna be there.

Before we got there, we seen a big house and it had a garden that looked like it was growin' real good. I thought, We is gonna have us a nice house and we can grow us 'nough vegetables to hold us the winter.

Wife, she saw that house and she asked, "Blucke, who owns that house?"

Colonel, he didn't want to answer, but wife planted her feet as tight as that garden was planted and put her hands on her hips. When she does that, she ain't a goin' nowhere till she gets a answer.

"That is my house," he said and started walkin' past it faster then b'fore and he wasn't stoppin' for nobody.

Wife, she whispered to me, "We better have us a house nice as that or there is gonna be hair a flyin' and it ain't gonna be mine."

"Hush, now, wife. We is here now and we'll make the best of what we gets. If it ain't a big house like that, then it ain't."

When we got there, we got us a big shock. All we seen was a lotta them pits and some huts that looked to be made outta straw and other stuff. Where was the houses? And there was a lotta black folks already there.

When we was lookin' all 'round we seen a man runnin' to us. When he got close to us, we seen it was our boy, Sam.

Mam and daughter they runned to him and put their arms 'round him. All I seen was, he was like a cripple runnin' with a walkin' stick. What happened to our boy?

Blucke, he was watchin' us and he said, "You know this man, Sam?"

"That's my boy."

Mam and his sister wasn't lettin' him go. I think they was 'fraid he was gonna be gone again.

I walked to my boy and pat him on the back. "You said you was gonna find us, but I guess we found you."

"Pap." was all he said.

We would have us plenty time for talkin' later, but now we has to see 'bout a shelter.

I looked 'round again and I said to myself it would'a been better for Colonel to bring us in dark night then we wouldn'a seen that the land was no better than the shore we passed in the boat when we was comin' to Port Mutton. It was bad. There was more rocks than there was dirt. They was stickin' right up outta the ground. Least that's what it looked like to me. How does Colonel 'spect us to plant anythin' here?

Wife, Sarrah, she just looked at him. She never said nothin', but she shore was thinkin'.

We was shocked at what we seen. Colonel called them shelters? We wasn't gonna tell him that we had to live in one almos' like them in Port Mutton. We wasn't tellin' him nothin' and I made signs for nobody to say nothin', even my boy. I was fin'lly learnin' from wife that you don't tell nobody nothin' less you has to.

"What is them things? Is the roofs just sittin' on top of the ground?"

Colonel looked like he was gonna be 'fraid to answer. He didn't say nothin' 'bout the pits to us when we was in Shelburne. He hadn'a dared to. Now he had to. He looked to where I was pointin'.

"Those are roofs built over trenches. We didn't have enough boards and nails so some of the people had to dig trenches and put roofs made of cloth and tree boughs. These folks call them pit houses. The huts are no better made and are not as warm."

I looked to where the huts was. I could see what he meaned. The huts was made with some kind'a straw, it looked like, and the roofs was covered with birch bark and was kind'a pointy. That wasn't gonna keep the winter out. Best to live in a hole in the ground with a roof on it. We has to keep warm, don't we?

I know my Sarrahs ain't gonna like that, livin' in a hole in the ground like a mole again, but it's better'n tryin' to build a hut without boards.

I didn't have to say nothin', wife ignored Colonel and said to me. "Sam, does Blucke 'spect us to live in one of them? An' does we have to build it our self?"

She never said nothin' to Colonel cause she was mad 'nough to say, "We know what they is." But she wasn't tellin' him nothin'.

Then she put a shock on me again when she said, "Well, if this is gonna be our new home, we best get to it."

She turned to Colonel and he backed up when he seen the look in her eyes. He was 'fraid she was gonna slap at him cause she raised her hand. That's what she wanted him to think. He seen her on the battlefield and he knew what she could do. He was prob'ly thinkin', she was thinkin', he was the enemy and if she could, she would kill him like she did the Patriot solders. He better be careful when he's 'round her, cause if she gets mad 'nough she'll hit him with somethin'.

Wife looked him square in the eyes. "Blucke." She still ain't callin' him Colonel. "You gonna get us somethin' to work with or does you 'spect us to dig with our bare hands?" she said with her hands on her ample hips and fire in her eyes. Seems like that's her fav'rit way to stand.

I didn't think she was gonna want to live in one of them pits again. I 'spected her to say she wasn't livin' in no hole in the ground and here she was tellin' Colonel we needed tools.

"Sarrah?" I asked.

"Sam, we has to live somewhere an' if this is how it's gotta be, we'll make the best of it for the winter. Then we'll find us a way to build us a good hut."

She turned to Colonel again. "Blucke, you get us somethin' to work with and get it now."

"Yes, ma'am," said Blucke.

He turned and runned off like the devil was chasin' him.

"If he don't come back with tools, he better not come back at all," she said.

I think my Sarrah put the fear of God in him, cause he wasn't long comin' back. He had us two shovels and two buckets.

Well, the shovels was good and we would need the buckets to haul the dirt we dug outta our pit and to make mud in to put on the roof. But that's all he bringed us. He didn't bring us no supplies. What he 'spect us to do?

Me and my Sarrahs, we got busy diggin' us a hole in the ground. It was hard work and we took turns with the shovels. My boy and a man he called Prince, they helped us. My boy, he was workin' hard as us.

I told him we would do it, for him to rest, but he said he ain't no cripple just cause he walks with a walkin' stick. I didn't ask no questions then, but I was shore gonna ask plenty after we was settled in.

It took us more'n a week to get our shelter ready, cause we had to cut us some logs for the roof. My boy, he had a hatchet Blucke gived him when he first come and that was good. Him and Prince, they cut the logs while me and my Sarrahs was diggin'.

Seems like we had to move more rocks than dirt. It had to be deep 'nough for us to stand up in. We ain't tall so it don't have to be too deep, but we had to dig b'low the frost.

The deeper we digged the hole, the dirt seemed like it was gettin' warmer. The wind can't blow through the dirt. If we made the roof strong 'nough, It might not be too bad in the winter time.

Till we got it dug, we stayed with my boy and his fam'ly. My boy got him self a wife and two young'uns. We shore had us a lotta cetchin' up to do.

My Sarrahs brought some dishes we had and all our clothes. We didn't have a lot, but we was hangin' on them coats. They was gettin' purty thin, but they still kept most'a the cold out. Sometimes. I didn't know what this winter was gonna be like, but if it wasn't no worse than the last winter in Port Mutton, we might be okay.

If I had to find us warmer clothes, I would, even if I had to steal them. I is purty good at stealin', but there ain't no point lookin' in the garbage boxes here cause the Blacks they ain't got nothin' for them selfs. The white folks' houses that I seen when we got off the ship, it looked like they was just gettin' by, too. But if I need stuff, I'll find it.

It rained one night and we thought the rain was gonna come right through the roof, but it didn't. My boy had his roof made strong. I was gonna make shore mine was strong 'nough to keep the rain out, too. We don't need rain leakin' on us.

14

Blucke, he come back and gived us some supplies to last us for a time. Then the British gived us six months' supplies and when they was gone they gived us more.

We couldn't keep dependin' on that, so in the winter, when I could, I tried to cetch some fish by makin' a hole in the ice. Sometimes I caught a coupl'a fish, but most times I didn't. And it was cold on that ice.

I couldn't hunt no meat cause I didn't have no gun. I found a piece of wire and I made myself a snare to cetch a rabbit and I think I caught one, but when I went lookin' the wire and the rabbit was gone. I seen some blood on the snow and some tracks walkin' away. Somebody stealed my rabbit.

When I first seen my boy again, I almos' didn't know him. He didn't look like he did when I last seen him. I seen this man runnin' toward me and he was like he was crippled cause he was usin' a walkin' stick and his face looked like somebody beat on him bad. When his Mam hugged him, I seen pain in his eyes that he was tryin' to hide.

When we was settled some I asked him, "Sam, boy, what happened to you?"

He told me 'bout a riot that was b'fore we come here and what the white men did to him and a lotta other black folks.

"I wish I could'a been here, they wouldn'a done that to you."

"You couldn'a stopped them, Pap. They might'a done to you what they done to me. Maybe worse."

"They wouldn'a got the chance, boy. Me and your Mam and sister, we was guerrilla fighters in New Jersey durin' the war. We knows how to fight and they would'a had a hard time doin' to us what they done to you."

"You all was guerrilla fighters?"

"Yes, we was and we was good fighters. We was called the Black Brigade."

"Pap, you is gonna have to tell me 'bout that."

"I will one day. Wait till you hear some of Mam's stories. When she had her sword in her hand, everybody better get outta her way. Colonel Blucke, he was 'fraid of your Mam."

"Colonel Blucke? No!"

"Yup, he shore was, still is cause he knows she don't like him and she don't trust him. He thinks she's gonna find out somethin' 'bout him that nobody but the white man knows. That's what I think."

When me and wife was by our self, she cried cause of how our boy looked. She wished she could'a been here to doctor him. He might'a been all healed by now. Liz and her Papa and Mamma, they did a good job, but they didn't know how to make the medicines wife knew how to make. Didn't she doctor his cuts what Henry put on his back all them many times?

Our first winter in Birchtown was hard, but it wasn't hard like when we was in Port Mutton. We was kind'a used to livin' in a hole in the ground, but it was still hard cause we never had to live like that where we come from.

I always knew my Sarrahs was strong. They had to be, bein' slaves and all, and even fightin' in the war, but livin' like this, in a hole in the ground, they was stronger than I knew they was.

One long winter night, the wind was a howlin' and the snow was a blowin'. We was sittin' in our hole in the ground. It sounds funny sayin' it like that, but that's what it was, a hole in the ground.

I said to them, "Where does you get the strength from? You is stronger than some of the men here. And I don't mean body strong, I means mind strong."

"We gets our strength from you, Sam. You is the strongest person we know. If you wasn't strong, we wouldn't be," said wife.

"Yes, you would," I said to her. "You was only young when I met you at Master Bulloc's, but you had a strength I never seen in a young girl b'fore. You made me want to be strong. And I was. Cause of you."

I took her hand. "And our daughter, she is strong cause we teached her she had to be strong and she seen the strength her Mam has."

"And her Pap," said wife.

Daughter, she looked at us and said, "I gets my strength from my Pap and Mam."

We held hands as the wind howled and the snow kep' blowin' 'round outside.

Me and my Sarrahs, we soon learned what Blacks had the strength for. I bringed my family to this New Land cause I wants them to have better'n what we had in New Jersey. We might be free, but it wasn't givin' us the better I was hopin' for. When we was there we had us food to eat and we could hunt us up some animals and cook them. Here, there is so many Blacks we is lucky we can find us some fish to cetch cause they is all fishin' too. And they steals any animal that is trapped, don't matter if it b'longs to somebody else.

I guess I don't mind, cause they gotta eat, too. Least here, we is our own Master and I like that.

We was only in Birchtown a little while when we heard how things was between some of the white folks and us black folks b'fore we got here. They didn't want us here and I heard they tried to take Birchtown for them selfs. They said that some white men tried to give a Mister Marston, whoever he is, some turtles to take the land for them.

What good is turtles, 'cept for makin' soup sometimes? And you is gonna need more'n one.

But I guess this Marston fellow he wouldn't give our land away. That was b'fore everybody moved on it. Good thing, cause where would we go then?

For now, we is livin' in a pit, but I promised my Sarrahs that we would have us a hut 'bove ground next year, and I was hopin' I could keep my promise, but I didn't know how hard things was gonna get.

Black folks wasn't wanted in the church, and when they got in, they had to sit in the back where no whites was. If there was more white people gonna be in the church, then the Black folks wasn't 'llowed in.

Preacher George, a black man, built his church in Shelburne Town and was baptisin' white folks. Some of the other white folks took 'ceptin' to it. No white folks should be baptised by no black preacher.

Them white folks, they must'a not liked the black folks buildin' shelters on preacher's land either. It would'a been too close to the church for them. I wondered why them Blacks they didn't come to Birchtown with the rest of us.

After the riot in the summer, that my boy told me 'bout, and all their shelters was tore down, them Blacks, they had to come to Birchtown and now they is livin' in holes in the ground same as us. Their huts and pits prob'ly ain't built no better'n ours was when we first built it.

Water runned in on our heads cause, even though I said I was gonna make it so it didn't leak water on us, I couldn'a put 'nough mud on it. I fixed it right off and nothin' comes in now.

Them blacks from Shelburne Town prob'ly had to do the same cause they wasn't used to livin' in no pit.

Me and wife was talkin' one day and I asked her, "Wife, does you think Preacher George will 'llow us to put up a shelter on his land?"

"Sam, didn't our boy tell you what the white soldiers did to the shelters that was there? Them black folks what owned them is livin' in Birchtown now. We ain't wanted there. If you wants to try to build a shelter in town, you'll be doin' it by your self. Me and Sarrah, we ain't goin' with you this time."

"I know they don't want us there, wife, but it might be better'n livin' where we is now, in a pit."

"Some of the white folk in town thinks we is gonna steal from them and they gives the jobs to the white man and pays him 'stead of givin' a job to us. And you know what? We ain't 'llowed to have dances, but the white folks can. You wanna live in a place like that?"

I looked at her and asked her where she heard that.

She shook her head. "Sam," she said, "where has you been that you didn't hear that?"

"I been right here, wife, but that ain't what I heard. I heard that the white folk will give us work cause we'll work for a little bit of money. The white man wants more. That's why the soldiers caused that riot b'fore we come here. And I know 'bout us not bein' 'llowed to have dances. We can't gamble neither."

Wife shook he head again. I know she was surprised that I knew that. "Where you hear that, Sam?"

"When I was in town the other day I heard the baker, I don't know his name, and 'nother man talkin' 'bout the riot and he said he was gonna hire the Negroes cause they work for less money and he don't care if them soldiers liked it. The soldiers want more money and if they riot again, they was gonna be in more trouble than they was durin' the riot. Who told you the white men think we is gonna steal from them and that's why they gives the jobs to other white men?"

she pat me on the head. "It was Miss Mabel what told me. She said she heard it from her man, Harry."

"Mabel? And she said her Harry told her? You can't talk after Harry. He never gets nothin' he heard right. Always mixes it up, he does."

Wife never said no more, cause I think she knew I was right. Harry better get things right b'fore he tells it to other folks.

One day Mabel come visitin' again and I wondered what Harry told her this time. Cause we only had us one room and it was cold outside, I sat in a corner and listened to everythin' they was sayin'. And I ain't 'shamed to say so. Wife ain't gonna tell me no more that I don't listen, and if Mabel tells her somethin' her Harry said and I knows it's wrong, I'll tell her quick.

"Sarrah," Mabel said, "did you hear that Jacob and George was 'rrested for gamblin' an' dancin' an' they was throwed in the gaol?"

"Well," said Sarrah, "they'll be lucky if they is only throwed in the gaol and not whipped, too. That's not gonna be good for George, cause he don't like bein' put in a cage."

Mabel clicked her chipped and rotted teeth. "Can you blame him? He was put in a cage when he was taked by the white man to sell in Africa. And what he says is he was there a long time. Like a animal."

"I didn't know he was borned in Africa."

"That's what he said. And, Sarrah, you know when they come b'fore the judge he's gonna say, 'Twelve stripes on the bar back in the town squar'. If he gets whipped and they puts him in the gaol, he's gonna be sick. If that was a white man he wouldn't even be 'rrested."

"You're right. You're right. Can you 'magine what would happen if you stole somethin'? You would be hanged prob'ly."

"Let me tell you," said Mabel. "A young girl in Shelburne town stole two things an' the judge said three hundred an' fifty lashes."

"What did she steal? Gold?" asked Sarrah.

"Don't know. All I heard was two small things. That poor girl."

"How can they be 'llowed to do that?" Sarrah asked.

"They cin do anythin' they want. You know Thomas what does odd jobs for some of the white folks in Shelburne an' gits paid almos' nothin'?"

"I heard of him," said Sarrah, "but I don't know him."

I was sittin' listenin' long enough. I said, "I know Thomas. What happened? I ain't seen him for a week."

"An' you ain't gonna see him for a long time," said Mabel. "I heard he was gived what they call forced labour. I ain't shore what that means, but they said he had his eye on a white man's tater garden. I guess they figgerd he was gonna steal some."

"Forced labour for lookin' at a garden?" I asked. "That can't be right. You must'a heard wrong."

"I didn't hear nothin' wrong," huffed Mabel. "My Harry told me and he don't lie. That's jest how it is for us black folks."

I looked at Sarrah and she looked at me. She shook her head cause she knew I was gonna say somethin' else.

I got up, I wasn't sittin' there listenin' no more. "Sarrah, I think I is gonna go to town to try to find some work."

"Okay, Sam, I hope you does, cause we is gettin' down on supplies. You be careful."

"I will."

When I got home, Mabel was gone. I couldn't wait to tell wife 'bout what I seen when I was in town.

"Wife, they was whippin a young girl they said stole somethin' from somebody's house. They was gonna give her a hundred and fifty stripes on her back. They was givin' her fifty today and fifty nex' week and fifty the nex' week after that. Wife, she was screamin' so and b'fore the first fifty was half done she was saggin' almos' to the ground. She stopped screamin' and I think she was unconscious, but the gaoler, he didn't stop, he whipped till he got to fifty. Wife, if she has to have a hunderd more, she ain't gonna live, if she ain't dead after today. And that girl that Mabel said was gonna have three hundred and fifty, she is shorely gonna die when they put the whip to her. Wife, all I could think 'bout was the day Henry was whippin' our boy b'fore we was sold to Master Stoffle."

15

Summer was almos' over and I was comin' home from workin' in Shelburne. I was whistlin' and almos' dancin' down the dirt path that was takin' me home to my Sarrahs.

I was passin' by a big patch of bushes when three white men jumped out from b'hind them and beat me with sticks and pounded on me with their fists.

I got away and started runnin' fast as I could. They only chased me a ways, and when I got close to home, they runned the other way cause they prob'ly figgered the Blacks in Birchtown would give them a good beatin'.

When I got home my right eye was swelled almos' shut and my lips was cut and bleedin' and I had a bad pain in my left shoulder. When wife seen me she got battle ready. I seen that look in her eyes b'fore when we was fightin' the Patriots. She wanted to hunt them men down and show them what it feels like to be set upon with sticks and fists.

I had to stop her b'fore she got outta the pit. We wasn't in New Jersey no more, where she had a sword. Strong as she was, her fists wouldn'a hurt them too much, but their fists would'a hurt my wife, then I would'a had to kill them.

I said, "It's okay. I cut one of them's lips real bad and I gived 'nother a swelled eye like he gived me. One of them was bloody as me."

Wife was still wantin' to go after them, but I told her, "No, Sarrah, They is big men and what is you gonna fight them with? And b'sides, you would be throwed in the gaol and they would hang you for killin' them white men. There be 'nother time and we can find a way to get at them tagether, cause two 'gainst three is better'n one 'gainst three."

She knew what I was sayin' was true, but she had to have her last say. "I could do it if I had my sword."

It was gettin' harder and harder to find work and the British was only givin' us half the supplies what they gived us b'fore. When I could find work I had to work longer times, but I didn't mind doin' that. I would'a done any kind of work cause I wasn't gonna sell myself to no white man to be his slave. I was a slave and it ain't no fun. Some of the Blacks was in-denturin' them selfs to the white man cause they can't find no work. My two Sarrahs would kill me b'fore they let me indenture myself to any man.

~

Colonel's soldiers, that be me and my fam'ly, we was valu'ble cause we knew how to dig trenches and cut wood. When they was talkin' 'bout buildin' a road outta Shelburne, they come to us cause we knew what to do.

We got paid some money, not much, but it kep' us in supplies for a time. The white workers didn't like us workin' and gettin' most of the work cause we was workin' for less money than they was use'ta gettin'. We did better work, I think.

They come down on us hard sometimes. They would beat up bad on us and call us Nigger or you black bastard. I know them's not nice words for me to say, but that's what they called us. We could'a called them names, but that would'a made us bad as them. They figgered we wasn't good as them, but I figgered we was better. The ones what come from the South in America, they was always like that. We was used to bein' called names, cause we was called them all the time b'fore we come to this New Land that was s'pposed to be better, and it ain't.

We didn't like the beatin's, but if we hit them back and they com-plained to the p'lice, the p'lice b'lieved the white man cause what we say don't mean nothin'. They prob'ly figgered we was lyin' anyway. Some-times the black folk got whipped, but I was lucky those white men what jumped me didn't complain to the p'lice when I bloodied one of them like they bloodied me.

There wasn't a whole lotta work for nobody. I could'a gone and worked on a fishin' boat like Mr. Boston King, but he had to go far away to do that. I guess he got paid purty good money and they even gived him some of the fish, but I wasn't leavin' my fam'ly.

My boy, Sam, he said he wasn't goin' on no boat no more, didn't matter how much money they gived him, cause he was 'fraid of the boats. He thought they was gonna sink.

I told him, "Boy, if you fam'ly needs food bad, is you gonna let them starve, just cause you is 'fraid to get on a boat? Is you? You gotta get over that, boy, cause I think things, they is gonna get real bad and we don't know what we is gonna have to do to feed our selfs."

He never said nothin', just stared at me. I think he knew what I was sayin' was true. We is black folk who ain't wanted here or nowhere and we can't be 'fraid of nothin'. We had 'nough of that when we was slaves. We is free now, but sometimes the way we is treated, it feels like we is still slaves.

Things wasn't gettin' no better for us. Winter, it come and gone again and it was almos' time to start plantin' so we could have us some taters and maybe some other veg'tables for the nex' winter. We was give a small piece of land, but the land we was give, I been sayin' to anybody who is listenin', that it ain't no good for nothin'. Never seen dirt poor as that and there seems to be more rocks than dirt what we has to move away. I don't know if we is gonna get them moved b'fore we is old.

Some Blacks, they turned to the sharecroppin' thing and me and my boy we talked 'bout doin' it cause we would'a had us some of the crops we planted on the white man's land. One man, name of John Brown, he did it and he told us they thought they was gonna go right over to that man's land and plant a big garden, but when they got there the land was all growed up and there was a lotta rocks.

He said to me, "Sam, don't you do that sharecroppin'. It took me and wife a whole year to get it all cleared and we thought we was gonna plant when we was done, but that white man, he sent us to 'nother piece of his land he wanted us to clear. We never got us no garden planted. You can't trust no white man."

Well, me and my boy we didn't do that sharecroppin' thing. We had to find a way to get us a garden planted some other place, but we didn't know where that was gonna be, cause the land was no good nowhere. Some of the Blacks was still indenturin' them selfs to the white man so they could have 'nough food to eat.

My boy he said to me one day, "Pap, when Liz was with child with John, I asked Mr. John if he would sign us back on, but he told me he couldn't. He didn't tell me how come and I didn't ask and I ain't gonna ask no more. Mr. John, he was good to us when we was with him, but I wouldn't trust no other white man like I did him."

"Boy, maybe you should be thinkin' 'bout goin' to Mr. John again. I hear he got his land now. Maybe if it ain't cleared you can work for him. And maybe we can get jobs, too."

"I ain't seen him in a long time. I can go to town and ask him, but Liz was in town with her Mamma tryin' to get us some bread from the bak'ry and she seen him talkin' to some black men she thinks lives in the town and she seen him give them some money. She thinks they might'a been workin' for him. I guess he must'a forgot that me and Prince said we would come back and work for him when he got his land."

"Boy, ask him anyway. If he don't want you, he'll tell you. You got to be careful who you indenture you self to cause they can up and sell you when they wants to, cause you is no better'n a slave to them and they can do what they want."

"Pap, did you hear 'bout the fam'ly what signed their young'uns over to a man cause they thought they would learn a trade with their master? You know what their Mamma and Papa got? They got a paper from the Master sayin' they owed him money for keepin' their young'uns. I heard it said he had them for a lotta years. Now, Pap, where was they gonna get money to pay him? He up and sold them young'uns for slaves to some-body else. I tell you, Pap, I ain't gonna sign my young'uns over to nobody. I is gonna find a way to look after my own."

"These is hard times, boy, and some folks, they don't have no choice. They might'a thought they was doin' good for their young'uns, they didn't know that Master was gonna do what he did. Maybe they should'a, cause there ain't too many white folks us Blacks can trust."

"Maybe, Pap. Maybe. But I still ain't a gonna do it."

Sam the Son

Sharon Robart-Johnson

16

Sam the son says:

It seems like a long time ago. I don't know where I fin'lly got the courage to leave, but I knew I had to go. I should'a left when my Pap and Mam and sis runned away. I told them I wasn't goin' cause we was the only slaves Master Stoffle had and if we all runned away, he would shorely be mad and hunt us down and make us suffer.

I wasn't tellin' Pap and Mam that I was 'fraid. 'Fraid of bein' caught and brought back to Master or bein' sold to 'nother master who had a overseer worse than Henry. Slaves ain't really safe nowhere, but I was kinda safe on Master's farm. He ain't got no Henry and he wouldn'a sent no dogs after you, least I ain't seen him do it. If Pap knew that, they would'a never went.

I wasn't with Master Bulloc no more, but I remembers the sting of the whip when it come down 'cross my body everywhere. When things wasn't the way the overseer, Henry, said they was s'pposed to be, he would take it out on the slave what was close by and a lotta times it was me.

I fight him one time and I got me 'nother whippin' and it was worse than the last one. If you touched the overseer, you got punished.

The last whippin' Henry put on me b'fore we was sold to Master Stoffle, Pap hollered at Henry and called him a liar. He told Master that his boy never stole nothin'. I never heard my Pap holler like that b'fore.

After we was sold to Master Stoffle, Pap, he told me I had to forget 'bout that and go on, we wasn't with Master Bulloc no more, but it ain't easy to do. Them beatin's, nobody forgets. They stays with you forever.

~

It was spring time in Bergen County, New Jersey and I was ready to run like my Pap, Mam and sis did. I wasn't 'fraid of bein' caught no more. I was tired of bein' a slave. It seems like ten years 'stead of two that they been gone and I wondered if they made it safe to the British.

Master, he was mad when he went to their cabin the next mornin' and they was gone. He didn't blame me for my fam'ly runnin' away like Henry would'a.

Now, I is goin' and ain't nothin' gonna stop me. I don't know what's gonna happen to me after I run away and I don't care. I heard the talk what people was still sayin' 'bout the Bitish promisin' freedom to us Blacks if we fight with them same as Pap heard and that was why we planned to run away. Pap always said he wondered if we could trust the British and I wondered too, but I knew that anythin' had to be better than stayin' where I was and always bein' a slave.

I got nothin' to lose cause bein' a slave I already losed my life. If I died tryin' to run away, well, then, I would die and I wouldn't be in this hell no more. All us slaves we had the same dream, to be free. If runnin' away, other than dyin', was the only way to be free, then that's what I was gonna do. I was 'termined I wasn't gonna be caught. I was gonna get to the British and be free.

I sat starin' out over Shelburne harbour, thinkin' 'bout that day when I made up my mind that I was gonna run away. It was a long day and the sun seemed to come up b'fore the roosters crowed, and it set later. That meaned we had to work longer times than we did b'fore. I was real tired, but I knew I had to go now and stop bein' 'fraid. I been 'fraid long 'nough.

17

I knew I had to wait for the right time to leave. I went to my cabin after I was done workin'. I didn't want to go to sleep, but I couldn't keep my eyes open no more. I was so tired.

When I waked up my heart was beatin' thump, thump, thump in my chest like I already runned ten miles. I looked out the little hole in the wall that was my window 'spectin' to see a sky all full of black clouds that was sposed to make it easy for me to run without bein' seen.

While I was sleepin' the black clouds was gone and the sky was clear as day. The moon was so big and yellow, it lighted up the sky like mornin'.

"I can't go now," I said to myself. "I is gonna be caught for shore."

But I knew I had to go. If I didn't, I wouldn't be goin'. I would be a slave till I died. Why didn't it rain like it was sposed to?

I put the few belongin's I had in a old raggedy sack. I had some food that I hid in my cabin cause I was gonna need eats. Good thing Master didn't go lookin' through his workers' stuff, cause he would'a found it. Then I would'a been in big trouble cause he would'a knew I was plannin' somethin'.

I didn't have a lot, but I thought if I only ate a little bit at a time and maybe only one time a day, it might last me till I can find me some more. I had to remember to hold it high over my head so it don't get wet when I goes in the river.

My heart was still poundin' in my chest, but I sneaked outta my cabin and runned 'long the edge of the woods, lookin' every way, till I come to the path that the young'uns used when they was goin' fishin' in the river. I thought I heard somebody comin' b'hind me.

"I ain't gettin' caught. I ain't gettin' caught," I said to myself over and over.

I jumped in the cold water and almos' runned down the river. I know I must'a looked a sight tryin' to run in the water, but I couldn't take no chances. I kep' movin' fast as I could. I almos' falled a coupl'a times and if

I had'a my food would'a been no good. Good or not, I would'a still had to eat it cause where was I gonna get more?

I didn't know how far down the river I was when I crawled up on the shore. I laid in the mud a little while.

I was so cold I was shiverin' and I was almos' 'fraid to breathe cause I didn't know if there was somebody close by and they could hear me. My old and raggedy clothes wasn't much pertection from the cold and they was wet clean to my skin. Maybe when the sun comed up they might dry some. I was hopin'.

It would be daylight soon and Master would be roundin' everybody up to get their breakfast, then get to work. I didn't know if he already knew I was gone, but I had to keep movin' case he did. I had to make shore I was far 'nough away that he wouldn't never find me.

I wonder what Master will say when he finds I is gone. That was gonna be four slaves what runned away in two years.

I got up outta the mud and started to run. It wouldn'a maked no diff'rence if my clothes had'a dried some, cause I was in the water and outta the water, hopin' to confuse anybody who might be lookin' for me. But I was gettin' tired. My legs, they didn't want to go no more.

The sun was high in the sky when I falled down dog tired. I don't know how far from Master's I was, but it must'a been a ways.

I knew I couldn't stay there for a long time, but I was so tired from all the runnin'. I listened, but I didn't hear nobody or nothin' comin', so I took a small crust of bread outta my sack and ate it like I never had nothin' for days. I was hungry, but I couldn't eat no more cause I needed to save some for 'nother day. Least I had water, cause the river was right there and it was fresh clean water.

I never thought to bring me a jug so I could'a filled it so I'd have some water when I was runnin'. I figgered long as I stayed by the river I'd be okay.

I jumped up. What was that? I thought I heard dogs. I listened some more, but it wasn't dogs, it was the birds in the marsh makin' a noise to each other. I was really 'fraid if I thought that birds was dogs.

I listened again, but I didn't hear nothin' else.

I had to get movin', I couldn't stay there no more. I drank more water and splashed some on my face to wake me all the way up.

I was used to bein' tired cause we had to work from daylight till it got dark, but I never had to run miles and miles, in and outta cold water. It wasn't only the runnin' that made me tired. I was tired cause I was 'fraid.

I said I wasn't 'fraid no more and that's why I runned away, but it's a good thing I was 'fraid too, cause it kep' my legs movin' when they didn't want to.

I knew I had to rest, I couldn't keep runnin' till I dropped. Then I would'a runned away for nothin'.

I pulled some marsh grass out and covered my self cause I was still cold from bein' in and outta the water and it would keep me a little warm and hide me from folks goin' by on the river. All they would see would be a lump of marsh grass, least wise I was hopin' that was all they would'a seen. I knew I couldn't stay there too long, just long 'nough to rest my body and legs.

But I was so tired I fell asleep and must'a slep' for hours cause when I waked up it was dusk.

Boy, was I shakin'. Not from the cold, cause that wasn't so bad no more. I was gettin' used to that. I was shakin' cause I could'a been caught and if I was, I could be dead now.

When we was on Master Bulloc's farm, all us slaves learned to sleep with one ear always uncovered so we could hear any sound that was made. You never knew when Henry was gonna come in your cabin and the alder, that he stripped the bark offa to wake you up if he thought you was sleepin' too long, would come down on whatever part of your body that wasn't covered with the woolly blanket. He come in my cabin a lotta times, but I always heard him comin' and I'd jump up and be standin' next to my cot when he come bangin' through the door. A couple'a times he used that alder on me anyway. Smacked it on my leg.

I gots to stop thinkin' 'bout Henry. He ain't here no more and he ain't gonna be comin' lookin' for me.

I looked 'round, but I didn't see nobody. Dark was soon gonna be settin' in good and I wished I could'a waited till dark to sleep, but I was so tired from all that runnin'. Nex' time I sleep I is gonna make shore it's in the nighttime. I had to get movin'.

I took 'nother bite of my crust of bread then started runnin' again. I was runnin' all bent over cause the grass wasn't very high and somebody would'a seen me if they was on the river. It might'a been gettin' dark, but the moon was risin' in the sky and it was bright as it was when I runned away. It lighted up the marsh like day.

I runned and rested, runned and rested for days till I los' track of how long I was runnin'. My food was gone, I ate the last piece of dried meat two days b'fore. And I didn't have no more water to drink. I thought I was still runnin' longside the river, but I was runnin' the other way. I was gettin' tired of runnin' but I couldn't stop cause I would'a been caught.

Now, I was hungry and thirsty, but I couldn't trust nobody to ask for food and water and there was no farms that I could see where I could steal somethin' to eat. I knew I was gettin' weaker and weaker and I had to find somethin' to eat purty soon.

I was so tired, I was gettin' careless. I wasn't watchin' where I was goin' and I tripped over a log and fell through some bushes into a open field. I was layin' on my belly and I couldn't get up cause the wind was knocked outta me.

The sun was high in the sky and it was warm on me, but I had to get outta the open and back in the bushes again.

When I tried to get up, somethin' heavy was pressin' in the middle of my back. I couldn't move. I tried to fight whatever it was, but I was so weak all I could do was lay still and wait for my end to come. I thought for shore Master found me.

"Get up, man."

I couldn't move.

"Get up," come again.

I turned my head and looked up into the eyes of the biggest, blackest man I ever seen. He reached down and picked me up with one hand like I was a child.

I started to shake, I was so 'fraid. He didn't have no whip in his hand, or alder, but that didn't mean nothin'. His hands, they was big as cast iron fryin' pans. If he hit me with one a them I would be dead. I b'lieved that I was gonna die that day in more pain than I ever got at Henry's hands.

I falled down on the ground again and curled up in a ball cause I was so 'fraid I didn't know what else to do.

He turned me 'round and he was kneelin' b'side me. He had somethin' in his hand. I didn't know what it was cause I only looked quick like. He put his hand on the back of my head and put a bottle to my lips that was dry and cracked.

"Drink this," he said.

Water, he was givin' me water. I drinked it so fast, I was chokin'.

"Easy now," he said as he pat me on the back. "Easy."

He picked me up again. He was almos' carryin' me. He might'a gived me water, but I was still 'fraid of what he might do. I did what I was told, but I kep' my head down.

Tired and weak as I was, I still looked for a way to 'scape. Not that I had the strength to, but I would'a tried. I come too far to be caught and sent back to Master's. I would fight to my death if I had to. If I was gonna die, then I was gonna die fightin'.

We didn't go very far when we come to a farm with a lotta buildin's. He taked me inside a big hut where there was men and women sittin' at long wooden tables, eatin'. The smell comin' from that food made me fall on my knees, I was so hungry.

The big black man picked me up and took me to one of the tables. "Sit down," he said.

The black folks, they must'a been slaves, looked at me one time then they ignored me like I wasn't there an' kep' right on eatin'. I was just 'nother slave, they prob'ly thought. And, well, I was.

I looked up into the big man's eyes, black as his skin. When he smiled at me, I was more confused than ever. Nobody but my Pap and Mam and sis smiled at me. Henry would'a never smiled at me. He would'a showed his teeth b'fore he whipped me unconscious.

The big black man pat me on the shoulder, but I was watchin' every move he made just in case he got mean. He told 'nother slave to bring me some food.

A big plate of hot food was put on the table in front of me. I just looked at it, wonderin' to myself. What is I sposed to do with this? I ain't never seen so much food b'fore and why was it bein' gived to me?

There was what looked like beef on the plate. I had meat before, but only the wild meat me and Pap caught. On Master's farm we was 'llowed to cetch rabbits and squirrels and other wild animals that we could eat and we could cook them in our cabin cause we had us a stove. But we never had no beef.

I seen a black hand come in front of my face, puttin' a big jar of steamin' black coffee nex' to my arm. I was thinkin', what does it matter if this is gonna be my last meal before I is whipped to death for runnin' away?

When that big man said, "Eat," I didn't need to be told again. I ate like it was my last meal!

My plate was soon empty and took away, then 'nother was put down. I almos' swallowed that food whole.

That big black man, he sat nex' to me, watchin' every bite I took. When I was finished he got up and said. "That's enough for now. Follow me."

I looked up in his face and I got up. I was shakin' cause I didn't know where he was takin' me. I wondered how come he didn't have my hands tied and was leadin' me on a rope so I couldn't run away.

I followed him outside and was took to a two-storey white house with a little house 'ttached to it. How come they is two houses put tagether? Why not make one big house? I thought.

This house was almost two times as big as Master's. The top and bottom had what they call balconies goin' from one end to the other. And the bottom part of the house had big poles holdin' the balconies up. Least I thought that's what they was doin'.

He took me inside the house in a room with big yellow flowers on the walls. I knew it must'a been some kind'a paper, but they shore looked real.

I was lookin' 'round till I seen a man sittin' b'hind a long wooden table. He was starin' at me, never blinkin'. He had eyes blue as the sky and he stared at me so long, I was gettin' 'fraid again. I never seen nobody with eyes that colour b'fore. His face was round and his hair was white as snow.

Then he talked and I was s'prised how soft his voice was. He wasn't yellin' at me. "My name is Peter Franklin. What is your name, son?" he asked.

"My name is, Sam, Massa." I said tryin' to sound like I wasn't 'fraid.

He kep' starin' at me and I couldn't tell what he was thinkin'. Is he gonna send me back to Master or have me whipped like runaway slaves is always whipped? I wish he would get on with it.

"From where did you come?" he finally asked.

Should I lie and tell him I come from some other place and I was free? Cause I ain't goin' back. But if I lie and he finds out, will he have his man whip me. And with them hands the big black man had I was prob'ly gonna die after ten strikes on my back. I better tell him the truth.

"I come from the farm of Master Stoffle Van Nostrant, Massa."

"Ah," was all he said.

"George," he said to his man, but still lookin' at me. "Take Sam and give him some clean, warm clothes and he can bunk in with Joseph."

He said to me. "Sam, you go with George. He will give you clean clothes, and shoes."

He was lookin' at my raggedy pants cut off at the knees, with a rope that was tied 'round me holdn' them up, and my shirt was almos' as raggedy and they was full of mud from the marsh. And I didn't have no shoes, I los' them in the river.

He was lookin' hard at my feet cause they was scratched and blistered. I ain't gonna be able to put no shoes on my feet 'till the blisterin' was gone. If he was gonna 'llow me to stay, then I could work in my bare feet. I done it b'fore and I can do it again.

He was talkin' again and I almost didn't hear what he was sayin'. "I will not send you back to Mr. Van Nostrant. My workers are free to leave when they choose, but it would be wise for you to stay until the hunt for you is over. You will be safe here. Do you understand?"

"Yes, Massa," I said, eyeing him up. I was s'picious and I didn't understand why this white man was bein' so kind to me. I wondered if I can trust him. I never had no reason to trust no white man b'fore. Words, they meaned nothin' to a slave when we was betrayed and treated no better'n animals most'a the time.

He was still talkin'.

"You will be safe here, Sam," Mr. Peter repeated. "You are within the British lines. And I am not your Massa," he said as he got up from behind that long table. "You can call me Mr. Peter, as the rest of my workers do."

I had to look way up in the air to see his face. He must'a been more'n six feet tall and he was a big man, too. Not fat heavy like me, them was muscles under his shirt. I bet mos' men is 'fraid of him cause he's big.

"Yes, Mr. Peter," I said, thinkin' this gotta be a trap. No white man was gonna talk to a slave the way Mr. Peter talked to me. And I ain't never been gived so much food and now he was givin' me clothes and shoes. 'Stead of bein' happy that I was behind British lines all I could think was, *It's gotta be a trap!*

I could tell that Mr. Peter, he was a smart man and he knew I didn't trust him, but he didn't say nothin'. Prob'ly none of his slaves trusted him when they first come here, but seems like they must now cause they was all sittin' in that big hut, eatin' his food and none of them looked 'fraid.

18

Me and George we left the big house. I walked b'hind him down a dirt path to a small cabin where a older white-haired black man sat on a rickety three-legged stool in front of it. He was whittlin' a small piece of wood. I seen a wooden crutch leanin' nex' to the door that looked to be made outta a tree branch.

When I got close I seen that he had but one leg and his face had so many wrinkles you couldn't see no smooth spot.

"Whatcha starin' at, boy? Ne'er see'd a man wid one leg b'fore?" he said in a deep boomin' voice.

George just laughed. "Brought you some company, Joseph. He'll bunk here for a while."

Pointin' to the stool, George said, as he must'a said to him every time he seen him, "When ya gonna get rid of that old stool before it breaks under ya and your ornery ass is sittin' on the ground?"

Joseph grunted. "Ne'er nee'd no company b'fore an' muh stool be jes fine."

I stood b'side George and listened to them talk. I could tell that Joseph wanted to make people b'lieve he was a hateful man and he might try to sound like he was mad at George, but I seen his mouth turn up in one corner like he wanted to laugh, but he was holdin' it back. I wondered if I was the first runaway who was brought to stay with Joseph. I didn't mind cause I kinda liked the old man.

I looked over at George and he was starin' back at me. "You'll bunk here with Joseph for a bit and he'll tell you and show you what you have to do 'round here. He knows a lot, so you be shore you listen to everythin' he says. If you got questions 'bout somethin', you ask him. Don't be afraid cause he don't bite."

"Does you, Joseph?" George said to him.

"Sometimes I does and sometimes I doesn't. 'Pends how hungry I is."

George laughed, and as he was walkin' away he said, "You can't do much bitin' with them teeth." And to me he said, "Sam, you listen to Joseph."

Then he was gone.

There not be much Joseph can teach me cause I was workin' on a farm for a long time and I know what I has to do. But maybe they does some things different 'round here. But I was willin' to learn whatever they want to teach me.

I looked at George walkin' away and wondered when he come here. Was he a runaway and where did he come from? I was gonna ask him one day, if I stayed here. I could tell by the way he talked that he was educated some, maybe he could read too. I was thinkin' maybe he'll teach me. I think I is gonna like George.

I could tell by watchin' George and Joseph that they was good friends. I don't make friends too much cause I don't trust nobody. You can't even trust some of the slaves who is like you.

But I don't think Joseph and George is like that, least wise I hope they ain't. Maybe Joseph will tell me 'bout the other slaves here and who I can be friends with and who I should stay way from.

I kep' starin' at the crippled man. I wondered what happened to his leg, but I wasn't gonna ask him. Not yet, anyway. Maybe one day.

"Ne'er see'd a man wid one leg b'fore?" Joseph said again.

"Yes, sir."

"Then stop starin' an' sit yo'sef down, I ain't a gonna bite ya," he snapped.

I think me and Joseph was gonna get 'long just fine. I sat down.

Joseph on his rickety stool, still whittlin' away, and me on the stone step b'side him, we never said a word as the sun set. I kep' lookin sideways at Joseph, hopin' he would say somethin', anythin'. I was beginnin' to wonder if he remembered that I was sittin' there. But all he did was keep on cuttin' off pieces of that wood that was gettin' smaller and smaller. I was waitin' for the old man to miss the wood and cut his finger off, but Joseph's hands was steady. I knew if it was me whittlin' away at that little piece a wood, I would'a cut my finger off a long time ago.

I looked over Joseph's head and seen two men comin' our way. I got up to run, but Joseph grabbed me by my arm with a strength that s'prised me and pulled me back.

"Sit down, boy. They's no' gonna hurt ya."

As the men come closer, I seen they carried a big pot between them. When they was in front of us they stopped. I could see the steam comin' outta it and I smelled somethin' that made me hungry all over again.

"Evenin', Joseph, brought you and your guest some supper."

"What slops ya bring me t'nite?" said Joseph without any of the steam that was comin' outta the pot.

"Chicken stew," they said with smiles on their faces, cause it must'a been the same thing Joseph said to them every time they bringed his food. They didn't pay him no mind.

I seen that little smile on his face when he said it, like he had when he was jokin' with George. Seemed like it was a game he played with all a them.

Chicken stew. I ain't never had me no chicken stew. My mouth was waterin', but Í didn't say nothin'.

I watched the men go inside the cabin and put the pot on top of the wooden table. They made a fire in the little pot-bellied cast iron stove that was sittin' in the middle of the floor.

The sun was almos' gone b'hind the trees and the cold was settlin' in like it did in the evenin's when the men come outta the cabin, tellin' Joseph his supper was ready.

I wasn't gonna ask Joseph if I could go inside. If his old bones didn't mind the cold, then I wasn't gonna complain.

Joseph fin'lly got up, grabbed his crutch and hobbled up the stone step into the cabin, that was nice and warm from the fire the men made in the stove. I looked 'round and thought, it was good to come inside, away from eyes that might be watchin' me.

"Stop starin' 'round and git dem plates o'er der," Joseph said. "We ain't gonna eat dis outta de pot, ya know. We ain't animals."

I got the plates and put them on the table. I had me two big plates full of food when I first got here, but my belly was makin' more noise than that rickety old wagon that passed by a while back.

Joseph looked at how I set the table, while a big pot of coffee boiled on his little stove. He moved the plates 'round, I don't know what for cause they was the same kind'a plate. I shook my head, but I guess he has his way of doin' things and that's what he wants. Who is I to say anythin'? It's his cabin.

"Sit down, man," he said. "We best eat this b'fore it gets cold."

We sat down to eat. I sat 'cross the table from Joseph and didn't notice that he didn't eat much. I was still hungry and I ate almos' all that was left. I was gonna make sure my belly was full if I had to make a run for it. My belly was so full, it hurt.

I cleaned off the table and washed the dishes in the bucket Joseph had there. He didn't tell me to and he didn't say nothin' when I did, but I could see him watchin' me outta the corner of his eyes.

When I was done cleanin' up, he showed me the bunk I was gonna sleep on. It was in the corner on the other side of the cabin.

"You kin sleep thar an' you betta not snore, or out you go," he said. "Thar's a extra blanket on my cot iffen you needs one."

"Thank you, suh. I won't need none," I said.

Eyein' the skinny body of Joseph I said to my self, *You is gonna need it b'fore me.* Out loud I said, "I doesn't snore."

Joseph covered his mouth with his hand, but I seen the smile on his face b'fore he did. "How you know you doesn't snore? You is sleepin' when you does it, ain't ya?"

I had no answer to that

I was tired. I didn't re'lize how tired I was, but I was runnin' a long time and I only had sleep a coupl'a times. When you is runnin' away you eyes is open more'n they is closed.

I laid down on the cot, but I wasn't gonna cover my self with the blanket cause I didn't want to get my legs all tangled up in it if I had to get up in a hurry and run. It was bad 'nough that I was 'fraid they was gonna take me when I was sleepin', I wasn't gonna let nothin' get in my way if I had to get up fast.

But I was so tired I didn't hear nothin'. I think they could'a took me and I wouldn'a knew till it was too late.

When I waked up in the mornin' the blanket was tucked under my chin.

I didn't know where I was at first and I was gettin' ready to jump up and run. Then I seen Joseph sittin' on the end of his bunk with both elbows on his one knee, his chin in his hands and he was starin' at me.

There was a fire in the stove and I could feel the warm soon as I put my legs over the side of the cot to sit up. The warm was shore welcome cause I was only used to the cold mos' days.

"Son," Joseph said with strong clear words, "as soon as your feet are healed you will be put to work. George will bring you clothes and shoes."

I know my mouth must'a fell open to my knees when I heard Joseph talkin'. He shore wasn't talkin' like he was yesterday. Today his words, they sounded almos' as good as Mr. Peter's.

Well, I figured I owed him to talk good as him, or almost good as him. "Yes, sir," I said. "But my feet is fine. I never had no good shoes b'fore. They was always full of holes so I didn't wear them. I only weared them if I had to go through some bushes or walk on some rocks."

I was starin' at Joseph and I was wonderin' what he was thinkin' 'bout when he was starin' at me. He was quiet a long time and he was makin' me nervous.

~

Joseph stared at Sam and thought, *A long time ago I was where Sam is today. A brave, cocky, young man what ain't so brave. Nobody never heard me cryin' out in pain, no matter how bad the beatin'. Not even when the dogs got hold'a me on one of the farms I was at and my leg had to be cut off. That shore was some pain I had that time. I was determined that I wouldn't let nobody see me cry out in pain. That means weakness. All they seen was a strong man. Or maybe they thought I was stupid for not cryin' out.*

Then he said, "You have no worries here, boy, Mr. Peter, he is good to his Negroes. His workers are men and women and he ain't gonna tol'rate cruelty toward them by his overseer. Not that George would 'buse any of the workers, he's gentle as a baby cow. But don't you tell him I said so," Joseph said with a chuckle.

"Here he comes now. If you think you can work today, after you have your breakfast, he'll show you what to do. George said you can eat with me for a few days, unless you want to eat in the big hall with the other workers."

~

George sat on the stone step outside the door and waited while we ate our breakfast. He brought some awful-smellin' ointment to put on my feet. It smelled worse than what my Mam used to make. And that smelled purty bad, like rotten fish.

But I told him, "I don't need none of that stuff. My feet will heal by them selfs, they always does. I is ready to go to work."

They didn't always heal, I said that so him and Joseph wouldn't think I was weak. My Mam always used her special medicine she made from things she found in the woods and my feet got almos' better after a few days.

I saw George lookin' at my feet and he was prob'ly thinkin', "His feet look like old bark." And they did, too. They was really rough to feel, but they didn't hurt, not much, and anyway I was used to my feet achin', I didn't notice it mos' days.

Joseph just looked at my feet. I knew he didn't b'lieve me when I said that my feet got better by them self.

Before we went out the door, he said, "Put them shoes on your feet, boy. You ain't that strong. If you don't put somethin' on them feet, the way they is now, they is gonna get worse."

I nodded at Joseph, took the shoes from George and put them on. I didn't want to make Joseph angry cause he was right, my feet would get worse if I didn't have somethin' on them.

Them shoes felt good and they fit good! I never had shoes that I didn't have to tie on with rope b'fore. Prob'ly why I didn't wear them much, 'cept in the winter when it was cold.

I followed George to the door. Joseph said that I didn't have to worry, I would be safe on Mr. Peter's farm. It helped to calm me some, but I was still nervous cause I didn't know what the day was gonna bring.

19

It wasn't so bad here. George gave me my chores and I did my work. I wasn't no fool, though. I was always lookin' over my back cause I never knew when Master would come and say I was a runaway and I b'longed to him.

One day Mr. Peter told me that Master did come 'round to see him and asked if he had seen his runaway slave name of Sam. I freezed in my tracks till Mr. Peter said he told him there was no man by the name of Sam here, but he was free to look over his workers to see if his man was there. Master, he didn't come lookin' and I think it was cause everybody knew Mr. Peter to be a honest man and I learned that he would lie heavy to pertect his workers. I was glad for that cause Master, he left.

Now I know why George took me to the other side of the farm and kep' me there all day. They didn't want Master to see me.

"George, I is glad you took me way on the other side of the farm so Master couldn't see me."

George said, "I do what Mr. Peter tells me to do."

"I is glad he told you that or Master would'a been leavin' with me in his wagon."

George sighed. "Do you think Mr. Peter would'a let him take you? He would'a bought you from him first."

"He ain't gonna change his mind, is he?"

"You is still here, ain't ya? You been here long 'nough to know when Mr. Peter gives his word, he don't change it."

"George, can I ask you a question?"

"What kind'a question?"

"I didn't want to ask Joseph, cause I don't think he would'a told me. Was you a runaway when you come here? You talk better'n the other slaves what is here."

"I was a runaway, and when I come here my back was just like yours. All marked up from the whip. Where I was b'fore, master had a overseer, a big white man name of Bubba, who liked hurtin' the slaves. B'fore I left, two of the other slaves got tired of bein' beat on all the time, and one night when Bubba was makin' his rounds them two slaves set on him and crushed his head with a rock. They left him layin' in his blood and went back to their cabins. Nobody ever knew who done it, but I did, cause I seen them."

"George, I has 'nother question."

"You is full of questions today. What is it?"

"Joseph likes to make people think he's a stupid old slave, but he talks purty good for a slave. Did he learn to talk good from Mr. Peter?"

"No. The people what owned this farm before Mr. Peter bought it, the Mistress taught most of her slaves to read. He can't write cause he said 'what does I need to write for? Who is I gonna write to?' Is that all your questions?"

"For now."

"Okay. Now, let's get back to work."

~

I knew from the minute I met Joseph that we was gonna be friends. He was almos' like a Pap to me. No one could take my Pap's place and I hoped that one day I would see him and Mam and Sarrah again, but Joseph was as close to a Pap as I was gonna get now.

One night Joseph was sick in bed and I wanted to stay with him and help him with his supper, but he told me to have supper in the big hut with the other workers.

"I'm not much hungry tonight," he said.

I waited for a time cause I didn't want to leave him 'lone.

"I don't needs no babysitter. Now go," he said, but he didn't sound strong as he usu'lly does.

I was worried 'bout him, but I left him 'lone and went to the feedin' hut. There was some new workers there I never seen before. George said that sometimes some of the kitchen help comes down and has their food with the rest of the workers after they served up the food.

I looked 'round when the workers bringed in the supper and I seen a girl in a purty green dress with a white apron over it. Her long black hair was hangin' almos' to her waist. I couldn't take my eyes offa her. She was beautiful!

George seen where I was lookin' and said, "That's Miss Elizabeth. She works in the big house for Mr. Peter's family. She come to us a while back.

She was born free and needed a place to stay for a while, but I think she's gonna stay. We shore hope she does cause she's the cook and you tastes how good the food is you has been eatin'."

George must'a took pity on me, cause I couldn't find my tongue when that purty girl, she come to our table and put a plate in front of me. "Elizabeth Princes, this here is Sam. He bunks in with Joseph."

She looked at me and said, "Hello, Sam. I is happy to meet you."

I couldn't hardly find my tongue. All I could say was, "Ma'am." I never been 'round a lotta young women, 'specially none beautiful as Miss Elizabeth.

I watched her till she left the feedin' hut. A couple a' times I was shore she was lookin' back at me, but I could'a been wrong. She was prob'ly lookin' at somebody else. I wasn't purty to look at like some of the other workers was, so why would she wanna to look at me?

I jumped when George tapped me on the shoulder. "Man, I think Miss Elizabeth has took a shine to you. She keeps lookin' at you like you is lookin' at her."

"I ain't lookin' at her," I said, tryin' not to look, but my eyes, they had a mind a their own.

"Who does you think you is talkin' to, Sam? That's all you been doin' since you first set eyes on her. But that's okay. She shore is a looker."

I looked at George and balled up my fists. I would'a punched him if he had'a made a move to her. I would'a punched him right in the nose. And she wasn't even my girlfriend. But I shore was gonna try to make that so.

"Un-ball those fists, Sam. I ain't got no intrest in her. I is too old for her, anyway. She's only eighteen. I'd say you is too old for her too," George said to me with a smile on his face.

"I is only twenty-six," I said. "I is not too old for her. She wouldn't want me anyway."

"For someone who wouldn't want you, she shore is spendin' a lotta time lookin' at you."

I didn't say no more, but when I looked where she was, shore 'nough, she was lookin' at me. And she was smilin'.

~

Mr. Peter, he been good to all us workers. Not once did he have George take a whip or stick to us. If any of us did somethin' wrong, and it wasn't nothin' serious, we was gived a good talkin' to.

I only heard of Mr. Peter losin' his temper with one of his workers one time. He's a big man and if he gets mad and has to raise his fist cause one of his workers did somethin' bad, you don't want it to land on your face. It happened one time with a fella named William. With one blow Mr. Peter knocked him right out. He was layin' on the ground.

I wasn't there when it happened, I was workin' in the back field, but news travels fast on the farm and soon everybody was talkin' 'bout how Mr. Peter hit William and knocked him down. Nobody knew 'xactly what happened, but it had to be bad for Mr. Peter to raise his hand to a body.

When I went back to Joseph's cabin and told him what happened, Joseph said, "'Bout time."

"What you mean, Joseph? What did William do?" I asked.

"William is always mouthin' off, sayin' that Mr. Peter is like all the other white slave owners, tryin' to make his workers b'lieve he's a good man, then he sells his slaves to the highest bidder. He can't get it in that thick head a his that Mr. Peter don't own no slaves. William could'a left any time he want, but he didn't. Today it comed to a head. William and Anthony, 'nother worker, got in a argament an' they got in a fight. When Mr. Peter got there he put a end to the fight. Then stupid as William is, he made the mistake of mouthin' off at Mr. Peter and raisin' his fist.

"William, he was a runaway and he only been here 'bout six months. He been bought, 'bused, and sold three times b'fore he fin'lly runned away. Whips, sticks and once the dogs was used to try to bring him in line, but he fought his masters all the time. When George found him layin' in a field, the overseer on the farm he runned away from had whipped him so bad his back was bloody hangin' flesh. It took him weeks to get better, but Mr. Peter he's a patient man and he 'llowed him to heal good b'fore 'ssignin' him his work on the farm, if he wanted to stay. We don't know how he come far as he did beat up like that without dyin' in some-body's field. He was lucky he was found by George cause somebody else would'a took him back to where he come from. Then, he would'a been dead.

"Nobody knows William good. He always kep' to his self. The other workers tried to be his friend, but he doesn't want nothin' to do with them, so they leave him 'lone. Nobody knows what happened to set Wil-liam off. Somebody said it was cause Anthony wouldn't run away with him, but they doesn't git 'long anyway so that ain't it. They don't know, but I do cause George told me and if I tells you, don't you tell nobody else, or I'll whup you."

Joseph caught me starin' at him. "Whatcha starin' at boy? I got food in my whiskers?" he said as he wiped his hand over his straggly beard.

"No, no food," I said. "It's just I never heard you say more'n ten words at a time, is all."

"Maybe it's 'cause I ain't never had nobody I wanted to say more'n ten words to 'cept Mr. Peter, his Missus and George. Now, is you gonna keep starin' or is we gonna eat this stew b'fore it gets cold?"

"We can eat and talk and I promise I won't say nothin' to nobody. Tell me what all you know 'bout William."

"Get them plates on the table and I'll tell you."

I finished settin' the table then we sat down. We had us a big plate of beef stew in front of us, but we didn't talk till we ate some.

Then Joseph said, "Do you think Mr. Peter was wrong for hittin' William?"

I thought for a minute. "I don't know what William did so I can't say if Mr. Peter done him wrong. He must'a done somethin' real bad for Mr. Peter to hit him."

"In Mr. Peter's eyes, what William done was bad. You know that young pretty half-white girl named Betty?"

I thought for a moment then nodded my head yes. "I remember seein' her in the feedin' hut b'fore Miss Elizabeth come there the first time. She was purty, but I think she was younger than Miss Elizabeth. She was only there a coupl'a times then I didn't see her no more. She must'a stayed in the house to eat stead of comin' to eat with us."

"Well, from what George tells me, William thought he was free to do with her what he wanted. That's how it's done on other farms he was on. If you wanted a slave girl, you took her. If you got her with child, more babies for the Master to sell. Anthony went after William cause Betty is Anthony's sister. Mr. Peter, he won't tolerate no man who forces his self on a woman, don't matter the colour of her skin. Some of the new workers was gettin' 'fraid cause they wasn't shore about Mr. Peter, 'specially after he knocked William out. He told his workers they had nothin' to worry 'bout and that George was talkin' to William and he would be back to work the next mornin'. That is, if he was gonna stay, he had the say so on that. Mr. Peter don't force nobody to stay if they don't want to. But if William's got any smarts at all, he'll stay put or he'll be in the same fix he was b'fore he come here, cause Mr. Peter heard that William's owner was still lookin' for him sayin' if he ever caught him, he would whip him within' a inch of his life. Well, seems to me he already done that b'fore George found him in the field."

I listened to Joseph and wondered if William ever tried to get at Miss

Elizabeth like that. I could feel my blood gettin' hot just thinkin' 'bout it, but I didn't want to ask Joseph if he heard anythin' 'bout that cause just thinkin' that William did, I might'a said somethin' I shouldn'a said.

But Joseph, he knew somethin' was on my mind. Can't keep nothin' secret from him. "What is it, Sam? What's on you mind?" he said, puttin' a spoonful of stew in his mouth.

I just shrugged my shoulders, then I couldn't keep it to myself. "Did William ever bother Miss Elizabeth like that?"

Joseph laughed. "So that's how the crow flies, does it?"

"What you talkin' 'bout, Joseph? I never said nothin' 'bout crows flyin'."

Joseph laughed again then he said, "When you get to know Miss Elizabeth, you won't ask nobody that. Miss Elizabeth, she can take care of herself and if William ever got up in her face she would knock him down. She be one strong woman. I shore wouldn't want to tangle with her." He patted me on the back when he got up to get some coffee.

"Joseph," I said, "all she got to do is blow on you and you'll fall down."

"You gittin smart with me, boy? I can still put you on you back with one hit, iffen I wanted to. Don't let this one leg fool ya." Joseph said, tryin' not to laugh, but I could hear it anyway.

He looked at me and said, "Let's clean up them dishes, boy. Miss Elizabeth outdid herself today with this beef stew. It shore was tasty. Everthin' she makes is tasty."

He eyed me with more curiosity. "Boy, you takin' a shine to Miss Elizabeth?"

Joesph knew I was, why was he askin' me? I could feel my neck gettin' hot and I didn't want to look Joseph in the eye. I shuffled my feet in front of my chair and stared at the floor.

I could still see him outta the corner of my eye when he put his head to the side and said again, "I ask you a question, boy. You takin' a shine to Miss Elizabeth?"

"Maybe a little," I said so he could hardly hear me.

Joseph just looked at me. "You never had you self a girlfriend b'fore? Where you been, boy? You is twenty-six years old. What's the matter with you, don't you like girls?"

I stared at Joseph and my mouth dropped open. "I had a girlfriend once, but I ain't never had none like Miss Elizabeth. And me and that other girl, we was more like friends, is all."

Joseph stared at me. He seemed to do that a lot. "If you wants Miss Elizabeth, you has to court her cause she's a lady and you don't just pick her up and off you go."

He was makin' me nervous, just starin'. "Stop starin'. If I has to court Miss Elizabeth, I will."

"Do you know how to court a woman?" Joseph asked me.

I wasn't 'bout to tell him no, he would laugh at me. Well, maybe he wouldn't, but I wasn't tellin' him just the same.

I was with the other workers the nex' day when Mr. Peter come to talk to us again 'bout William. The men who was there b'fore I come didn't blame Mr. Peter for doin' what he did. They knew the kind of man he was and they knew what he would tol'rate and what he wouldn't, but it was the ones what ain't been here a long time who was 'fraid that Mr. Peter was gonna have them beat the way their other masters beat them, if they done what they shouldn'a done. But when he come to the big feedin' hut and s'plained what really happened, you could see the fear go away.

"You have nothing to fear from me," Mr. Peter said. "Do your work and show me the respect that I show you and everything will be fine. And, never raise your hand to me like William did, or the outcome will be the same. You are free to leave whenever you choose. You will not be stopped."

20

The first year I was with Mr. Peter, me and Joseph, we bickered and argerred and told each other 'bout some of things we each been through. I laughed at some of the things Joseph said he done on the farms where he was b'fore he come on this farm that he been on for a lotta years. Cause Joseph only had one leg, the masters would b'lieve Joseph 'stead of the overseer cause the things the overseer was sayin' that Joseph done, the masters didn't b'lieve that a one-legged man could do them things.

But I knew what Joseph can do. I seen the things that Joseph done here and I is still shakin' my head. Some of the other stories he told me was so crazy that nobody would'a b'lieved he done them. Not even me.

One time Joseph told me 'bout the time he climbed the ladder up to the hayloft in the barn and throwed ten bales of hay to the ground. "I was in a mood that day cause the overseer called me a stupid ole man and ain't nobody callin' me a stupid ole man. The overseer blamed one of the new slaves and was gonna take a strip offa his back with the whip when I grabbed his arm and told him I did it. He called me a liar and that's somethin' else ain't nobody gonna call me."

"What did the overseer do when you grabbed his arm?" I asked.

"He told me to climb the ladder and prove it. I told him I ain't doin' nothin'. The Master he come outta the house and he told the overseer that the slave couldn'a done it cause he was workin' in the back field all day and he was the stupid one if he believed I did it, even if I said I did. He looked at my leg, then at me, right in my eyes cause he know'd I done it, then he looked at the overseer and told him to go 'bout his business. He would get to the bottom of it and punish the one who did it. After the overseer left he told me I had to stop doin' what I was doin'. If the overseer don't cetch me, I is gonna break my dang fool neck."

I laughed cause I could see Joseph doin' it.

That night we talked for hours, 'till we was too tired to talk no more. But it was a good time cause the more time we was together, the more he reminded me of my pap. I was shore missin' my pap.

I was just startin' my second year on the farm when Joseph got sick. I was gettin' really worried 'bout him.

Me an Elizabeth was boyfriend and girlfriend now. Joseph was right, I had to court her, after I found out what courtin' her meant. George, he laughed at me when I asked him. But he told me what I had to do to make her mine. He must'a been right, cause now she's mine and ain't nobody else gonna have her. I can talk to her 'bout anythin'.

One night when we was walkin' 'round the farm I told her, "Liz, I is worried 'bout Joseph. I think he's sick. He don't say nothin' and when I asks him he says he's fine and stop frettin' over him."

"Have you talked to Mr. Peter 'bout it, Sam? If you is that worried, talk to Mr. Peter. If Joseph is sick he'll find out what's wrong."

"I knows you is right, Liz. One day I comed home and he was coughin' and he was spittin' up blood. Joseph, he said it was just a cold and don't tell nobody. He always kep' how he feels to his self. Sometimes he would send me to the feedin' hut, leavin' him 'lone. He would say, 'When I gits hungry, then I will eats.' When I got back to the cabin a empty bowl was on the table and he was sleepin' on his bunk and I cleaned up so he wouldn't have to. A few times he didn't eat nothin', and the food was cold in the bowl. I talked to George 'bout it and George said he would keep a eye on Joseph. I ain't heard nothin' from George and he prob'ly told Mr. Peter anyway. I'll wait to see if Joseph don't get no better, then I'll go to Mr. Peter, I don't care what Joseph says."

"You do what you think is best, Sam."

It was 'bout a month later, I was spendin' my evenin' with Elizabeth after supper like I usu'lly do. Joseph had been in good spirits for a coupl'a days. He seemed to be back to his old self. He was eatin' like he wasn't eatin' b'fore, but sometimes I don't think he ate nothin', just put 'nough food in the bowl to make me think he did.

I tried to get him to go to the feedin' hut with me, but he'd say. "You know I don't go to the feedin' hall, ain't been there for years. And why does you call it a hut? You ever seen a hut that big b'fore? You go, have your meal with Miss Elizabeth and then take her for a nice long walk by the river. When's you gonna ask her to marry you, boy? Mr. Peter, he can do it, he can marry folks."

I remembered that day and the talk we had. He sounded like my pap cause my pap would'a said the same thing.

"Joseph, I can't ask Elizabeth to marry me."

"Why not? You love her, don't ya?"

"Where is we gonna live? Mr. Peter ain't got no more cabins."

Joseph was silent for a minute. Then he said somethin' that set me back. "Well, when I is gone you can have my cabin. It's not big 'nough if you wants to have chillins, but it'll do till you gets your self a bigger one."

"Then that's gonna be a long time, cause you ain't a-goin' nowhere no time soon. So, we ain't gonna talk 'bout it no more."

Joseph never said no more. He looked at me, smiled and went outside to sit on his rock step cause his rickety old stool just falled over one day and he never got it fixed. It's a good thing he wasn't sittin' on it cause, like George told him, his ornery ass would be sittin' on the ground.

I left to go to the feedin' hall, cause Joseph said it ain't no hut, but I looked back at the cabin a coupl'a times. I had a uneasy feelin' in my belly. When I turned 'round, Joseph was still sittin' there, whittlin' that little piece of wood.

Me and Liz, we went for our walk like we us'ully does, and when I got back to the cabin I found Joseph layin' face down on the floor. I tried to wake him, but I knew, soon as I touched him, that he was gone.

I runned to the big house. "Mr. Peter, it's Joseph. I think he's dead. You gotta come quick!"

I runned outta the house with Mr. Peter right b'hind me. I knew I was runnin' fas', but Mr. Peter, he runned right on by me.

When George seen us runnin' he come a runnin' b'hind. He caught up with us when we was goin' in Joseph's cabin.

Mr. Peter got on his knees nex' to Joseph. As soon as he touched Joseph's cold skin, he knew he was gone. He kep' his hand on Joseph's chest and put his head down.

When he looked up at me and George, I seen tears in his eyes. "He's gone. Joseph's, gone. George, will you help me prepare him for his final resting place? I want the best for him."

I knew how close Mr. Peter was to Joseph, cause George told me one day when we was talkin'. Losin' his friend was gonna be hard for him.

"Mr. Peter, let me an' Sam take care of Joseph for you," George said. "You go on up to the house now, leave it to us. We'll take good care of him. Go on now. You gotta tell Missus Annabelle."

He put his hand on Mr. Peter's back and turned him to the door.

Mr Peter looked at Joseph one more time, then he turned 'round and walked outta the cabin. We never took our eyes offa him till he went in-side his house.

George said, "He loved that old codger, ornery as he could be at times. There was nobody who knew the farm and the best way to run it better than Joseph. When Mr. Peter bought the farm twenty years ago, Joseph already been here for thirty years before that. They had some loud arg'ments sometimes 'bout how things should be done, but Joseph wasn't gonna change his mind and Mr. Peter knew Joseph was right. He was new to farmin' and Joseph worked on farms for seventy years. He never told nobody how old he was cause he wasn't sure his self, but he thought he was 'bout eighty-five years old and only cause his Mamma told him how old he was when he was fifteen. He used to mark down every year so he would know how old he was as he got older. Far as Joseph knew he might even be older than eighty-five. Mr. Peter seemed to think so, too.

"Like clockwork Mr. Peter would visit with Joseph two or three times a week. They would talk 'bout farm business and he would ask Joseph what he thought of doing things this way or that. Joseph knew more 'bout the farm than it seems anybody did. Now, Joseph is gone. Mr. Peter is gonna miss his friend."

Me and George, we got Joseph ready for his buryin'. The workers was gived the day off to mourn for Joseph.

The day of his buryin' there was singin' and preachin' and prayin'. It was nothin' but the best for Joseph, surrounded by his friends. Some of the newer workers they was s'prised cause no slave is 'llowed to mourn a dead slave. It didn't matter if it was your family, the work still had to get done. There was no special burial, dig a hole, build a wood box, put the body in, and cover it over. No time for grievin'.

But for Joseph, Mr. Peter had a special box made outta a special wood and he 'llowed his workers to cel'brate their friend. Them new workers, they couldn't get it through their heads that on Mr. Peter's farm, they wasn't slaves no more.

21

I was happy for the first time since I was old 'nough to remember. I been with Mr. Peter three years now and for the firs' time since I was borned, I wasn't a slave. We was free to leave any time, but I wanted to stay cause I had no wheres else to go. B'sides, I loved Miss Elizabeth and I wasn't goin' nowheres that she wasn't gonna be.

I wished Joseph was still here so he could see how happy we was.

Me and my Liz, like I called her, we was so much in love, sometimes it scared me.

She asked me, "Sam, why is you so scared? You is safe here, ain't nobody gonna take you away."

I told her, "I is scared cause I don't know if Master is gonna find me and make Mr. Peter give me back to him. George, he told me that Mr. Peter would buy me from Master b'fore he'd give me back, but I is scared anyway, cause you never know."

"Sam, if George told you that, then you don't have nothin' to worry 'bout."

I never said no more. I kep' them thoughts in my head since I been here and I never told nobody, not even Joseph. I was happy with my Liz, but I was still scared that we would get sep'rated.

One day when I got home from workin' in the back field, I went in my cabin and Liz was there. It was my cabin now cause, after Joseph died, Mr. Peter, he said I could have it if I wanted it cause I been livin' with Joseph up till he died.

I looked 'round the cabin and I never seen it look like that b'fore. I think Joseph would'a maked all kinds of noises if he could'a seen them fancy curtains and the covers on the table and the cot.

Cot? There was only one cot, but when I looked, it was the two that was there put tagether to make one. I never said nothin' cause I didn't know what to say.

Liz was standin' nex' to the table and she had a big smile on her face.

"Liz?"

"Sam?" she said, still smilin' at me.

"How come you did all this? I never seen it look so clean and ...purty."

"Don't you like it,?" she said.

When I looked at her hands, she had them tight tagether in front of her. "I loves it, but why did you do this? For me?"

"For us, Sam. I did it for us. I is movin' in with you, with Mr. Peter's blessin's,"

"Mr. Peter said it's okay?"

"He did. I love you, Sam, and I want to be with you in our own cabin."

I runned over to her and picked her up and swinged her 'round. We laughed like little young'uns playin' in the yard. I guess that was the night that our Jenny was made.

~

We been livin' together for almost two years and our little Jenny was walkin' and gettin' into all kinds of mischief. She had more energy than me and I spoiled her even when Liz told me not to. She said spoilin' was okay sometimes, but not all the time.

I said to her, "Liz, what does slave young'uns have that makes them laugh and be happy? They is sometimes sold when they is babies and their life is over. We has to give our Jenny and other young'uns we has somethin' to smile 'bout, if only for a little while."

Liz looked at me then she said, "Sam, you is forgettin'. You ain't no slave no more and our Jenny she was borned free, just like me."

"I was forgettin', cause it's hard to forget when you is born a slave and that's all you knows. I ain't gonna forget no more."

When Liz went to work at the big house, she took Jenny with her. Mr. Peter and Missus Annabelle, they spoiled Jenny more than I did cause there was only the two of them. Missus Annabelle, she couldn't have no babies of her own so she spoiled all the workers' babies. When Jenny was bein' born, she was right there helpin' the midwife.

She had to do it by herself for a coupl'a the other women on the farm when the midwife couldn't get there in time, so she would'a knew what to do if she was by herself when our Jenny was born. And she helped my Liz till she was well 'nough to go back to work in the big house. I think she wanted to take care of Jenny.

We was happy. We was. But it didn't seem like 'nough for me. I knew Liz didn't feel that way and I seen her watchin' me sometimes. She knew somethin' was botherin' me and one night after we had our supper and Jenny was asleep on her cot, she took me by the hand and we went outside and sat on the rock that was our front step. The same rock that me and Joseph used ta sit on day after day, tellin' jokes, talkin' farm business or him whittlin' away at that little piece of wood while I kept waitin' for him to cut his finger off.

Liz said, "Sam, why don't you make us a nice wooden step, 'stead of us havin' this old rock?"

"This was Joseph's step and I wants somethin' else to remember him by b'sides my memories. When I got to the cabin after I was done my chores, and we ate our supper, me and Joseph we would sit on that rock and talk 'bout all that was done that day. It's all I got that was Joseph's."

I think she seen how 'portant the rock was to me. She said, "Okay, Sam, we'll keep Joseph's rock."

Tonight the moon was full and the stars seemed to be twinklin' just for us.

She laid her head on my shoulder. "Is somethin' wrong, Sam?"

I didn't say nothin' right off, then I said, "Liz, does you want to stay here for the rest of your life?"

"What does you mean? Here we is free. What more could we want? Mr. Peter is the kindest man. He always gived us anything we asked for. And Missus Annabelle helped us when Jenny was born. Where would we go, Sam?"

I could hear fear in her voice. She prob'ly thought I wasn't happy, but someday I wanted a house and a farm for us.

"I been hearin' that ships is gonna be leavin' from New York and travellin' to a New Land 'cross the water. They'll take anybody on them ships who can prove they is free and has a special pass."

"How can you prove that you is free? You is free livin' here with Mr. Peter, but you is a runaway. If your old Master hears 'bout that and wants you back, he might find you in New York. He won't give you no paper sayin' you is free."

"I is behind British lines, now,, and that means I is free. I'll get a paper somehow."

I could see that she was 'fraid of what might happen if we leaves Mr. Peter's. She could get that special pass to this new land cause she was borned free and she got her papers that says so. I said I would get that paper somehow, but how is I gonna get it? Maybe Liz, she don't want to go to this New Land.

She was starin' at me. "Is this what you want to do? Where you want to go?" she asked, her voice shakin'.

"I want a big house for you and me and Jenny and more babies. This cabin ain't big 'nough now and there ain't no bigger ones on the farm. Liz, I always dreamed of bein' a free man, havin' a wife and many babies that nobody can take from us. I wants that more than anythin'. And I wants my fam'ly to be safe."

We never said nothin' for a long time. Then she said, "We'll talk to Mr. Peter tomorrow. Sam, I ain't never told you 'bout my family, did I?"

When I shook my head, she said, "I ain't seen my Papa and Mamma and brother for almos' five years. My Papa, Prince, he has his papers cause he bought his freedom from his master, a man named Stokes. He worked hard and saved his money for a lotta years b'fore he had 'nough money. My Mamma, Margaret, and my brother, Nicholas, they was born free like me. I wish I could see them again. I miss them so much. Sam, has you heard of any other fam'lies that is gonna go on them ships?"

I know she was hopin' that maybe her Papa and Mamma's names was said, but I couldn't tell her that.

"No, I don't know who the people is. I only heard that there was gonna be a lotta folks goin'. Is you hopin' your fam'ly is gonna be in New York?"

"Yes, I is hopin', but how is we gonna get there? Is we gonna walk? Sam, maybe your Pap and Mam and sister is gonna be there, too. Won't that be somethin' if we was all tagether again?"

"It would be somethin' wouldn't it, Liz?"

I think Liz maybe seein' her family again was all the convincin' she needed.

The next day we went to see Mr. Peter. He listened to what we was sayin'.

"I think I knew this day was going to come," he said. "But I wished it were later instead of now."

He looked at us. "Your whole lives have been one battle after another, but, Sam, I can understand why you would want to settle in a New Land where you wouldn't have to be forced to fight and where you would be safe. I want what's best for you and your family. As long as you are sure that this is what you want."

Me and my Liz we looked at each other, and she said, "Yes, we is shore. Thank you, Mr. Peter."

Mr. Peter put his hand out to me, I didn't know what he wanted. Was I s'pposed to give him somethin' to let us go?

But he laughed. Then he took my hand and shook it up and down. I kep' shakin' his hand and it was a wonder his arm didn't fall off, I was shakin' it so hard. Nobody ever shook my hand b'fore. I liked it. I knew my smile was wide as my face.

Me and Mr. Peter, we laughed, and when we looked to our women, we seen tears runnin' down their cheeks. It was gonna be hard to leave, but it was time.

22

We didn't know when we was gonna leave, but we thought it best we wait till after winter, cause where was we gonna stay? We'd have to find lodgin's and if other Blacks was there lookin' to go on them ships, how was we gonna find some place to live?

Mr. Peter, he said. "I hear the ships are going to start leaving in early spring, maybe March."

"What is we gonna do, Mr. Peter?"

"If you leave a month before, you should be alright, because it should only take a few days to get to New York from here and that will leave you with plenty of time to get yourselves ready for when the ships are leaving."

"What is we gonna do if we has a lotta snow?"

"I wouldn't worry too much about that right now, Sam. That's still a ways off. You don't have your papers that say you are free do you?"

"No, I doesn't and I don't know how I is gonna get me some."

"When the time comes, Sam, I'll take care of that. I have a good friend who lives in New York and he will look after you when you get there. You don't have to worry."

But I was gonna worry!

We had to start gettin' ready for our trip. It might'a been months away, but we was gonna need all the money we could save. Mr. Peter, he paid us workers real money. He said that was cause we wasn't his slaves, we was his hired help.

He told me one day, "Sam, if you want to do extra jobs, I can pay you a little more money. It wouldn't be much, but it will help."

"Yes, Sir, Mr. Peter, I can do the extra jobs you wants done. Thank you. You is a nice man, Mr. Peter."

~

Every time I got paid, when I got to our cabin, I would go to my special hidin' place where I kep' a old coarse bag to put my coins in. Then I would shake the bag. Liz would laugh at me every time.

"What is you laughin' at, Liz?

"Sam, you does the same thing every time you puts coins in that bag."

She was right, I does and I laughed with her.

It seemed like winter was never gonna go, but the day fin'lly come for us to leave. It was cold and George said we might get a late snow. I shore hoped not cause it might not be a long ways to New York, but I didn't want to do it in the snow. If it was only me and Liz, we could'a done it, but we got little Jenny now.

Mr. Peter and Missus Annabelle gived us clothes that was warmer than what we had and Missus Annabelle she had a basket full of food for us to take with us and Mr. Peter, he put some coins in my hand.

"What is they for, Mr. Peter?" I asked. "I didn't work today."

"It is a gift from me and Missus Annabelle."

I didn't know what to say cause nobody ever give me a gift b'fore.

I grabbed his hand and shook it. "Thank you, Mr. Peter. Thank you."

Me and Liz, we was happy we was gonna be startin' a new life where we wouldn't have to look over our backs all the time to see if somebody was gonna take us away and sell us. Liz might'a been borned free, but freeborn people, they was took and sold too. If you had a black face, you was gonna make somebody some money.

We was still sad to be leavin' our friends on the farm, but it was time. Mr. Peter shook my hand again and Missus Annabelle and Liz was holdin' each other and cryin'. And Jenny, she was standin' there wonderin' what all the fuss was 'bout.

"Papa, why Mamma c'ying?" she said in a voice that was too big for her little body. It made everybody laugh.

Liz picked her up and took her to Missus Annabelle for one last hug and kiss. "Mamma is sad cause we is leavin' Mr. Peter and Missus Annabelle."

"Why's we leavin'?"

I went over and put my arm 'round my Liz and baby girl. "We is goin' to a new land and have our own farm, a farm just like this one," I said.

"Oh," she said, not quite understandin' what I was sayin', but she knew it had to be alright cause her Papa said so.

"Kay," she said.

Mr. Peter, he told George to take his best horse and wagon to take us to New York. I was s'prised cause when me and George was talkin' b'fore he said, "I can only take you to the edge of the city cause we got word that Patriot soldiers is all 'round there and if I try to go in the city, they might stop us and who knows what they'll do. We has to be careful cause the Patriots is always waitin' to grab any Blacks they think is runaways and sometimes it don't matter if they is runaways or not, they'll take any Blacks and sell them."

But Mr. Peter, he told George to take us right to his friend who would be waitin' for us. He still didn't tell us what his name was, but every time he said 'my friend', he had a smile on his face. He must'a been a special friend to make Mr. Peter smile.

But George, he must'a knew who he was cause how else could he take us to him? Well, I wasn't gonna ask who he was. I guess we'll find out when we gets there.

We left Mr. Peter's and was on our way. We had to leave the trail sometimes to miss the Patriot soldiers, but George knew where to go.

One time they come out of nowhere, it seemed, and stopped us right in the middle of the trail. Liz was holdin' Jenny on her lap and she reached over and squeezed my hand.

"Where you people going? You got any papers?" one soldier asked.

George said, "I got their papers right here." And he took papers outta his shirt.

The soldier, he snatched the papers outta George's hand and it seemed like he was takin' a long time lookin' at them.

Then he looked at us. "You is slaves of Mr. John Moore?"

"Yes, Suh, they is," said George. "I belongs to my master, Mr. Peter Franklin."

What did George mean, me and my family is the slaves of Mister John Moore? Did Mr. Peter sell us? I opened my mouth to say somethin', but Liz squeezed my hand so hard it hurt.

I looked at her and she shook her head just a bit so I would know not to say nothin'. I was confused.

The soldier said, "Okay, you be on your way and no stopping till you get where you're going."

"Thank you, Suh," said George.

Then we was movin. When we was far 'nough away from the soldiers, I said to George, "Did Mr. Peter sell us to this Mr. Moore?"

"He didn't sell you to nobody, Sam. You knows better. How long you been with him? These papers ain't real, they is to get us to the city without bein' taken."

I didn't know what to say but, "I is sorry, George. I guess I does know

112

better, but I is scared."

"We is all scared, Sam, cause to some Patriot soldiers, all they think 'bout is tryin' to make some money by sellin' Blacks whether they is slaves or free. If we is lucky we won't see no more soldiers less they is British.

We had to sleep in the wagon two nights cause we couldn't keep the horses walkin' without restin' and we needed to sleep sometimes. George was tired, I could see it in his eyes, but he didn't say nothin'.

When we waked up in the mornin' after the second night we had us a little bit of the food that was left from what Missus Annabelle gave us.

George said, "We is almost there."

We got there without seein' no more soldiers. And we was lookin' for them. I looked all 'round and I could see a lotta black people and I wondered if they was waitin' to go on them ships too.

We got down from the wagon and George give Liz a hug and he shook my hand. I felt somethin' cold in my hand and when I looked it was coins that George gave me. I looked up at George's face.

George said, "I had a little money saved for a special day and I guess today is that special day."

"I can't take your money, George," I said.

"I didn't give you all my money." He laughed and closed my hand over the coins. "Just hang tight on it so nobody steals it."

I thanked George cause I knew it was no sense argerrin' with him. George give Liz one last hug, a kiss and a squeeze for Jenny then he grabbed me in his tree trunk arms and squeezed me so hard I almos' couldn't breathe.

George let me go and he was lookin' up the road. Who was he lookin' at? I wondered. Was the soldiers comin?

George had a big smile on his face when he seen some people comin' our way. Liz seen them too and she gave a shout and she started runnin' with Jenny in her arms. She run right in the arms of the man and woman who was with the white man, squeezin' Jenny in the middle.

"Mamma, Papa, Nicholas," I heard her say.

Her fam'ly. They was her fam'ly! She was fin'lly with them again. I was so happy for my Liz.

George was standin' nex' to the tall white man and they was talkin'.

"Sam," George said. "This is Mr. John Moore, Mr. Peter's friend."

"Sam," Mr. Moore said. "I am happy to meet you. And he put his hand out to shake mine.

I shook his hand, but I didn't say nothin'.

"Sam," I heard Liz say. "This is my Papa and Mamma and brother."

Mr. Moore, he was starin' at me and he was makin' me nervous, just like Mr. Peter did when I first seen him. I turned away and went to Liz who was standin' nex' to George.

George put his hand on my shoulder and said. "I has to go now, Sam. Mr. Moore he will take good care of you if you lets him."

What George mean by that? If I lets him. I didn't want to see George go cause he was my friend.

"It's gettin' dark, George. How you gonna see where you is goin? Can't you stay and go tomorrow in the day light?"

"Yes, George," said Mr. Moore. "You can stay with me. I have plenty of room."

"I could see that George didn't know if he should stay cause he told Mr. Peter he would come d'rectly back and he said that to Mr. Moore. But when Liz grabbed him by his arm, he had to come 'long with us cause my Liz, she don't know what the word "no" means.

I said to her, "Liz, we best find us a place to stay, it's gettin' dark."

She turned and reached out her hand for her Papa. "Papa, this is my Sam. Sam, this is my Papa, Prince Princes. Papa told me that Mr. Moore is lookin' to hire more servants and he might be willin' to hire us."

She looked at Mr. Moore. "Is that right, Mr. Moore?"

"Yes, Elizabeth, it is."

He looked at me. "Sam, would you be interested in working for me as an indentured servant?"

I could feel my chest swellin' up with anger. "That's a slave and I ain't gonna be nobody's slave no more."

"Sam," said Liz.

"No, Liz. I ain't no slave no more."

George, he come to me. "Sam, does you want to get on the ships that is goin' to the New Land? Does you?"

"Yes, I does, but I ain't goin' as no slave."

"You won't be no slave, but you gotta have a paper sayin' you is free or you b'longs to somebody. Where is you gonna get one that says you is free?'

George was right. Where is I gonna get one? I is a runaway and if Master wants to get me back somebody will sell me to him.

I never said nothin' for a time. I looked at Liz to see what she wanted me to do. Her Papa, Mamma and brother, they all worked for Mr. Moore so he must be a good man. And if we was with him we'd have us a place to stay and food to eat. I had to think 'bout Jenny now. Me and Liz, we'd be alright, but our Jenny, she's a baby.

Liz put her hand on my arm and nodded.

"Sam," said Mr. Moore, "you will not be a slave. This indenture is a formality so all of you can go with me to Nova Scotia. Do you understand? I will release you and your family from the indenture as soon as I can after we arrive."

"Sam, does my fam'ly look like they is treated like slaves? They is happy. You got to do it, Sam, for me and Jenny. Please!"

Liz, she never asked me for nothin', but I still wasn't shore. I knew she was right. She wouldn'a asked me to do nothin' that would'a hurt us. I guess I knew what I was gonna do.

I looked back to Mr. Moore and said, "Thank you, Suh." Then I shook his hand.

"Thank you, Sam."

Mr. John, he had a big house; he must'a had a lotta money.

Me and Liz and her fam'ly, we was talkin' one night after supper and I asked Prince, "What does you know about Mr. John? He must have a lotta money to buy a big house."

"He didn't buy it, he is only rentin' it 'till we leaves. Other folks, they has to stay in them compounds that holds a lotta the British folk, but he said he ain't gonna stay there. He prob'ly got some money, but things, they wasn't always easy for him. He fight with the British and was taked prisoner by the Patriots. He lost most all his passessions and he tried to get them back, but they wouldn't give him none. So he is goin' to this Nova Scotia place like the other Loyalists."

"How does you know all this?" I asked.

"I knows cause I listens when people is talkin and they don't know I is listenin'."

"My Mam and sister they do that, but my Pap, he never hears nothin'," I said. "Not the good stuff anyway. Did you hear if Mr. John was mad cause they took his stuff? He don't seem to be. Me, I would'a been fightin' mad if they took my stuff, what little bit I got and wouldn't give me none back."

"I heard he said theys not much point bein' mad cause the British, they lost the war and he was fightin' for them."

I couldn't say nothin' to that cause I guess he was right. Not much point to fightin' the ones what won if it wasn't you.

I liked Liz's fam'ly. Her Mamma reminded me of my Mam, she seems to know everythin', but Liz's Mamma she's quiet most'a the time. And they loved little Jenny, their first grandbaby, and they spoiled her more'n

I did.

Liz tried to stop them, but they wasn't gonna listen to her. They told her, "You hush, she's our grandbaby."

Liz, she never said nothin' else. I laughed and she looked me in the eye with that look she gives me when she's gonna get mad. When she put her hands on her hips, I laughed some more.

"And what is you laughin' at, Sam?"

"I is laughin' at you, Liz. You is a mamma now, but when you Mamma tells you to hush, what you do? You doesn't say no more. They prob'ly spoiled you like they is Jenny."

I could see she was thinkin' 'bout that. When she looked at me again, she said, "I doesn't know if they did, Sam. I doesn't remember."

"I say they did or they wouldn'a been spoilin' our Jenny."

~

Spring was finally here and the ships was beginnin' to fill the harbour. Mr. John told us to get our stuff tagether cause we would be leavin' soon.

We had more'n we come with cause Mr. John and Missus Jessie, they bought us new clothes. I felt like a king with new britches and shirts and shoes. New shoes. I never thought I would see the day. Mr. Peter, he give me shoes when I first went there, but they wasn't new.

Cause I knew how to fix broken tools and do some carpenter work, I was hopin' Mr. John would 'llow me to do work for other people after I got his done so I could make money to get the wood to build a big cabin for me and Liz and Jenny.

We thought we was gonna be able to walk right on the ship when it was our turn, but we was told that all the Negroes had to be counted and their names put in a book. It would say what we looked like and who we was with. Mr. John told me that mine was gonna say that I was in his pos-session, but I was the property of Stoffle Van Nostrant of Acquackenack, New Jersey and I left him four years ago. That means I was a runaway.

I was scared and I told Mr. John, "If it says I is the property of Master Stoffle, can't he come and take me away? What is I gonna do if he comes?"

Mr. John looked me square in the eye and said. "Don't you worry, Sam. I have the papers that say that you are indentured to me. He can demand your return, but I will fight him if he tries."

And I knew he would. He was a lot like Mr. Peter. He would fight for his workers, too.

I was still worried cause some of the other runaways wasn't lucky. Some of their owners come and took them away, sayin' they owned them even if they didn't. There was one woman whose name was Elizabeth, like my Liz, but everybody called her Betty. A man named Thomas Smith went to some men who was s'pposesd to deal with slaves and they own- ers. He said Betty was his and she argerred that she wasn't, she was free. It didn't make no diff'rence, she was made to go with him.

I know she was gonna suffer bad for runnin' away. Poor Betty.

I never gived up hopin' that my fam'ly was gonna come and go on them ships and go where we was goin'. I asked all the black folks I seen, but nobody heard the name I said. They would'a remembered a name like Van Nostrant. I kep' hopin' that they was safe b'hind the British lines, but maybe they was captured and taken back to Master.

He got them now, he don't need me.

23

I couldn't wait to get on the ship. When it was movin', Master, he wouldn'a been able to get me.

But when we got on the ship we wasn't movin' nowheres. We was told we couldn't leave till everybody was on all the ships. We was on them ships what seemed like weeks. Might not a been that long, but it shore felt like it.

I heard one woman sayin' 'bout babies cryin' and it might make her crazy. Well, she must'a been crazy anyway cause babies cry. I remember how much my Jenny cried. Almos' blew my ears out.

The day finally come when we was told the ships was gonna leave. We was hopin' for good sailin' cause the captain said it was gonna take nine days.

There was a lotta ships, I don't know how many, cause I couldn't see all a them. But I was 'fraid that one was gonna hit 'nother one cause they seemed awful close together.

We wasn't far out to sea when a storm seemed to come outta nowhere. It was rainin' and the wind was blowin' somethin' fierce. The waves was goin' over the ships. We was scared.

One of the ships got caught bad and it sunk in them waters and nobody could be saved. We could hear the Blacks screamin' for help, but we couldn't help them. I wish I could'a helped them.

I got worried and scared that the ship we was on was gonna get sunk, too. Was we gonna die? The ship was shakin' and rockin' and I thought one time we was gone, but we must'a had us a good captain, cause he kep' us from sinkin'.

When we was almos' to where we was goin', 'nother ship got sunk. I heard talk that they was all disbanded soldiers, whatever that means. None of them could be saved either.

I was shakin' in my shoes. I didn't want me and my fam'ly to die. I didn't want nobody to die.

We didn't have no more storms and it was time to land. When we seen what we come to, we wondered if we was in the right place. There was nothin' but trees and rocks. There was no houses and no roads that I could see. Maybe on the other ships they could see more'n us, but I don't think so cause that's all I could see for a long ways. And there was snow on the ground.

What was we gonna do?

Mr. John, he told us not to worry, he would take care of us, but how was he gonna do that when there wasn't nothin' here? I think Mr. John better look 'round and see what we sees. Nothin'

We got offa the ship with the little bit of b'longin's we had and we was standin' on the dock starin' 'round at what wasn't there.

We watched some of the other folks run offa the ship like they was locked in it for months 'stead of nine days. Some of them falled on their knees and put they foreheads to the ground, right in the snow. They was happy to be offa the water, they didn't care if there was snow on the ground.

~

Me and my Liz and Jenny, we was one of the lucky fam'lies cause we got to stay in the town cause we was indentured to Mr. John. He didn't have a house like he did in New York, so we had to live in tents. That wasn't too bad cause it was better'n bein' outdoors. We didn't have no cots for sleepin', but we'd make do.

It's spring, but it's still cold outside. There ain't no stove, but maybe they'll bring us one so we can be warm. And how was we gonna cook if we don't get us a stove? I guess Mr. John will know all 'bout that.

Mr. John was gived supplies cause he was a Loyalist, and some other folks got some too. It was like heaven. They was gived bread, flour, beef, pork, butter, rice, oatmeal, peas, vinegar and molasses. I know Mr. John would give us some cause we was indentured to him. He wasn't gonna see us go hungry.

I don't know what the vinegar was for, but I is shore Liz would know. They wasn't gonna give us no rum like the white folk got, but we didn't need none.

I heard that some Blacks, who was slaves, their owner kept half their supplies for themselves. That ain't right. I'm glad Mr. John, he didn't do that.

Then he told us he didn't get the land he was promised and I think he was gettin' mad, but he didn't say nothin'. I never seen him mad and I don't want to cause I think cause he's quiet most'a the time, when he gets mad, he gets real mad. And I heard that nobody was gonna get no land cause the Gove'nor he wanted all the good land with the pine forest next to the harbour and it didn't matter if the white folks wanted to build there or not. What does it matter what kind'a trees they is?.

And cause we is indentured servants, fancy name for a slave, far as I can see, we can't get no land of our own. If Mr. John says we is free, then maybe we can get us a piece of land. I hope that is soon cause I wants my own land to farm on like I told Mr. Peter. There ain't nothin' like growin' you own garden and harvestin' the crops. I is gonna plant taters and cucumbers and carrots and anythin' else I can plant. But I has to make shore I plants crops that is gonna last all winter without goin' bad. That won't be good if that happens.

On Master's farm, sometimes I would sneak in the garden and get me a coupl'a cucumbers and carrots and have me a good feed. I was lucky I never got caught.

I didn't know what we was gonna do. We couldn't clear no land for Mr. John till he gets it and he didn't know when that was gonna be.

Well, we didn't have to worry too much 'bout that cause he come to me and Prince one day when we was clearin' the land 'round our tent.

"I think it's time for you and your families to be free. I was hoping you would be able to help me clear my land for a house and a garden, but our land grants have been delayed."

"Mr. John.' I said. "We can help you do that. We be right here, won't we?"

"I'm afraid not, Sam. All freed Blacks have to go to Birchtown. It's a village for Blacks, about six miles from here."

"We can still come and help you." I said. I was gettin' scared cause I didn't know nothin' 'bout this Birchtown."

"I won't be able to pay you."

I looked at Prince. He was starin' at Mr. John.

"Mr. John," he said. "does you know when you is gettin' your land?"

"I am told it might not be until next year."

"If we is still here," said Prince, "we'll help you when you gets your land. You bringed us here so we could be free, so it's only right that we help you some when you needs it."

I don't think Mr. John he knew what to say for a minute. He looked at Prince and said, "Thank you, Prince."

Me and Prince we turned and walked to our tents to tell our fam'ly. I didn't know what Liz was gonna say, but there's nothin' we can do. Blacks who is free has to go to Birchtown. That's what Mr. John said. We ain't wanted in Shelburne. White folks got no choice havin' us here when we was under Mr. John's care, but now that we ain't, we gotta leave.

It ain't right. I is just glad that it's almos' summer cause it's still warm.

I went in the tent. "Liz."

She just looked at me and she knew right off somethin' was wrong. "What is it, Sam" What's wrong? Is somebody hurt?"

"No, nobody is hurt."

I didn't want to tell her, but I better get it out cause if I didn't, her Mamma would come runnin' in and tellin' her. "Mr. John, he released us, we is no longer his servants, We is free. And your papa's fam'ly too."

"That's a good thing, Sam," she said, still starin' in my eyes.

"It's a good thing that we is free, but we can't stay in Shelburne. We has to go to Birchtown."

"Why can't we stay here?"

"The white folks, they don't want us here. All free Blacks has to go to their own village and that's Birchtown. It ain't gonna be easy for us. I don't know if they is gonna be a shelter ready for us when we gets there. We might have to build us one."

"Build us a shelter? Sam, how is we gonna do that? You gotta talk to Mr. John and ask him to sign us on again."

She stopped talkin' and just stared at me. I know my Liz and I know when she has somethinn' else she wants to say.

"Sam, I is with child again."

"Another babe, Liz?"

She nodded.

I had to talk to Mr. John. He had to sign us back on to work for him. I had to try to make him see that we needed him now that Liz was with child, but it wasn't like I was hopin'. He told me he can't. He never said no more.

If Mr. Peter knew that his friend, he ain't takin' care of us like he said he would, I bet he would'a found somebody else in New York to help us. But maybe Mr. John, he got no choice either, I don't know.

"What is we gonna do, Sam? What is we gonna do? We should'a stayed with Mr. Peter."

I put my arms 'round her. Maybe she's right. Maybe we should'a stayed with Mr. Peter. We had us a cabin, it was only little, but it was ours. And we had plenty of eats. Here we gets supplies, but they ain't gonna last forever.

What is we gonna find in this Birchtown? I was gonna ask some of the Blacks who lives there who comes to town to work.

I shore didn't like what I was hearin'. They said some folks was livin' in huts and the roof was tied tagether and covered with birch bark. And some was livin' in what is called pit houses. They is just a hole in the ground with a log roof over it. I ain't a takin' my fam'ly to live in them. A hole in the ground? We ain't animals that makes their home in the ground.

I was tellin' Liz and her Mamma and Papa, but Prince, he already knew what they was like cause he went there the other day and seen for himself.

"Why didn't you come for me? I would'a went with you." I said.

"I comed lookin' for you, but you wasn't here. Liz said you went to see Mr. John to ask him to sign us on as his workers again. Why you do that? I could'a told you he wasn't gonna."

"I do that cause my Liz, she is with child again. What we gonna do, Prince?"

"We is gonna go to Birchtown and we is gonna do the best we can. That's what we is gonna do. Not much point to worryin' over somethin' b'fore we is even there."

"You said not much point to worryin', but you didn't say what you seen. Is the shelters like I was told?"

"We'll get by, Sam. We'll help each other to build our shelters when we know what kind we want and what is best for us. We has to build shelters that will keep us warm in the winter. This is gonna be our first winter in the New Land and we don't know what it's gonna be like. We'll get by, Sam," he said again.

I knew we was gonna have to start gettin' our things ready to go to this Birchtown, but that didn't mean I wasn't gonna keep it clean 'round our tent and Mr. John's. I didn't mind hard work cause I knew there wasn't gonna be no whip at the end of the day.

In this New Land I could sing again. Even though we was gonna have to leave and I didn't have nothin'to sing 'bout, I was gonna sing. .

When I was cleanin' up 'round Mr. John's tent, I remembered a song some of the Blacks was singin' cause they was fin'lly gonna be free. I looked 'round to see who was there to laugh at me, then I said, "They can laugh all they wants, I is singin' anyway."

> Now farewell my Massa my Mis-sey a-dieu.
> More blows more strikes will me e'er take from you.

Or will me come hither or thither me go
no help make you rich by the sweat of my brow.
Yankee doodle Yankee doodle dandy. I vow.
Yankee doodle Yankee doodle how wow wow.

I near jumped off the ground when I heard someone b'hind me.

"Where you learn to sing like that, Sam?" said Prince.

"Where you come from? Don't come on a man from b'hind. You near scared me to death."

"You have a very nice voice, Sam," said Mr. John. "You should sing more often."

"Where you come from? You been hidin' in the bushes?" I asked him.

"Prince and I have been right here, over behind that pile of rocks," he said with a smile on his face.

Prince said. "That's not the whole song. How come you don't sing the whole song?"

"Cause if you knows the whole song, it says there won't be no more snow or mosquitoes or black flies."

"Well, that sure doesn't apply here," Mr. John said, laughin'. "I have the bites to prove it."

Me and Prince we laughed cause the black flies has been havin' us for dinner all week.

"Next time you sing it," said Mr. John, "will you sing the whole song?"

"Maybe," I said. But I said to myself, the next time I sing, I is gonna make shore nobody is 'round.

The nex' day I said to Prince, "Prince, I wants to go see this Birchtown for myself, b'fore we has to go there to live, but I can't see there will be much buildin' if some of them is only a hole in the ground with a roof over it."

"Okay, Sam, me and Margaret will go with you. She ain't been there, so we'll all go together."

We went and when we got there I got a big s'prise. There was a lotta black folks livin' there and a lotta them huts and pit houses all over. It didn't look like there was none that nobody lived in. We was gonna have to build our own.

When we seen how big some of them was, I said, "They is only 'bout five feet wide and not two feet deep. How's anybody gonna live in that? It looks like a grave, only it ain't deep 'nough. I ain't gonna live in that. When I digs ours it's gonna be a big one and it's gonna be deeper."

Liz, she was just lookin' and I seen the fear in her eyes. I was holdin' her hand and I could feel it shakin'.

"Liz, we is gonna have us a big one. Don't you worry none. And I is gonna have it on a hill cause it's dry up there and it'll be sheltered by the trees."

"We'll talk 'bout it later, Sam. Let's go back to Shelburne," she said, lookin' all 'round. "We still got us some days b'fore we has to come here. Is we gonna have any tools to help us?" She didn't sound like she was worryin', but I knew my Liz. I knew she didn't want me to worry 'bout her, but I will anyway.

"I was talkin' to Colonel Blucke who is in charge of the black folk in Birchtown and he said he was gonna get us what we need, if he can find some. The white folks has been takin' all the tools and wood soon as it's brought to Shelburne. But he's gonna try."

We went back to Shelburne. I said to Liz, "Tomorrow we is doin' nothin'. We is gonna go down to the harbour and see if 'nother ship is gonna come in."

"Sam, is you still hopin' that your Mam and Pap and sister is gonna be on one?"

"I is always hopin', Liz. I told them I would find them and I will."

"My Mamma will look after Jenny. What day is we goin' to Birchtown?"

"I guess we has to wait for Colonel Blucke to come and get us and bring us our tools."

24

My Liz, she was thankful every day for what we had now, even though we didn't have much. I think Liz, she just wanted to talk 'bout anythin' so she didn't have to think 'bout us goin' to Birchtown and livin' in a hole in the ground, a hole that looked almos' like a dug grave.

"Sam, remember the time I told you 'bout a slave owner's mistress who spit in the food that was left in the pot so the slave couldn't take the scrapin's that was in the bottom? It didn't make no-never-mind that most'a the time, the slave was hungry. She would'a ate what was in the pot, spit and all! She prob'bly ate worse."

"I remember you tellin' me. We is lucky, even though things ain't good as they was at Mr. Peter's. We is free and seems to me that's all that matters. We don't have to look over our backs cause we is 'fraid of bein' snatched up and shipped back to America or the sugar plantations in the West Indies. I think it's cause people still thinks we is indentured to Mr. Moore, so they don't dare take us. If we wasn't we might be snatched up too and you never know where you is gonna be sent. Some free Blacks wasn't lucky as us.

"Remember I was tellin' you 'bout that Dick Hill. He had his Certificate sayin' he was free, but he was snatched right offfa the street in Shelburne and put on a ship that was goin' to the West Indies b'fore he could be saved. A letter was writ sayin' that Dick was a free man, but b'fore it got to the captain the ship was way out in the harbour and the captain never got the letter. Least, they don't think the captain got it. I think maybe the captain got paid a lotta money to take him."

"You is right, some ways we is lucky, but I think from now on we is gonna have to make our own luck.'

"I think you is right, Liz. I think you is right."

Me and Liz, we set out to go to the harbour. It was a cool day when we sat on the end of the dock and watched a ship comin' in.

When the ship was tied up at the dock, I seen a young girl bein' pushed down the gangplank. I couldn't hear the words the man b'hind her was sayin', but I could tell they was angry words. I couldn't tell how old she was cause, with slaves, even young'uns looked older than they was.

I watched her and when she got closer, the look in her eyes when she looked at her Master said that she was gonna fight him every time. There was trouble ahead for her, I could see it. I wondered how she was gonna survive. She might'a had a Master, but I could see he didn't care much for her. She was gonna get what he wanted to give her and nothin' else.

I felt sorry for that child. I wondered when she was sold away from her Mamma. I don't know what I would'a done if our Jenny was taken from us. I think I would'a tried to kill them for takin' her.

I watched the ships unload their cargo of black folks. I was always hopin' to see my Pap and Mam and sister comin offa a ship. I was beginnin' to lose hope that I would ever see them again and I b'lieved in my heart they was captured and carried back to Master. I miss them so much.

But I wasn't gonna give up hopin'. I wasn't.

~

B'fore we went to Birchtown, things wasn't good for the Blacks who was free and livin' in Shelburne Town. They wasn't 'llowed to do nothin' for joyment. They couldn't dance or have parties or do the gamblin' and they wasn't 'llowed to drink no liquor.

Where they got the money for gamblin', I don't know cause the little bit I made doin' them odd jobs was to take care of my fam'ly. Maybe they didn't have no fam'ly. If they was caught doin' them things, they might'a been throwed in gaol.

They didn't have to worry 'bout me doin' none of them things, cause I wasn't gonna do them. B'sides, my Liz, she would'a hit me right upside my head.

We was almost ready to move to Birchtown. Me and Liz and Prince and Margaret was sittin' down talkin' 'bout what we was gonna do when we got there.

Prince said, "Sam, the first thing we gots to do is dig our pits. Maybe we should do that b'fore we moves there and gots no place to live."

"Will they 'llow us to do that?" I asked. "What if somebody says they is theirs b'fore we gets to move there?"

"I never thought 'bout that, but we still has to have us a place to live

126

till we gets them dug."

I didn't want to live in no pit, but my Liz, she said it might be warmer cause it's under the ground. I was still kind'a worried 'bout her, but that's what she wanted, so I'll dig one.

We didn't talk no more 'bout that, cause Prince he didn't like it either. He started talkin' 'bout somethin' else.

"Sam, remember the day me and Mr. John heard you singin'?"

"You can sing?" said Liz. "How come I never heard you?"

"You never heard me cause I never singed where you was and I didn't have nothin' good to sing 'bout."

"What you mean you never had nothin' good to sing 'bout? You had me, didn't you?"

"You is my good thing, Liz, but when you is a slave and you thinks you is gonna always be a slave, you don't think you got nothin' good."

She never said no more.

Prince was gonna say somethin' else when we heard music comin' from outside. We went out cause we thought some of the town Blacks was havin' them selfs a party and was gonna get throwed in gaol like they always does, but it was the white folks all dressed in fancy clothes who was havin' them selfs a big party.

All 'round the tents and trees and other bushes they had fires made, so they could see what they was doin', I guess. They better watch out they don't set fire to them. They was singin' and dancin' and drinkin' plenty of liquor. Boy, if that was us black folks, we would'a been in plenty trouble.

"What they havin' a party for?" I asked. "They didn't ask us to come. A party ain't no party without black folks showin' them how to sing and dance."

"You gonna sing and dance, Sam?" Prince asked me, and he was laughin'.

We had us a good laugh 'bout that.

I still wondered why they was havin' a fancy-dress party. What was they celebratin'? We listened to the music and watched them dance and some of the men falled down cause they was so drunk they couldn't stand on they own two feet. We went back inside the tent cause it was a pitiful sight to look on.

The nex' day I heard Mr. John say that they was celebratin' the King's birthday. I is glad they didn't ask us to come. I wouldn'a celebrated the King's birthday. What did he ever do for the black folks, but sell them as slaves? Black folks don't talk 'bout that and maybe some of them don't know 'bout it.

~

We been in Birchtown since b'fore the big riot. Me and Liz and her Mamma and Papa, we got us our pit houses made. Liz said it would keep us warmer in the winter cause it's below ground, but I don't know 'bout that.

We had us a lotta hard work to do to get our pit dug. We didn't stay in Shelburne cause we knew somebody was gonna say that the pits we was diggin' was theirs. We wouldn'a blamed them, cause they didn't have no more'n we had.

A man and his woman let my Liz and Jenny stay with them till our pit house was ready. They didn't have a lotta room, but they was older folks and they didn't mind helpin' out.

Me and Prince, we worked till our fingers was sore and we could hardly hold the shovel. Cause Liz was with child, he wanted us to get ours ready first.

Liz, she wanted to help, but I asked her, "What is you gonna do, Liz

"I can dig."

"You is with child, you can't do no diggin'."

"I is with child, but I ain't sick no more."

I remember her bein' sick when she first got with this child and it wasn't a purty thing to see. She never got sick like that with Jenny. I was kinda worried and scared that somethin' might happen to my Liz. I just stared at her.

"Sam, you let me help or I'll smack you."

And she would'a, too.

"Okay, but don't you go liftin' the bucket when it's got dirt in it. You just put it in the bucket a little bit at a time and me and Prince we'll come an' get it. And if you gets tired, you stop."

"Sam!"

That's all she said. I knew the way she said my name she was gonna get mad at me. I never said no more, but I watched the dirt she was movin'.

My Liz, she was a hard worker. She filled the wooden bucket to the top then she called me or her Papa to empty it. And she knew where she wanted some of it to go.

"Sam, empty this bucket over there nex' to the wall so's we can make us somethin' to sleep on. We ain't got us no beds so we has to make some. I wonder," she said, "do we make us a bed for each of us, or one big one so's we can be warmer in the winter time?"

She was standin' there with her hands on her hips and her belly stickin' out.

"I think only one," I said. "We'll be warm that way. And with a baby comin' in the winter, we has to keep our selfs warm the best we can."

"Okay," she said. "You is right, but we don't want to make it direc'ly cross from the door openin' cause the wind might blow right in. You see what side is best, Sam. If you ain't shore, you can ask somebody who lives in one already, cause they'll know."

Then she went back to diggin'.

After a little while I made her rest. She would'a worked 'longside us all day, but I seen her put her hand to her back a coupl'a times.

"That's 'nough for today. You is gonna get too tired, but you did good. You did real good."

"Okay, Sam. I'll do some more tomorrow."

Maybe she will and maybe she ain't. I is gonna talk to her Mamma, Margaret. She'll know what to do. And if we can, me and Prince will have all the diggin' done our self, if we has to dig all night.

Liz, she didn't do no more diggin'. Margaret, she took her daughter to hand and Liz, she ain't gonna do what her Mamma says she can't do.

Them folks what took my Liz and Jenny in till we got us a shelter built, they lived in one of them huts made of grass and plants and it must'a been mud, looked like, and it was covered with birch bark. It didn't look like it would be too warm, 'specially when the wind was blowin'.

Liz, she asked them, "How come you didn't dig your self a pit house?"

They said, "We is gonna be in the ground soon 'nough without livin' in a hole in the ground."

"Is your hut warm?"

"It be okay now cause it be warm out, but we ain't never bin in it in the winter."

Margaret said she was in it the other day when the wind was blowin' and it was comin' right through the walls in some places. If that's so, they is gonna freeze in the winter time. I talked to Prince and me and him, we is gonna try to fix it so the wind don't come in. They helped us, we is gonna help them. It's only right.

Me and Prince, we got 'nough logs cut for mine and his pits. It took us a long time cause we only had us a hatchet. Colonel Blucke said the white folks took all the big axes. But that's okay, cause the hatchets, they was sharp.

We had to make sure we got us 'nough moss and grass and mud to put b'tween them so's the rain and wind and the snow don't come through. Prince, he knew how to mix the mud and moss and grass so it was good and strong when it dried. Liz, she was s'prised when she seen what we done.

We built under the trees so we would have some pertection from the wind and snow. Liz, she was a smart one when she told me to make piles of dirt that looked like a bed cause we didn't have no beds, and we used the rocks we moved from the land to make us a fire pit so we could cook our food and keep warm.

We was ready to move into our pit. Liz, she made it as comf'table as she could. We had us some quilts cause, Mr. John, what he give us when we was livin' in a tent next to his, he told us we could keep. Cause we only made us one big bed, we might be warm in the winter.

I don't know where Colonel Blucke was. We never seen him after he brought us the buckets, shovels and hatchets. Somebody said he was buildin' his self a big fancy house. I bet people was wonderin' where he got the money or wood boards to build his house. I bet he had his self some big axes. He wasn't gonna use no little hatchet.

25

We been livin' in Birchtown for a time. I knew it was dangerous to go to town cause there was white soldiers there tryin' to find work, too, but I had to have me some work so I could get us some food.

Them soldiers, they got it in their heads that they didn't like us Blacks and didn't want us there cause we was gettin' all the jobs. We would work for a little bit of money and they wanted more. They didn't like that. No, siree.

I heard one soldier tell his friend that he made more money in the war than they is makin' here. Well, we ain't in the war no more and they can't s'pect to make the same money.

Most of them soldiers, all they know was how to fight and we learned how to fix tools and do carpenter work and cut wood. And some of the other Blacks, they knew how to build buildin's with real boards.

I wish I knew how to do that. I can do a little bit a carpenter work, but I can't build no buildin's. Maybe someday.

I was almost to Shelburne when I seen some white men wavin' sticks and muskets and some of them had them big hooks offa the boats. They was headed straight for Preacher George's house.

I ran and hid b'hind a tree and watched them put ropes to the poles of his house and down it come. Then they tore down the shelters of the blacks what was built on the preacher's land. They beat some of those Blacks who couldn't run away fast 'nough, somethin' fierce.

The Blacks who was bein' chased outta Shelburne started runnin' my way, I knew where they was goin'. Birchtown. There was no place else for them to go.

I turned and runned for home. Some of them was runnin' right by me. I never seen nobody run fast as that b'fore.

I runned fast as I could to get home, I didn't want them crazy white men gettin' at my Liz and young'uns. My John, he was but six months old.

I seen Liz comin' down the hill from where our pit was and I hollered loud as I could, cause there was so much yellin' and hollerin' b'hind me, she might not hear me. "Liz, get back in the pit. Get back in the pit. There's some crazy white folks comin' and they is beatin' on all the black folks they see. Get in the pit and hide."

She seen them comin' b'hind me and she runned with the young'uns back up the hill and in the pit. I wasn't gonna go up cause they already seen me, but I don't think they seen Liz and our young'uns. I was hopin' they couldn't see our pit 'mongst the trees. I runned the other way so they wouldn't go after my fam'ly.

Them white men, they meant to kill us if they could, I know it. They was runnin' some fast, swingin' their weapons over their heads and yellin'.

B'fore I knew it, two of them was on me. One of them had a long gun and I thought he was gonna shoot me, cause I heard shootin' b'fore, but 'stead, he hit me upside my head.

I fell down on the ground, holdin' onto my head. I knew it was cut cause I could feel blood runnin' down my face.

He kep' hittin' me with the gun and the other man, he was kickin' me in the back and in my side. He even stomped on my legs. I guess he wanted to cripple me so I couldn't go to town lookin' for work no more.

I fight like I never fight b'fore, but I didn't have the strength to fight them off. I was hollerin', but they was hollerin' louder.

"Die, you nigger bastard. Die."

They was 'termined I was gonna be dead when they was done with me, but I wasn't gonna die. I wasn't. All I could think 'bout was my Liz and our babies. What is they gonna do if I ain't there for them?

I figgered it wasn't much point to fightin' them no more, so I just laid still as I could, hopin' they would think they killed me. They must'a thought they did cause they left me layin' on the ground. One of them kicked me again b'fore they went runnin' after somebody else.

I knew my cut was bleedin' bad and I had me some broken bones. I couldn't move cause I was in a lotta pain.

I waited till it was quiet 'round me b'fore I opened my eye that wasn't closed shut where they pounded me in the face. I didn't see nobody and I didn't hear no more yellin'.

I tried to crawl up the hill to our pit, and Liz come runnin' down the hill. I didn't see her at first and I thought it was them men come back for me when they seen me movin', but it was my Liz hollerin' when she seen me.

I looked at my Liz and she had a big iron pot in her hand and she was wavin' it over her head.

I tried to smile, but my face, it hurt too much. I don't know if she heard me, but I said, "What you gonna do with that pot, Liz?"

She just looked at me like I was crazy. And I was. Crazy in pain.

"Sam. Sam. What they do to you?"

"I is hurt bad. I think some of my ribs is broke and my head hurts somethin' fierce. My legs, they be painin' too, but I think I can walk."

"Stay still. Let me see how bad you is hurt."

We heard somebody comin' and Liz, she grabbed her pot and was gettin' ready to fight whoever it was, but she seen it was Prince and Margaret and she put it down.

Prince, he kneeled down b'side me. "They shore did a job on you, boy. We is gonna get you up the hill and in your pit. Can you walk?"

"I don't know, Prince. They stomped on my legs. I think they wanted to cripple me."

I tried to get on my feet when Prince and Liz was helpin' me to get up, but the pain was so fierce I cried out. I felt like I was dyin' all over again.

"I guess I can't walk, Prince. I feels like I wants to die."

"Don't you die on me, Sam. Don't you die on me," Liz said.

Her hands, they was warm when she put them on my face. They felt so good, but that's all I remember cause I must'a passed out. It was almos' two days, Liz told me, b'fore I waked up.

"Is I dead?" I asked. "Is I dead? I is lookin' at a angel. I must be dead."

"No, you ain't dead, Sam. I wasn't gonna let you die. My Mamma and Papa, they helped take care of you. We was worried when you wasn't wakin' up, but you kep' callin' for me in your sleep and we knew you was gonna be okay cause you wouldn't leave us to be 'lone. I was scared, Sam. I was scared."

I tried to sit up, but it hurt real bad. It felt like them white men, they was still beatin' on me. I put my hand to my head and felt a rag tied 'round it and there was rags tied 'round my chest.

We had to learn to be our own doc, cause if the white folks that we worked for wasn't gonna help us when we was bein' beat on, they wasn't gonna doctor us. We has us a doc in Birchtown, Mr. John Brown, but he was tendin' to so many of us Blacks what was hurt by them white men, he couldn't come to me. My Liz and her Mamma and Papa did good as any doc could'a.

The riots wasn't over. Some of the Blacks who went lookin' for work after was beat if they was caught 'lone and the white folks even come to Birchtown again and pulled down some of the shelters. I was glad we lived in a hole in the ground cause there was no walls to tear down. Our roof was tore up once, but we fixed it.

We didn't know when the white folks was gonna stop beatin' up on us black folks. Then more soldiers come in and I said, "Oh, oh, we is in for it now." But they was there to stop the other soldiers what started the riots from beatin' up on us.

That shore looked funny. White folks stoppin' white folks from beatin' up on black folks. Never thought I would see the day. But it was good, cause the riotin' stopped.

My legs, they is healin, but it seems like it's takin' a long time. I didn't think they broke nothin' but they must'a. They jumped on one of my legs hard and the pain was somethin' fierce.

I couldn't put one foot on the ground to walk for almos' two months, and when I did, I had me a limp. My left knee it was still swelled two times bigger than my other knee and it still hurt real bad.

I had to use a walkin' stick and somebody had to walk b'side me for a time cause I would'a falled down. If I did, I prob'ly would'a broke it again.

Liz, she was always tryin' to stop me and tellin' me to sit down. "Sam, you can't go to workin' for nobody. Not yet. Your leg ain't healed. Sit down for a spell and rest."

"Liz, I ain't sittin' down. Who is gonna get us money so we can buy food?"

"I will get 'nough food for all of us," said Prince as he come through the door. "Margaret is in the woods now lookin' for what she needs to make the medicine for your leg."

"Margaret? What does she know 'bout makin' medicine?"

"She used ta make it all the time for me when I got hurt. If she can find what she wants she can fix your knee up right good."

I didn't say nothin', but I didn't think she knew how to make it like my Mam. "Prince, where's you gonna get 'nough work to get food for all of us?"

"Don't you worry 'bout that, boy. You just worry 'bout gettin' better."

But I wasn't gonna let my legs keep me from doin' what I wanted to do. Days when I was feelin' down, cause of the pain, I thought 'bout my friend Joseph and how he must'a had a lotta pain when his leg got cut off. Havin' one leg never slowed him down none and I wasn't gonna let nothin' slow me down. I got me two legs and when my bad one is better so I don't need nobody to walk with me, they is gonna take me where I wants to go. If I got pain, then I got pain. Shore wouldn't be the first time.

Margaret, she found what she needed to make her medicine. I don't know what she put in it, but it shore smelled bad. It smelled almos' worse than what my Mam made.

"It don't make no never mind how bad it smells, it's gonna make the swellin' in your leg go 'way," she said.

Margaraet's medicine taked the swellin' down, but I is still walkin' with a walkin' stick and sometimes it hurts bad if I walk too far, then it swells again. I think I is always gonna have a limp, but's that's okay. Least, I is still livin'. I shore thought I was gonna die that day.

~

We thought it was gonna get better, but with all the Blacks livin' in Birchtown now and all of them lookin' for work same as us, how was we gonna find jobs? And where was they all gonna live? They ain't a gettin'' my house. It's just big 'nough for my fam'ly.

After the riot, Preacher Mr. George, he come to live in Birchtown too, what was left of it. He was goin' from hut to pit tryin' to do his preachin'. Some folks let him come in and some of them sent him a runnin'.

Liz, she didn't like me chasin' him off. "Why you send him away, Sam? You know we ain't 'llowed in church in Shelburne. If he can give us a church where we lives, that's good."

"I don't like him," I said. "But if you wants him to come here with his preachin', if I sees him again I'll tell him he can come. But I ain't stayin' when he does."

She didn't arger with me, she just said, "Okay, Sam."

26

It ain't got no better for us. We is free, what we wasn't b'fore, but we ain't got much as we had when we first come here. We been here a while now, but I don't know how long, cause one day is the same as the other.

We didn't have us much food and people was gettin' sick all 'round us and some was dyin'. Some of the Blacks got the small pox, that was ugly to see. They had some bad sores on their face and body and I had to keep away from them so I didn't get it and bring it home to my fam'ly.

I forgot to say that my Pap, Mam and sister come to Birchtown. That was a s'prise. He was here when the small pox was and he got it and he was sick. I don't know how come Mam and sis didn't get it, but they didn't. I stayed away from my Pap for nigh on three weeks, till he was better. That was a time.

When we was gettin' supplies from the British, we was only gettin' half the supplies we was gettin' b'fore and to get them we had to work almos' a week. The white folks only had to work two days. It wasn't right, but I guess it was cause we had brown faces. Makes me mad sometimes, but I can't do nothin' 'bout it. Now, we ain't gettin' none and folks is doin' what they gotta do to have food in they bellies.

We was all poor. Real poor. Some of the Blacks in Birchtown was indenturin' them selfs to the white man. I was gonna work much as I could and hard as I could cause I wasn't gonna sell my self to no white man to be his slave for no time. That would be what you is, his slave.

Some of us was lucky, we had us a trade. I knew how to fix farmers' tools cause my friend Joseph, he teached me, and I can do some carpenter work. I was a little bit slow learnin', but Joseph, he was patient. He smacked me up side my head one time, he said I wasn't payin' 'ttention. I shore did after that time.

Pap, he could fix tools too cause he learned it on Master's farm. And Mam, she could sew and fix clothes for people and she cleaned houses when they wanted somebody to clean their dirt.

I asked Mam one time, "Mam, why does you want to clean those white folks dirt?"

She looked at me and said, "If they is too lazy to do it they self and they wants to pay me, I'll clean for them. I prob'ly cleans better than them anyway."

Sometimes it didn't matter if you could do nothin' or not, if the white man wanted his self a slave he would do what he wanted to get one.

When some of the black folks indentured them selfs, sometimes they didn't know when they was gonna be let go. They put their X on that paper thinkin' that in 'bout a year or two, they was gonna be free again. We heard 'bout one woman who put her mark on a paper and didn't know it said she was gonna be his slave for thirty-nine years cause she couldn't read and nobody told her what it said. I think her name was Lydia Jackson, but I is not shore. Liz, she will know cause she knows everythin'.

"Liz, does you remember me tellin' you 'bout the woman who was tricked to signin' a denture for thirty-nine years? Does you remember her name?"

"It was Lydia Jackson, Sam. Why does you want to know?"

"I was just thinkin' 'bout other times and how Blacks is indenturin' them selfs to the white man cause they can't get work and they is poor."

"Why you thinkin' 'bout that? You ain't thinkin' 'bout goin' to see Mr. John again, is you?"

"No, I ain't. I ain't gonna indenture my self to nobody. I was a slave b'fore and I ain't gonna be none again. I'll do what I gotta do to get us what we need. I wonder what happened to Lydia? You never heard nothin' did you, Liz?"

"I heard some and it ain't purty. The man who bought her, sent her to 'nother man who beat her bad with sticks and rope and a month b'fore she was gonna be birthin' her babe, he stomped on her when she was on the ground. I heard his wife beat her almos' as bad."

"That poor woman. Did her baby die?"

"Never heard nothin' 'bout that."

Me and Pap we was talkin' one day and he asked me, "Boy, you hear how some of the Blacks is indenturin' them selfs to the white man cause they can't get no work and they is des'prate?"

"Yes, Pap, I heard that. You ain't thinkin' 'bout doin' that, is you?"

"No, I ain't and you know you Mam would smack me good if I said I was gonna. But things is gettin' hard, boy. Things is gettin' hard. I walked all the way over to Beaver Dam to pull the weeds from my little tater patch and all that was left was the weeds. Somebody took the taters. I don't know why they gave us land all the way over there. That is almos' ten miles away."

"They took the taters? But they wasn't full grown cause the growin' season ain't done."

"That don't make no-never-mind when you is hungry."

"You got any left from last year?"

"Now, boy, you know they ain't none left."

"What you gonna do, Pap?"

"I was thinkin' 'bout cetchin' me some fish and saltin' them down."

"Where's you gonna get the bucket and salt to do that?"

Pap didn't answer right away.

"Pap," I said again. "Where is you gonna get the buckets and salt to do that?"

He looked at me. "I is gonna steal them. I got purty good at stealin' when we was in New Jersey workin' with Colonel Tye. I can still do it if I has to."

"Pap, if you gets caught they'll throw you in the gaol and you'll be whipped. Didn't you hear 'bout that woman who stole a bag of taters? They killed her, Pap. And there was 'nother woman who stole a old dress. She was with child and they killed her and the baby. Pap, you gotta be careful, or you be dead, too."

"Boy, sometimes you can work your fingers raw for the white man and they ain't never gonna be satisfied. Look at that King fella what made a wooden chest for a man in Shelburne. A right fine one it was, too. He walked all the way to Shelburne in snow past his knees and he didn't have no warm clothes to wear. He got to that man's house and that man told him it wasn't good 'nough. He bringed it all the way back here and made him 'nother one. He was lucky he didn't freeze to death. If it had'a been me, I would'a hit him over the head with the chest and told him to make one his self."

Pap would'a, too. I wanted to laugh at Pap, but he would'a hit me over the head with somethin'.

"Boy, me and you Mam and sis, we was a good team in New Jersey. We never got us caught, not once. Almos' did a coupl'a times, though."

"You is gonna get Mam and sis to help you steal? You ain't only gonna steal salt and buckets, is you? What else is you gonna steal?"

"Now, never mind. It's best you don't know what we is gonna do, cause you might get your self in trouble if you know. But, boy, we'll bring back 'nough for you and your fam'ly. If we don't steal what we needs we'll have to go beggin' the white man to give us food and I ain't beggin' less I has to. We waits 'till it gets dark then we'll see what we can get."

I never said nothn' to Pap, but I was thinkin' we was prob'ly gonna have to go beggin' the white man anyway. Pap was sittin' there quiet a long time and I was wonderin' what he was thinkin'.

"Boy, Birchtown is a terrible place to live now. Even the white man is sayin' it. I wants to see them live in huts or holes in the ground that rain comes in more'n it stays out."

"You is right, Pap. You is right."

Pap left to get Mam and sis and when they come back that night, all they had was some old bread the baker put in a can behind his bak'ry. I don't know why cause people, they can eat it. Most'a the time it got some green stuff on it, but you can cut that off and the rest is good.

~

The time it come that I had to go to Shelburne town and beg for food. I had me four young'uns now and I couldn't get me no work and the gardens they wasn't growin' with all the rocks that was there. And I don't know where they got the dirt from, we couldn't get hardly nothin' to grow and what was growin' was stole b'fore they was ready to come outta the ground.

We never had nothin' to eat for a coupl'a days and my young'uns was cryin' most all of the time.

I got my self to town and went to the bak'ry hopin' he throwed some of that old bread out in the can. When I got there, I said to myself, I is goin' inside and ask him for some bread to feed my fam'ly.

I seen him watchin' me when I come in his store. He never took his eyes offa me, prob'ly thought I was gonna steal somethin'. I went to where he was.

"Sir, I can't find me no work and my four young'uns is hungry. Can you spare some old bread so I can feed them? If you wants me to work for you to pay for the bread—"

He didn't let me say no more. "Get out of here, you black beggar. You get nothin' from me. Go work like everyone else."

"Sir, they ain't no work or I would be workin'. Please, Sir, my young'uns is hungry. I needs to feed my fam'ly. I don't wants it for me, Sir, I wants it for my young'uns. Please, Sir?"

He stared at me for a long time. He took a loaf of bread outta a can and threwed it at me. It hit me in the chest and falled on the dirty floor.

I picked it up, and if my young'uns wasn't hungry, I would'a throwed it back and hit him in his head. I'm not a animal you throw food to. But I didn't throw it at him cause I needed it. I looked down at the bread so's he didn't see how mad I was. I didn't want him to take it back from me. The bread, it had some green on it, but I took it off b'fore and I can take it off again.

I was walkin' past the butcher shop and I was gonna go in to see if Mister Wood had some meat he could give me. He had young'uns and maybe he would give me some meat for my young'uns. I got almos' there and I seen him throw somethin' in the can nex' to the door then he went inside.

I looked all 'round case he come back out or someone else was comin', then I runned to see what he put in the can. It was a big piece of meat, big 'nough to feed my whole fam'ly. It had a funny smell, but I grabbed it and I runned fast as I could to home.

On my way outta town I seen a tater garden all big and growin'. I figgered I would get Pap and we would come back after dark and get us some.

Liz, she seen me comin' on a run and she come runnin' to me cause she thought somebody was chasin' me. I bet she was rememberin' the day when them white soldiers beat me so bad I couldn't walk.

"What you runnin' from, Sam?" she said when she didn't see nobody b'hind me.

"I is not runnin' from nothin'. I got us some bread," I said holdin' it up for her to see. "The bread it got some green on it, but I think it's okay."

"Let me see," she said, takin' it from my hands. "I can take it off. The rest is good. What is that smell?" she said, sniffin' the air.

"I took my hand from b'hind my back where I was hidin' the meat.

When she seen that big piece of meat in it, she shouted, "Where you get that and why does it smell funny?"

"Butcher, Mister Wood, he was throwin' it out when I went by and I waited 'till he went back in his shop and I grabbed it and runned fast as I can to home." I wasn't tellin' her my leg was painin' somethin' fierce.

She took it outta my hand and smelled it up close.

"Liz, does you think you can cook it so it's okay for us to eat?"

"Sam, food is food and we has to eat what we gets. We got us nothin' else."

My Liz, she cooked it good and it didn't make us sick. It tasted a little funny, but we had us a feast that day and she saved us some for the nex' day.

27

I kep' tryin' to plant us a garden. When it would grow sometimes, somebody would steal what was growin' b'fore we could get to it. Me and Pap, we thought the white folks was doin' it cause they didn't want us there. They didn't need our gardens cause they had big gardens that growed like weeds.

Liz, she asked me, "Sam why does you go there if you ain't gonna be able to plant nothin' and when you does somebody steals it b'fore it's ready?"

"I gotta try. I can't get no more food from the town, they runs me every time I goes there. They says that us Blacks is dirty and lazy. I tells them, I ain't lazy, I'll work for the food 'stead of the money, but they just runs me outta their shop. What else is I gonna do?"

Liz, she knows same as me that I ain't gonna get no vegetables outta dirt that wasn't made for growin'. All the good land was gived to the white folks. I think they knew what they was doin', givin' us land that wasn't good for growin' nothin'. They don't want us to have nothin'. They want us to work for them all the time and they gives us what they wants. They lives all 'round us plantin' their vegetables and gettin' good crops.

I tried to steal outta their garden and I got somethin' once, but then they kep' a good watch so we couldn't do it again. But I think, one day, they is gonna be poor as us and if I is still alive, I'll laugh. Maybe.

~

Every time I looks at my boy, John, I thinks of the day my Liz was ready to birth him. It was in the winter and it was cold. Never thought we was gonna keep warm, but we did.

"I is goin' outside to move the snow from the door."

"Okay, Sam. OOhhh!"

I turned 'round and Liz was a holdin' her belly. I runned to her.

"Is it time?"

"It's time," she said. She was bent over, holdin' on her belly. "Get my Mamma and Miss Hannah. Hurry!"

I runned out the door and was shoutin' for Margaret and told her to get Miss Hannah.

"Go back inside, Sam. you can't leave Liz 'lone. Let's hope she don't have that baby b'fore Miss Hannah gets here. I ain't never delivered no baby," she hollered as she was runnin' through the snow, "but I will if I have to."

It seemed like days 'stead of a hour b'fore Margaret and Miss Hannah come through the snow that was almos' up to their knees. Liz's pains was gettin' harder and harder I was just pullin the deer skin from 'cross the openin' when Miss Hannah and Margaret come runnin' in.

"Outta our way, Sam. Outta our way. We got us a baby to born," Miss Hannah said.

Little Jenny, Prince took her to his house cause he didn't think she should see what was gonna happen. And he didn't want to either cause it scared him. All that screamin' and such.

But I wasn't goin' nowhere and I told Miss Hannah so when she told me, "Go outside, Sam, you is in the way."

"I ain't goin' nowhere. I is stayin' right here with my Liz. Now, do what you come here to do," I told her.

"You stand over there and don't get in my way."

I was walkin' back and forth from one side of the pit to the other. My Liz had a lotta pain, it seemed to me. She was doin' some yellin'.

Then everythin' got quiet.

I stopped still, but I couldn't see nothin' cause Miss Hannah's big round ass was in my way.

Then I heard what I was waitin' for, the wailin' of a new born baby. Miss Hannah was standin' there with a big smile on her wrinkled brown face.

I was tryin' to look 'round her to try to see my Liz. Miss Hannah wasn't makin' it easy for me. I wanted to yell at her to get outta my way, but she might'a smacked me.

'Stead she put her hand on my arm and pulled me to my Liz. She pulled me so hard I almos' falled on top of Liz.

"Get over there, Sam, and see your Liz and son."

Liz was half sittin' up and sweat was runnin' down her face. She was holdin' the most beautiful baby I seen since our Jenny was born. It's a boy, Sam. We have us a son."

"We has a son?" I said.

I took my son from her arms and cradled him to my chest. I stared in his beautiful brown face. His eyes was open and I know he couldn't see his papa, but I was hopin'.

Soon as Liz knew that she was gonna have 'nother baby, me and her, we said that if it was a boy we was gonna name him John. We wouldn'a gived him no other name cause Mr. John and Missus Jessie, they brought us here so we could be free. Wait till I tell them.

~

I had to go to town one day to fix some tools for one of the farmers. I figgered b'fore I went home I would go down to the harbour to see if some more ships was comin in.

I was walkin to the dock when I seen a black man with woolly reddish brown hair that was all 'round his face. He was sittin' on the dock, lookin' out to sea, and he didn't hear me comin'. His shoulders was bent over and he looked like he didn't have no friends.

I watched him for a time. wondering if he was wishin' he could go back to where he come from. Then I walked up to him.

"The sea is calm today," I said.

He looked 'round quick. Prob'ly thought I was his master come lookin' for him. I figgerred he was still a slave cause I ain't never seen him in Birchtown and most all the Blacks in the town what was free, I knew most'a them and I ain't never seen him b'fore.

His funny colour eyes was movin' back and forth like he s'pected somebody to jump out at him with a whip. It prob'ly wasn't the first time it happened and it ain't gonna be the last I think. He looked at me.

"My name is Sam," I said, starin' right in his eyes. I knew the look in his eyes, the look of fear that his Master was gonna cetch him talkin' to other folks when he was told not to. I knew cause it was the same look that was in my eyes for a lotta years. How many times, at Master Bulloc's was we warned 'bout talkin' to the other slaves too long when there was work to be done? How many times did Henry put the whip to me cause I did?

I kep' starin' at him. He was starin' at my hand that I put out for him to shake.

"My name be James," he said

"Can I help you carry those sacks?" I asked, givin' a nod to what he had under his arms and in his hands.

"Tank you," replied James, "but I'se cin carry dem."

I didn't want him to leave just yet cause he looked like he needed a friend. Prob'ly didn't have any.

"Where you come from?" I asked him when he started to walk away. "I come here two years ago from New Jersey. My fam'ly was indentured to Mr. John Moore, but now we is free. We live in Birchtown, over that way," I said, pointin' to the Southwest.

After a minute James answered, "I'se com'd here with ma Marster, Major Sam'l Anderson from Florda. We's only ben' here a little while."

"Was you born there?" I asked.

"I was borned on da Singletery plantation in North Carlina. Me an' ma fam'ly was sold to Major Sam'l Anderson after the war. He got sent to Florda and he taked us with him."

I sat on the edge of the dock and pointed at the spot next to me for him to sit down. He s'prised me when he did and I figgered I best keep talkin b'fore he decides to walk away.

"Does you have any young'uns?"

"I'se had two girls, but one of dem, ma girl, Jude, was sold b'fore Major Anderson done buyed us. Ar marster's brother buyed her then sold her agin. Some slaves said a man named Marster Wood took her away."

"Master Wood?" I said.

I thought, I wonder if it's the same Master Wood who lives in Shelburne Town. He had slaves and one was a girl of about eleven years old.

"Do you come into town often?" I said

"Onc' a week," he said. "I has to git supplies fer da Marster and Missus."

"I'll keep an eye out for you next week,"

I wasn't lookin' forward to goin' back to Birchtown by myself. Other blacks who had to go from Birchtown to Shelburne Town to work was sometimes jumped on and beaten bad. I been lucky, I ain't, been jumped on since the riot, but I always kep' my eyes open and was ready to run if I had to. I can't run fast as I once could, but I was gonna do my best so they didn't cetch me no more.

When I was 'lone, it seemed like I was always thinkin' 'bout how things was b'fore I come here. Now I got my new friend James and sometimes I worries 'bout him. I shore wish they never took his girl from him.

When I think 'bout James and losin' his girl, Jude, I 'ppreciate all I got. I might not have a lot, but I still got my young'uns. I don't know what I would'a done if they was sold away from me. I think I would'a killed the ones what bought them, that's what I would'a done.

Well, I best be gettin' home, it'll be dark b'fore I get there.

I got up to go, and 'cross the street I seen a older woman and she had two black children with her, a girl and a boy. I wondered if they was hers cause that girl, she remind me of the girl who come offa the ship the day me and Liz was watchin' the ships come in. She was hangin' back, draggin' her feet and I knew she didn't want to be where she was.

The woman kep' lookin' back at her and she said somethin' to her, but I couldn't hear what she was sayin'.

Her hair was done up in braids and they was wrapped 'round her head with hair stickin' up all over. I seen them b'fore and I think they was the slaves of Mister Wood, the butcher.

I was too far away to see her good, but somethin' told me I was lookin' at James's girl, Jude.

I would have to think on what to tell James nex' time I seen him. If it wasn't his Jude, I don't want to get him hopin' his girl was here if she wasn't.

James, he come back the nex' week and he was all excited. He told me that his Jude was with them again. The Major he bought her from Master Wood.

I guess that was his girl I seen last time James was here. I is happy for him.

He said he was gonna come back the nex' week, but I never seen him no more.

28

So much happened when we was in Birchtown. So many bad things. When we was there we didn't have no time to think 'bout nothin'. All you could think 'bout was survivin'. And the good mem'ries you has. Sometimes that's all that kep' us goin'.

The best mem'ry I had was meetin' up with my Pap and Mam and sister again. I never thought it was ever gonna happen.

Me and Prince, we was outside tryin' to plant a few taters in what little bit of dirt was close to our pits. That was b'fore we was gived land almos' ten miles away. We didn't know if they was gonna grow cause it was late for plantin' but we was gonna try.

Small taters was better'n no taters. When we was gettin' rations from the gove'ment, we didn't get no taters. You gotta have taters. Cause taters, if you can't cook them, you can eat them raw. They don't taste so good less you can put salt on them, but food is food no matter how you has to eat it.

Me and Prince we was in the garden for a long time. I stand up to stretch my back when I seen some black folks comin' up the path outta the woods. Now, where is they comin' from. I wondered.

"Prince." I said. "Who is them people comin' here? Does you know any of them? They is with Colonel Blucke."

Before he could answer, I seen three people, I wasn't shore I was seein'. It was my Pap and Mam and sister. They was lookin' all 'round and they eyes seen me the same time I seen them.

Pap grabbed Mam's arm and pointed to where I was, then we was all runnin'. Well, I wasn't runnin' too good cause I still had my walkin' stick, but I was runnin' my way of runnin'.

"Sam. Sam!" Pap and Mam and sis shouted. Mam and sis grabbed me tagether and they squeezed me so hard I thought my ribs was gonna break. Pap, he took hold of my arm and was starin' at me.

"Where you been, Sam? How come it took you so long to find us?" Sis laughed cause she knew that I was here b'fore them and they was the ones what found me. I give her a big hug.

We had so much cetchin' up to do, we didn't know where to start, but now that we was tagether again, we had plenty of time.

They was comin' here late, summer was almos' gone. They was gonna have to build a shelter right quick b'fore the weather got bad. There was no pits or huts empty, but with me and Pap and Prince workin' every day to get it done, we can have them a shelter built. I guess they is gonna have to stay with me 'til their shelter gets done. My shelter, it ain't big, but they gotta stay somewhere. We would be puttin' seven people where there was only four b'fore.

Mam and Pap looked 'round.

"Sam, boy," he said, "where does you live? Is there anybody livin in them huts?"

"All the huts is bein' lived in, Pap. You is just gettin' here, you will know purty soon that we don't get nothin' b'fore the white folks. If there is any left, we might get some and if there ain't, we gets nothin'. We has to use what we has."

I pointed b'hind me. "We lives in that one over there."

"You lives in a hole in the ground? Why didn't you build one of them huts? They look better'n a hole in the ground."

"Hush, Sam," said my Mam. "We lived in a hole in the ground when we was in Port Mutton and it wasn't bad as I thought it was gonna be. B'sides, them huts, they don't look like they is gonna be warm."

Mam looked at Colonel Blucke. "Blucke," she said, "you get us the tools we need to build our shelter. We needs them now."

Blucke, he took off a runnin'.

"Mam," I said, "he wasn't long gettin' way from here. You think he is gonna bring some tools for you?"

"He'a gonna bring them, if he wants to keep walkin'. Now, what was you sayin' bout them huts?"

"They ain't warm, Mam. When the wind blows, it blows through cracks in the walls. They is only made of plants and grass and mud and they is covered with birch bark. You was in Port Mutton? How long you been there?"

"We was there all winter and after the big fire they had there, they was gonna send us away to 'nother place where they was gonna build a new town, but we said we wasn't goin'. We had to wait a little bit b'fore we could leave and come here and we had to walk through the woods and 'long the shore. It took us a long time cause we couldn't go through the woods at night cause we would'a got our selfs lost."

"Well, I is glad you didn't get your selfs lost, but, Pap, you is gonna have to build a shelter for you and Mam and Sarrah and you is gonna have to decide what kind you wants."

We didn't have no choice with nothin' else, but least we could say what we lives in even if it is dirt, 'bove the ground or b'low.

"Till then you can stay we with me and my fam'ly."

"Fam'ly?" Pap said. "You has a fam'ly?"

"I does. I has my Liz and two babies, Jenny and John."

I almos' laughed when Pap's mouth falled open so much I thought it was gonna hit his chest.

Mam, she hugged me again. "I has two grandbabies? How old is they?"

"Jenny, she's three and John he's nine months. He was born the beginnin' of the new year."

"Where is they? I wants to see them."

'They is with their other grannie, Margaret, Liz's Mamma. They is over there in Prince's pit. This here is Prince, Liz's Papa."

I was so excited to see my Pap and Mam and Sarrah, I didn't see him runnin' b'hind me. They all shook hands.

Pap turned to Prince. "You shore you wants my boy with your girl? Look at that ugly face. Had his nose broke more'n once."

"Too late now," said Prince. "They already got them selfs two young'uns . Gotta keep him."

I laughed at my Pap. He never said nothin''bout me walkin' with a walkin' stick, but I know he will sometime, cause I seen him watchin' me.

"We gotta get started makin' you a shelter," I said. "Go look see what kind you want. Keep to mind we ain't got no good tools, only two buckets and a shovel. And I got a hatchet. Blucke said there was no more big axes."

Colonel Blucke, he come runnin' back with two more buckets and shovels. He looked at Mam and turned 'round and runned back down the path.

Mam looked at him and laughed. "Good thing he comed back when he did, cause if I had to go find him, he would'a been in trouble."

We got to work right away diggin' for Pap's shelter. He said he wanted the same one we had.

"We lived in one in Port Mutton and it wasn't too bad," he said

Me and Pap and Prince worked day and night and it only took us a week. Mam and sis, they worked right 'long side of us. I told them the men could do it and Mam and sis, they didn't like that.

They said, "We is used to doin' hard work. We was in the war. Get outta our way and let us do our job."

I got outta their way.

Me and Prince was cuttin' the logs for the roof while Pap, Mam and sis did the diggin'. Then we had to gather moss and other plants to fill in b'tween them. Mam and sis, I think they worked harder than us. I shouldn'a been s'prised, Mam always worked hard.

After Pap and Mam and sis come we did us a lotta talkin'.

Pap said, "Did you see the big house Colonel Blucke build for his self? I wonder where he got the money."

"I seen it," I said,

"Your Mam asked him and he didn't want to tell her. Your Mam, she never liked the Colonel. She said he's a crook. Maybe she's right."

We had us a lotta cetchin' up to do and I was gonna ask them plenty questions.

They told me all 'bout the fightin' they did durin' the war and 'bout Pap gettin' wounded in the leg. That must'a been somethin' to see when Mam was tryin' to sew him up. Pap was always 'fraid of a needle. You would'a thought that bein' a slave you wouldn'a been 'fraid of nothin' 'cept the whip and the stocks and the brandin' iron. There was more, but bad as they is, it's funny that Pap is still 'fraid of a needle.

Mam said, "Pap seen the needle, but he went unconscious and he didn't know I sewed him up like I do my quilts till he waked up after two days."

"Mr. Sam," said my Liz.

"How come you calls me Mr. Sam?" Pap asked.

"Well, there is two Sams, like there is two Sarrahs."

"Never thought 'bout that," he said.

"Mr. Sam," she said again. "How come you is 'fraid of a needle?'

Pap sighed. "It ain't only a needle, it's anythin' that is sharp on the end. I remember when I was little, b'fore I was sold the first time, one of the slaves did somethin' the overseer didn't like and he took a sharp stick and poked his eye out. The overseer was a mean bugger. The Master, he was mad as he could get cause he said a blind slave ain't no use to him. He was so mad he sold the overseer to the nex' farm and some of the other slaves said they heard that he was just a slave like them now."

"You never told us that, Sam," said Mam. "How come you never told us?"

"I didn't want to remember that time. When you is a young'un lookin' at that slave with one eye, it ain't purty to see. And I was a scared every time I seen him. And I is sayin' again, you ain't a sewin' me up no more. You let me bleed to death."

"You is bein' foolish, Pap," I said. "We ain't gonna let you die cause you is 'fraid of somethin' sharp. I guess we is gonna have to knock you out b'fore Mam does her work. She does good sewin', Pap."

We laughed at the 'spression on his face.

"Mrs. Sarrah," said Liz. "How come you could do all them things in the war, wasn't you 'fraid?"

"We was at first," Mam said. "But we had to survive the best we could and it kep' Master Stoffle from tryin' to get us back."

Sister, Sarrah, she said, "I wasn't 'fraid. I wanted to fight the Patriots for all they done to us. Keepin' us slaves. We is human the same as them, but sometimes I think they is more animal than they calls us."

Liz said, "I guess I would'a been 'fraid, but you is right, you has to survive the best you can. Mrs. Sarah, you and your girl, you is strong women. I hope my children will be strong like you is."

"They will be," said Mam. "They got themselves a strong Mamma and Papa."

"Mrs. Sarrah, can you tell me 'bout some of the things you had to do? It must'a been hard stealin' from folks. I don't think I could do it."

"Like I said, you do what you has to survive. It ain't hard, Liz, when you think 'bout it. I was thinkin' they took more from us than the food and old raggedy coats that we stole. The skin was took offa our bodies and some slaves, they died, but they didn't take our strong. All they done to us is make some of us stronger."

"Mrs. Sarrah, listenin' to you sayin' 'bout what you had to do, if I had to go fight in a war, I think I could."

"If you want to fight somebody, fight Blucke," said Mam.

"You don't like Colonel Blucke? He helped us when we first come here."

"How he help you?" Mam asked.

"He got us some buckets and a shovel and a hatchet."

"That's not helpin'. You see that big fancy house he's livin' in? That's not a hole in the ground like we is gonna be livin' in. He's only for his self and I is gonna hit him when I sees him again. When he brought us here, after we got to Shelburne from Port Mutton, he said, 'Mrs. Sarrah, I will get you the supplies you need to build your shelter.' You seen what he bringed us, buckets and shovels and we ain't never seen him no more. I said the first time I seen him he was a crook and I is sayin' it now."

Pap said, "Liz, Didn't you never have to steal nothin'?"

150

"No, I never stole nothin'. I don't think I could."

"You could if you had to."

Pap, he looked at me and I seen he was sad, and I thought it was cause he left me there. "Boy, what happened after we left. What did Master do?" he asked.

"He was mad cause you runned away and his men couldn't find you. Pap, you should'a heard him shoutin' at them. He told them they better not let nobody else get away or they was gonna be sorry. A couple of the men didn't like bein' called down in front of the others, but there was nothin' they could do 'bout it."

"I was worried 'bout that cause Master, he can be a mean one sometimes."

"He can be, Pap, but he said it ain't my fault you runned away. He asked me how come I didn't go with you. I told him cause he wouldn'a had himself no more slaves."

"What he say 'bout that?"

"He never said nothin', he just looked at me then went to the big house. Pap, does you remember Ben and Pack from Bulloc's farm?"

"I remember them. Somethin' happen' to them?"

"I seen them in New York, but they is here now. You'll see them sometime. I guess Bulloc's slaves is runnin' away, too. Ben, he said to me one day. 'Sam, you better watch you self cause, Pack, he told me he heard Henry say he was gonna get you and when he did, you wasn't gonna walk no more.' Henry would'a tried, Pap, and he might'a done it, but Bulloc would'a send him to the block for shore cause he always said cripples ain't no good to him on the farm. He always said that, remember?"

"How come you ain't never told me that b'fore? We was there, too, cause we wasn't sold yet. Boy, that is more than Henry dare do cause he knew he would'a been gone. I wonder if Henry is still there?'

"I don't know, Pap, but if any more slaves runs away, then Bulloc, he'll sell him shore as we is standin' here."

29

It wasn't good. People livin' in the pit, they was beginnin' to get upset and doin' things they shouldn'a been doin'.

'Bout a month after Pap and Mam come here, my Liz, she come to me one day and she said, "Sam, I don't know if I can live in a hole in the ground. I is 'fraid all the time and sometimes I feels like I is dyin'. I hears some of the women and they is cryin' all the time, it seems. We ain't animals, why does we have to live like them? My Mamma, she cries every day. Don't your Mam say nothin'? Sam, we gots to get us a hut."

That's the first time Liz said somethin' 'bout the pit. They bothers me too, but I wasn't sayin' nothin' to her cause I didn't want her to be worryin'. I guess, I best be the one worryin'.

"Liz, how come you didn't say somethin' b'fore? I'll see if I can find some logs to cut to make us a hut. I don't know if I can get us 'nough, but I is gonna try."

Liz, she cried.

Our Jenny, she asked, "Why Mamma cryin'?"

I said, "Mamma be sad, Jenny."

She went to her Mamma and put her head on her Mamma's legs. Liz put her head on Jenny's and held her tight.

It's hard on everybody, not just my Liz and her Mamma. Peggy, four pits past us, she ain't said five words since her man, Jacob dug their pit almos' two months ago. They got them selfs two young'uns what don't hear their Mamma talk no more. Sally, she is two and she don't know why her Mamma ain't talkin' to her. Baby Edward he was only borned 'bout a week ago.

She don't even talk to Jacob and he is gettin' sad too. I worrys 'bout him and the young'uns more'n I worrys 'bout her. He was always a strong man, but he ain't strong as he was.

There was a old man named Tobias who figgered he didn't have nothin' to live for and he let his self die. He wouldn't eat or drink nothin' and they found him in his pit dead as dead can be.

A lotta the women they screams at night, and one night Miss Dolly, she runned outta her pit screamin' like the devil was after her and she was runnin' right down to the river. Some of us we runned after her and we got her b'fore she jumped in, cause we knew she couldn't swim.

She was fightin' us and screamin', "Let me die! Let me die!"

We might'a saved her that time, but we knew she was gonna be tryin' it again and we wouldn't be cetchin'' her the nex' time. Miss Dolly, she had that wild look in her eyes, like a animal that's trapped b'fore it's killed. She didn't have no man to look after her, that's how we knew she was gonna get it done the nex' time.

There is so many folks who tried to do bad to them selfs, we couldn't save them all. After a while we didn't stop them, cause I think mos' of us feeled the same way. What has we got to live for?

I kep' a real close watch on my Liz and I told Pap and Prince to keep a look out for Mam and Margaret.

Pap said, "Don't you worry 'bout your Mam. She's a strong woman. She'll be okay."

"Pap, you was there when Peggy was gonna jump in the river. She wasn't screamin' like the other women did. We wouldn't'a knew she was gonna do that if Jacob wasn't runnin' b'hind callin' after her. What would them poor young'uns of hers done without their Mamma?"

"What did you Mam do, boy? She took Peggy to her pit and she stayed with her till the sun come up."

"Mam is strong, Pap, but seein' that all the time, gotta 'ffect her some. You watch after Mam. Anythin' can happen."

"Okay, boy. I'll keep a watch out."

Time went by and most folks 'cepted where they had to live, but some they still couldn't 'cept it. Some runned away and we don't know where they went. Maybe they jumped in the river and we didn't see them.

I still kep' watch on my Liz and with her Mamma and my Mam stayin' close all the time, it helped her Mamma, too. Pap was right, my Mam was a strong woman, but bein' with Liz and Margaret helped them all feel better.

'Bout two weeks later, Peggy, she walked outta her pit in the dark night when nobody seen her and walked right in the river.

The nex' day her man, Jacob, he come lookin' for her. Me and Pap and Prince, we went a lookin' with him. We kind'a thought she might'a done it this time, but we didn't want to say nothin' to him.

We found her on the shore. Dead.

Winter was comin' on and it was gettin' real cold outside. The screamin', it started again. I thought my Liz was gettin' better, but she put her hands over her ears and squeezed her eyes shut.

It was Miss Dolly again. She screamed almos' every night. I was almos' wishin' she would jump in the river like Peggy did so's my Liz didn't have to hear it no more.

My Mam, she helped Miss Dolly much as she could, but it wasn't doin' no good. She had my Liz and Margaret to look after, too.

It kep' gettin' colder and folks had to stay inside most'a the time. Liz said she was gonna be okay, but when you can't go outside cause the snow is up to your knees, it plays on the mind somethin' fierce.

I was gettin' worried 'bout some of the other folks, too.

It was a long winter. Some folks went missin' and nobody knew if they runned away or did away with them self. If they runned away, I don't know where they would'a runned to. They couldn't go to Shelburne, cause nobody wanted them there.

One day Peggy's Jacob found Miss Dolly in the woods, froze. The nex' day me and Pap found Tom froze stiff as a rock in his pit. Tom told me one time, "I don't care if I lives or dies cause this be worse than where I come from. I might'a been a slave in North Carlina, but if we minded what we did, our Master always seen to it that we had food to eat and a shelter that wasn't a hole in the ground. I might as well be in a hole that I can't come outta."

Maybe he done his self in, cause there was no wood in his pit and it was freezin' cold outside. I guess Tom, he's where he wants to be.

We couldn't bury him or Miss Dolly cause the ground was frozed. We put Miss Dolly in Tom's pit with him and I guess we is gonna have to leave them there till the weather warms up 'nough so we can give them a proper buryin'.

Spring was comin' on us and nobody else went missin or was found dead. That was good, I guess.

Liz and most all the other folks got better some cause they could go outside. They wasn't stayin' in a hole in the ground all the time. The folks what lived in a hut, they didn't seem to have no problem. I guess cause they was on top of the ground.

The ground was startin' to thaw some and we buried Tom and Miss Dolly. They'll be restin' better now, I guess.

30

I never thought I seen the day that there was gonna be a school in Birchtown. I don't know what good havin' a school is gonna be when we hardly got no food in our bellies.

Me and Mam, we was talkin' one day and I was tellin' her 'bout it. "Mam, there's gonna be a school in Birchtown!"

"A school? Where you hear that?"

"When I was in Shelburne this mornin' cuttin' wood for Mr. Burton, the baker. I heard him talkin' to the butcher, Mr. Wood. They was sayin' Colonel Blucke, he was gonna be the teacher at the school."

"What else did they say? Cause I know that ain't all what was said, much as they don't like us black folk. And Blucke, what he know 'bout teachin'? What he gonna teach?"

"Mr. Burton, he said what's the point givin' them niggers schoolin', what they gonna do after? And Mr. Wood, he said that they was gonna be teached knittin' and sewin' and other things."

"What's the good of knittin' and sewin'? And what does Blucke know 'bout knittin' and sewin'? They need them self a woman teacher if that's all they is gonna teach. Blucke a teacher? That's gonna be somethin' to see. The boys, they ain't gonna like that. Maybe Blucke is gonna teach them sewin' so's they can make them self some clothes, cause they is runnin' 'round almos' naked. And they got no shoes. Is they gonna knit them? Why ain't they gonna teach them readin' and writin' like they is the white folks' young'uns?"

"What they gonna need readin' and writin' for, Mam? The girls, they can get them selfs a job if they knows how to fix people's clothes."

"What 'bout the boys? What they gonna learn? Sam, they ain't gonna want to learn no knittin' and sewin'."

"Mam, you know there is a lot of black folks in Birchtown who has a trade. Maybe some of them will teach in the school. They can do carpenter work and wood cuttin' and you know Moses, he knows how to make shoes and I bet they ain't knitted. We even got us a doctor here, Mr. John Brown. He was the one who tried the sharecroppin', but I don't think he can teach the young'uns doctorin', they is too young. Miss Rose's man, he's a baker. He can teach the girls and boys how to do that. And we got us Mr. Roger Scott, he can teach carpenter work to the boys. We has a lot of folks what can teach our young'uns if they has what they needs to teach. That would be good, wouldn't it?"

"Yes, it would be, but where is they gonna get what they needs to teach? And if we has us a doctor here, how come he didn't fix your leg when it was hurt so bad?"

"Liz, she sent her Papa to get him, but he was busy with other folks that was hurt, so her Mamma and Papa did what they could for me. I wish you had'a been here cause my leg would'a got better real quick."

"Margaret, she did a good job of fixin' your leg, boy. I couldn'a done better, but I is sorry I wasn't here," Mam said.

She was quiet for a time then she said, "If Blucke lets them folks teach the young'uns a trade, they might be able to find them some work. Just knittin' and sewin' ain't no good. We'll see, Sam. We'll see. Did Mr. Burton and Mr. Wood know you was listenin' to them talk?"

"They wasn't payin' no 'ttention to me. I think Mr. Burton, he forgot I was there."

"Did he pay you when you was finished cuttin' his wood?"

I held up the bag I was carryin'. "He gave me four loafs of bread and it ain't got no green on it," I said, takin' one out and showin' my Mam.

"Here, Mam, this one is for you and Pap."

"You keep it for your young'uns, Sam, me and Pap we'll be okay."

"You take this, Mam, three is 'nough for us. Take it."

Mam didn't say no more and she took the bread.

~

It been two years since Colonel Blucke set up a school here. I thought my Jenny was gonna be goin' to it, but the Colonel said she wasn't old 'nough. It was for the older girls and boys to teach them a trade. Jenny, she was only seven.

I don't know what kinda trade knittin' and sewin' is, less it's like I told my Mam, the girls could fix the clothes of the people in Shelburne. A coupl'a the boys, they wanted to learn the knittin' and sewin' cause they wanted to have their own tailor shop one day. A man sewin' clothes, that don't seem right. He should be doin' a man's work. Hard work.

I guess that ain't gonna happen now, cause nobody got no money for nothin' and don't nobody know when they is gonna get some.

Blucke, he was tryin' to get some clothes for the young'uns who was goin' to school, cause they was runnin' 'round almos' naked. Now, ain't that what my Mam said? It took him long 'nough to try to get them some clothes. And I don't know how they is gonna keep the school when there ain't no money to get what they needs to learn whatever they is learnin'.

Mam said, "Sam, you should go to the school so's you can learn a trade. It ain't only for the young'uns."

"I ain't goin' to school with them young'uns."

"Why not? Don't you want to learn more'n farmin' and fixin some tools?"

"I gets by. I don't need to learn no more. Anyway, ain't they only teachin' knittin' and sewin'? I ain't gonna do that. And b'sides, if I wanna learn my self somethin' else, I'll go see one of the men what can teach me. Maybe carpenter work."

"Sam, if you does what you is sayin', that would be good, cause you know you can't do no farmin' cause the dirt ain't no good. And how many tools has the white folks got you to fix? We been beggin' and stealin' and goin' in the garbage boxes for food cause most'a the time we ain't got none. You ain't gonna get hired by the white man and paid money."

"I ain't goin' to no school."

I gave my Mam the eye so she wouldn't say no more 'bout me goin' to the school.

~

It was gonna get worse, I could feel it. Everybody was poor, black folk and white folk. There ain't no work and some of the white folks is leavin' and goin' back to America cause they is losin' everythin' they got.

I is gonna miss workin' for some of them, but I ain't gonna miss some of the other ones cause they could be right mean and they shore liked callin' us them names. They was so worried 'bout buildin' big houses they never thought 'bout their bis'ness they wanted. Now, they has to go back to where they come from cause they ain't got no money.

But there ain't nobody poor as us. When we could get us some work we didn't get much money as we usu'lly got. Sometimes they give us food, some was good and some of the bread it had that green on it. They never give us no meat, but sometimes I got me some meat again like I did b'fore from the can nex' to Mr. Wood's butcher shop. A couple times we couldn't eat it, it was so bad, but most'a time Liz could cook it.

Some of the white folks, they don't want to hire us no more cause they don't trust the black folks cause of the riot. But it wasn't us who was ri-otin'. We was bein' beat on. They think we is gonna steal from them.

Maybe that is why they don't trust us, maybe we thinks they owes us for what they done to us. That is some strange thinkin' if they thinks that. The way we been treated since we been here, we would'a been stealin' all the time. Well, I guess we is gonna have to steal if we want to eat. Most all of us got young'uns to feed.

Liz was gettin' what little bit of food we had left, ready for our young'uns. I said to her, "We gots to be careful, Liz. We can't be havin' us no more babies. We is havin' trouble findin' food for all of us."

"I know, Sam. I know," she said like she always says when our food is almos' gone. "I wish we never left Mr. Peter. We wouldn'a been lookin' for ways to get food for our babies."

I is sorry we left, too, but like Pap said to me, we gotta forget 'bout the past. They ain't nothin' we can do 'bout it now. But when they was sayin' 'bout this New Land I thought we was gonna have us a nice house and some land to have us a farm on, but what we got was nothin' and we has to live in a hole in the ground. And soon we is gonna have us no food. I'll get us some, Liz. My young'uns ain't gonna be hungry."

31

Me and Pap, we was talkin' one day. We does a lotta talkin'.

"Everybody is havin' it hard, boy. I is gettin' worried, but your Mam ain't. What little bit we is able to plant, in dirt that I ain't never seen the likes of b'fore, hardly nothin' grows in it. You know, cause your garden, it don't grow. I ain't wastin' no more time tryin' to plant in dirt that don't grow nothin'. If I wants me some vegetables, I is gonna take some outta the white man's garden."

"Pap, if you gets caught, you'll be whipped bad."

"They took everythin' else from us, they might well take my skin offa my back."

"You is talkin' crazy talk, Pap. What does you think Mam would say if she heard you sayin' that? And you ain't never had no whippin' b'fore, if you did, you wouldn't be sayin' that."

"You Mam wouldn't say nothin', she would hit me on the head with somethin'. Boy, don't you see what's goin' on all 'round us? The animals is goin' missin'. We figured a coyote or some other wild dog must'a got them. They would take a cat just like that if they could cetch them. Then Willie, in the pit next to mine, his dog went missin'. I knew it was no coyote what got him, cause he was a big dog and would'a put up a fight. Then I heard that Willie killed his dog cause he had no food and him and his family was starvin'. Willie got himself three young'uns and it must'a been hard for him to do that cause he loved that ole dog. I wonder what he told his young'uns where the meat come from."

I said, "Oh, Lordy, now that's hungry."

"Boy, I lost my supper on the ground after hearin' that. What little bit I had in my belly. Them poor people...but when you is that hungry and you can't find nothin' to eat, you gotta eat whatever is there. If it's your an-imal...."

Pap never said no more 'bout Willie and his dog.

"Boy, your Mam," he said, "I didn't think she knew 'bout this cause she was in town. She got herself some work in a old lady's house, cleanin' for her. She been there before and she said this ole lady lived 'lone and every time Mam went there, she didn't know what that woman done to get her house so dirty, but it was a lot for her to do for what little bit she got paid. One time the woman didn't pay her nothin' and Mam said she wasn't goin' back to clean no more, but she did cause she felt sorry for her."

"That's my Mam. She don't like seein' nobody needy."

"Boy, I was outside cuttin' wood when she come a runnin' home from town. 'Sam,. she said, almos' cryin'.

"'What's wrong, wife?' I said to her.

"'I just seen two people fall out dead in the street in Shelburne. They was starved. You could almos' see their ribs comin' outta their chest. Sam, it was awful.'

"I put my arms 'round her shoulders. 'Do you know who they was?' I said.

"'No, and I is glad I didn't, Sam.' she said.

"I could hear fear in her voice. You know you Mam, she ain't 'fraid of nothin', but she was 'fraid that day."

"No, she ain't never been 'fraid of nothin' that I knows of, Pap, but sometimes somethin' you see makes you 'fraid."

"You is right, boy. She said to me, 'What's gonna happen to us? Is we gonna fall down dead in the street cause we is starvin'?'

"'I won't let that happen, wife,' I said. 'I'll find us somethin'. We can get fish and maybe I can hunt us up some meat.'

"'And what is you gonna hunt with, Sam?' she said. 'You ain't got no gun and when you sets a snare somebody steals what you cetch.'

"'I got me a knife. I is purty good huntin' with a knife.'

"'When is you been huntin' with a knife and what did you cetch?' she said.

"Boy, I didn't have no answer, cause she knew I ain't done no huntin' with a knife. Then she says to me, 'Don't you go killin' nobody's dogs and cats.'

"'You know 'bout that, wife?" I said.

"'Course I know 'bout that. Maybe if you had'a said somethin' 'bout that to me, you would'a knew that I knew 'bout it.'

"'Wife, I ain't gonna kill nobody's cats and dogs. We been eatin' fish when I can cetch them and anythin' else I can cetch that will fill a empty belly,' I told her."

"Pap, we'll be okay. We can find us some food and you can go huntin' with your knife."

Me and Pap, we had us a good laugh 'bout that.

~

Things they got worse and worse. There was no more animals for people to kill and eat and I was glad 'bout that cause young'uns was cryin' all the time for their dog and cat. I is shore glad they didn't know they was in their bellies.

Most'a the time we couldn't find no food. We ate us a lot of berries in the summer time and one time, Old Joseph, not my friend Joseph what lived on Mr. Peter's farm, cause he's dead. Old Joseph, he found his self a patch of berries what he never seen b'fore and he seen the birds eatin' them and said, "If they ain't gonna kill the birds, they ain't gonna kill me."

He ate them berries and they almos' killed him. He was dog sick for three days. He throwed up nothin' but water and his belly was so sore he was cryin' from the pain. The rest of us, we made shore we didn't eat none of them berries. We only eat what we knew. We caught what fish we could cetch, but there was so many of us in Birchtown, most'a the time we didn't cetch us none.

We was hungry most all the time, but I had my Liz and young'uns to feed so I had to find food somewhere. Sometimes I did and sometimes I didn't.

Some of the older folk, they let them selfs lay down and go to sleep till they was gone. They didn't care no more. Some of the younger folks, they didn't have no say if they lived or died.

Sometimes I didn't care no more, but then I thought 'bout my fam'ly and I knew if I died, who was gonna look after them? Me and my Liz, we was always hungry cause we give most all the food I got to our young'uns. We only kep' a little bit for our selfs, 'nough to keep us goin'. We didn't want to fall down dead and leave them with no Mamma and Papa and we didn't want to bury our babies like some folks did.

Them was sad times.

Sometimes I still got us some of that green bread, I called it, when other folks didn't get there b'fore me and Pap. And the last time I went to Mr. Wood's, the butcher, the meat in his garbage box had them little white worms crawlin' on it, but I figgered if I scrape them off we can still cook the meat. It smelled real bad, worse than the other piece I bringed home, but I knew if I didn't take it, some of the other black folks would get it and we wouldn't have nothin' but green bread. Liz, she would know if it was good to eat.

But there is some things you can't eat, it don't matter how hungry you is. I took it home and Liz looked at it and smelled it and she said. "I don't know, Sam. I think this ain't good to eat. I think it might make us real sick. What is them little white things on it. They is movin'."

I looked at the meat and I seen some of them worms I didn't see b'fore. I looked at Liz. "There was some on it when I found it and I took them off. I guess I didn't see them ones. You shore we can't eat it? If you cook it real good like you did b'fore, can we eat it then?"

"All I can do is try," she said, lookin' at it again. "I'll try."

I could see she didn't think it was gonna be no good, but I hoped it was.

She cooked it real good and we ate it, but it made little John sick. He throwed it back up soon as it went down. It might'a been a good thing he did ,cause he might'a got sicker and died. I would'a killed my boy.

We thought Liz's Papa and Mamma was gonna be gone cause they never had no food for almos' a week and they never told us. They said they was eatin' 'nough.

"Papa," said Liz. "Why didn't you say you didn't have no food? We could'a give you some."

"We ain't takin' no food from you babies. And you and Sam, you need strength to take care of them. We would'a found us some food some-where."

"And how was you gonna find it when you doesn't go outside? Was you just gonna lay down here and let your selfs die? Sam, he got us some bread and Pap, he caught some fish and you is gonna eat all of it. You hear me? You is gonna eat all of it."

I got the bread that I took the green offa and Pap, he brought the fish. We give them the fish raw cause if we'd'a cooked them, the smell of them cookin' would'a bringed some of the other folks lookin' to have some. I don't like tellin' nobody they can't have no food when they is starvin' same as us, but we wasn't lettin' Liz's Papa and Mamma die. If they died then my Liz would'a died.

We don't talk 'bout Liz's brother Nick no more. His name was Nich-olas, but everybody called him Nick. Everybody but his Papa and Mamma and Liz. Nick, he liked bein' called Nick cause he said it made him feel like a man 'stead of a boy.

Anyway, like I was sayin. We don't talk 'bout Nick no more cause he died. When the small pox was ragin' through Birchtown, he got it and he got real sick. He come down with a fever and the fever, it took him.

We don't know how come his Papa and Mamma didn't get the small pox cause they was tendin' to him when he was sick. I guess it was a good thing they didn't cause they wouldn'a had to worry 'bout starvin' to death, the fever would'a took them too. His Papa and Mamma and Liz, they cried for two days and they is still sad.

'Nother winter come and it was hard cause we always got us a lot of snow. Nobody had no warm clothes to wear. Most all of us only had what we had on, and we had to wear them all the time. Sometimes we couldn't wash them and they got real dirty and smelled funny.

Where was you gonna wash them in the winter? The river was frozed over and even if it wasn't, how was we gonna dry them?

Pap and Mam and Sis, they was still wearin' them coats they said they got outta a rich fam'ly's garbage box in New York.

"Pap," I said. "Your coats, they got almos' as many holes in them as the sides of the huts."

"Maybe so, boy, but raggedy as they is, they is over our other clothes and keeps some of the cold out."

"How? Your other clothes is just as raggedy."

We ain't got us nothin' to laugh 'bout nowadays, but me and Pap, we always find us somethin' to laugh 'bout. Like the time we laughed at him huntin' with a knife. It shore helps us get by when we laughs.

With only the raggedy clothes we had on our backs we had to walk all the way to Shelburne in the snow and then we had to come back. One time the snow was almos' four feet deep. I ain't a tall man, and in some places it comed up to my chest.

The young'uns wanted to go, 'specially my John. He was still a baby, but he wanted to help. If he had'a went, he would'a been buried in the snow and I wouldn'a found him till spring. If I wanted to get us somethin' to eat, I had to go. It didn't matter how much snow was on the ground. I was hopin' what shopkeepers was still there would give me somethin' to feed my Liz and young'uns.

"You be careful," said Liz, b'fore I set off to walkin'.

"I will be, Liz. I is gonna bring back somethin'."

I had a hard time gettin' there and back to home, but I was lucky cause Mr. Burton, he was outside puttin' some green bread in the box. I grabbed that quick as I could.

One day, two women, they was goin' to town cause they had young'uns to feed. They went to Shelburne in all that snow to beg for food. The story that was told was Miss Betsy and Miss Debra was comin' home and they was so weak they couldn't make it to home. They falled in the deep snow.

Mr. Marrant, our black preacher, he was comin' back to Birchtown and he found them layin' in the snow. One woman, she was froze to death and the other, she was still 'live.

Mr. Marrant, he had some rum in his pack and he give her some to drink then he rubbed some on her face. She come to 'nough for him to get them home.

I know it wasn't Miss Betsy cause I seen her and her man, Daniel, in Birchtown. And it wasn't Miss Debra cause she ain't got no youngun's. I never knew who they really was.

Mr. Marrant, he had the small pox a while back and he couldn't carry the other woman home, so he had to leave her in the snow. Weak as some of the men was, they wasn't gonna leave her there for the animals to get. They followed the tracks back to where she was and bringed her home.

That poor woman. They said she had four young'uns. Who is gonna look after them now?

There was so many people who had to go beggin' in Shelburne and had to walk back in the deep snow. Sometimes it was snowin' when they left to walk and we was always hearin' 'bout somebody who didn't come back.

One day it wasn't snowin' when I went, but it shore was when I was comin' back. Liz, she told me b'fore I went, "Sam, it's gonna storm. You can't go today."

"I looked up at the sky and there was some clouds and I seen the sun. "It ain't gonna storm, Liz. They ain't even no wind blowin'. I has to go, we only got us a little piece of bread left and maybe Mr. Wood throwed out some meat that ain't like the last piece I bringed home. I won't bring none like that no more. I almos' killed my boy. I'll be careful. I got me my wife and four young'uns. I gotta come back."

Liz, she didn't like what I said 'bout almos' killin' my boy. "Sam, you didn't almos' kill our boy. We didn't get sick, did we? John got his self a weak belly and that's why he got sick. I don't want you talkin' like that no more."

It was a hard time gettin' there and gettin' back. It started to snow just like Liz said and I was real cold. The shoes Mr. John give me in New York had more holes in them that Pap's raggedy coat, but I wasn't stoppin'.

When I got to home, Liz had a fire in the pit and I falled down beside it and laid there till I could feel my bones again. Liz, she rubbed my feet and my young'uns, they was rubbin' my hands and arms and back. I falled asleep and didn't wake up till the nex' mornin.

Liz, she said, "I didn't think you was gonna wake up, Sam. I didn't think you was gonna wake up."

I looked 'round and there was my Pap and Mam sittin' there starin' at me. Mam was holdin' her hands so tight tagether her knuckles was white. Then she come over and hugged me.

Pap, he didn't say nothin, he kep' starin'. It looked like his eyes was shinin', but I knew my Pap wasn't cryin' cause I ain't never seen him cry.

I don't know if things is gonna get better, maybe they ain't. It can't get no worse. Folks was gettin' tired of havin' to beg and steal to live. We was all tired of people dyin' all 'round us.

32

The black folks, they was gettin' tired of not havin' nothin'. We all come here cause we was promised land and shelter and supplies. We got our supplies for a little while, then the gove'ment they stopped sendin' them and nobody got nothin', not even some of the white folks.

But I don't care 'bout them.

Them was real bad times, but me and Pap and Prince, we got us so tired of livin' in a hole in the ground that we cut us some logs. We was a long time gettin' them cut, but we 'ventu'lly had us 'nough to build us log huts.

I had my four young'uns so I had to build me a good size one and, even if it was small, it was on top of the ground. Liz, she was happy and so was my Mam and Liz's Mamma.

Some of the other folks, they built them selfs a log hut, but some of the others, I guess they was used to livin' in a hole in the ground, so they stayed in them.

The land they gave us was shore no good for plantin'. I is always sayin' it. I ain't never seen dirt like that b'fore, nothin' would hardly grow. We couldn't have us the veg'table garden we thought we was gonna have and if some did grow, b'fore it was all growed, somebody stealed it right outta the ground when nobody was lookin'. And it was hard to keep a watch on it cause the land they gave us for farmin' was almos' ten miles from Birchtown.

When the folks was hungry it didn't matter whose garden they was diggin' in. I think they digged in the white man's garden too cause they was all 'round us. I went in their garden a coupl'a times and I ain't 'fraid to say. The white man, they took 'nough from us, time we got somethin' from them.

Talk was goin' 'roumd 'mongst the black folk that a man by the name of Clarkson was tryin' to get people to leave and go to a place in Africa called Sierra Leone. I never heard of that place, but I guess some folks was thinkin' 'bout it.

I wasn't leavin' and I told Liz and Pap, "I ain't goin' to no Africa. The black folks is sayin' that it s'pposed to be better'n here, but I don't b'lieve it. We was promised good land for plantin' here and we never got none and I don't think there is gonna be none in Africa. I bet they is gonna have to live the same way they is livin' here."

We got us a church here in Birchtown too, cause we wasn't 'llowed in the one in Shelburne, 'specially when it was full of white folks. Mr. Moses Wilkinson, he was the black preacher. He was blind and cripple and people, they had to carry him from one place to 'nother so he could preach.

When he preached, almost' everybody went to hear him. Even my Liz and her Mamma and my Mam. Me and Pap and Prince didn't go cause we didn't want to hear none of that wailin' that some of the people did. Even some of the men who was there, and there was plenty, they took to wailin' when Preacher Wilkinson took to singin'.

He was a purty good singer, if I must say. But some of them others, I would'a put my hands over my ears if I was goin' by what my Liz was tellin' me.

"Sam, you should come to church and sing. Papa said you got a real purty voice."

"I ain't goin' and singin' nowhere."

Well, this Clarkson fella, he started holdin' meetin's in our church to get the folks to leave here and go to Africa. There was a lot of folks who was listenin' to what he was sayin' and wantin' to go and I think they might. Some of the white folks, they don't want us to go cause we work for only a little bit of money and sometimes for food 'stead of money.

But there is some white folks who wants us to go so they can buy our little pieces of land from us and give us almos' nothin' for it. They ain't gettin' mine. It might not be no good, but it's mine.

Pap, he come to me one day. "Boy, me and Pack we was talkin' the other day and he said he's goin' to Africa. He was tellin' me 'bout how he come to be in America. He wasn't borned here."

"Where was he borned?"

"He was borned in Africa. It's a sad story, boy, what he was tellin' me and it was hard for me to listen to what he was sayin'. He never told it to nobody b'fore and he wanted to tell me why he was goin' home, he called it. It made me sad hearin' it, boy, but this is what he said."

I was thirteen when me and my Mamma, Halima, was walkin'

home from the waterin' hole. We was almos' home when we was set upon by some black men from the neighbourin' village. I know'd they was, 'cause I seed them many times when we walked down that path to our village. Always watchin' us they was. They scared me and mamma would take my hand and we runned away from them. Now, them men, they was on us like bugs on dead meat. We screamed and my Papa heard us and come runnin'.

Pap said, "I knew he was rememberin' what happened, cause he stopped talkin' for a little while. I never said nothin'. I didn't think he was gonna tell me no more, but he did."

My Papa, his name was Adili. He seen the men grab us. He was runnin' to us, but he didn't see the ones jumpin' outta the bushes b'hind him. They had a big machete and they cut his head off and left his body on the ground for the animals.

Me and Mamma screamed and tried to run to Papa, but we was knocked to the ground and they put chains on us. I was scared. We din't know what was gonna happen to us.

They taked a lot of people from our village and they tied us together. We walked a long ways. Our feet they was raw and bleedin'. Some got sick and died. They wasn't buried, they was cut loose and their bodies left to rot in the hot sun. They hauled the rest of us 'long 'til we come to big cages made outta trees.

There was a lotta people from other villages there. Some we know'd and some we din't.

We was kep' there a lotta days, then we was bringed to a big hut. When we got there our feet was covered with sores and our bellies was as empty as the water bucket we had to drink from like animals. We was put in dark rooms that din't have no windows. The men was put in one and the women and young'uns in 'nother.

We heard the moans and wails of the women and the cries of the babes. Some men would come and take a coupl'a the young girls, we could hear them screamin' when they was bein' taked, and they wasn't seen no more.

Pap said, "He stopped talkin' again and he rubbed his achin' hip. I knew he had a bad hip cause he limped sometimes. I seen him put his hand on his left shoulder. He turned and moved his shirt to show me the scar that was there. I seen the scar b'fore, but I didn't know how he got it till he told me."

> They put the brandin' iron to us to mark us. Sometimes I can smell my burnin' skin like I is still there. It was a lotta pain and my mamma had to half carry me and drag me to the ships we was bein' put on. If we was too slow, we feeled the whip.
>
> The ships, they was bad. We was packed in them like fish in a barll. People was gettin' sick, and throwin' up and there was no bucket to use when you had to have one and people was dyin'. You don't forget the dyin'.
>
> I watched my Mamma dyin' from a fever that killed a lotta them. They throwed my Mamma's body offa the ship with the others what died. Throwed them off for the sharks to get. I wanted to die cause I didn't want to be there without my Mamma.
>
> Sometimes we was bringed up on the deck to get us some air and some of the slaves would jump in the water. I was gonna jump, but they cetched me and throwed me down in the ship again and tied me so I couldn't get out.
>
> After we got to America, I was sold four times till I runned away from Master Bulloc. I wants to go home now. I got me no fam'ly there no more, but it be my home and if I is gonna die, I is gonna die there.

"Pap," I said, "I didn't know that's where Pack comed from. He never said nothin' to nobody cause if he had'a, everybody would'a knew. But like you is always tellin' me, you gotta forget the past cause it ain't no good rememberin' it."

"Pack don't talk much anyway, if you remember, boy, and he stays by his self most'a the time. I guess now we knows why. But, boy, Pack been through a lot and it's kinda hard forgettin' that, 'specially if you was old as he was and seen you Mamma throwed overboard to the sharks. I hope he'll be happy when he goes to his home."

"I hope he is, too."

There was gonna be a lotta black folks who was goin' to Africa. Some-body told me more'n five hundred. They was gettin' ready, packin what little bit they had, and some of them didn't have nothin' but the raggedy clothes on their backs.

169

Me and Pap, we went down to the harbour to see how they was gonna go to Africa. We was s'prised to see all them ships waitin' to take the Birchtown folk to Halifax, cause I guess that's where they has to go first b'fore leavin' for Africa.

They come a marchin' in a big crowd and some of them seemed kinda happy to see the ships. There was all different kinds of ships. Some was big and some was small.

Pack, he comed to us to say goodbye and he said, "Them ships shore ain't like the one I was brought in from Africa. I hope you never has to go on one of them ships."

It took a little while till they was on the ships then they was sailin' away to Halifax.

Pap looked at me and said, "Boy, is you sorry you didn't go with them?"

"No, Pap. I told you, I ain't gettin' on no ship no more. If you and Mam and Sis wanted to go, there wasn't nothin' I could'a done 'bout it."

"Boy, I told you we wasn't goin' nowheres. You said you wanted to go to this Yarmouth place and when you is ready, we'll be goin', too."

"I hear tell that in Yarmouth they have good dirt for plantin' and we can have us a good big garden. But I heard if we wants land we has to put our names in for a piece like Mr. John did to get his land in Shelburne."

"Does you think they is gonna give black folks land to farm on?"

"I don't know, Pap. I never heard nothin' 'bout that, but when I decides to go, I'll ask 'bout it. I heard Mr. Burton talkin' to a man on the street and the man wondered how can we live in a hole in the ground. Mr. Burton, he said we has to cause we got no place else to live and we got no lumber to build our selfs a house. I never told Mr. Burton that we built our selfs a log hut now, so maybe he thinks we is still livin' in a pit. I never seen that man he was talkin' to b'fore. He must'a come here from some other place cause he would'a knew 'bout the pit like everybody else in Shelburne. Then he said, and I heard him loud as can be, 'There aren't any pits in Yarmouth. We wouldn't let anybody live in a hole in the ground. They aren't animals.' I heard him say that, Pap. I did. And if I'da knew he was from Yarmouth, I would'a asked him if us Blacks can get us a piece of land if we puts our name in for one. But they went in Mr. Burton's bak'ry and he wouldn'a liked it if I went in botherin' his friend. I'll find out when we is ready to go to Yarmouth."

When we got back to Birchtown, our boy, Sam, he went to his hut and I went to mine. Me and wife we sat there talkin'.

"Sarrah, you is awful quiet tonight. Is you bothered 'bout somethin'?"

"Sam, ain't nobody safe nowhere. We come here cause we was s'pposed to be free."

"We is free."

"Is we? Did you hear 'bout that woman, Mary Postell? She was s'pposed to be free cause she worked for the British b'hind their lines and had her paper sayin' so. Then she was taken and brought to a place outside of Yarmouth town by a man who said he owned her. He selled her for a hunderd bushels of taters and he took her young'uns, Flora and Nellie from her. Sam, if anybody had'a took our Sam and Sarrah when they was young'uns, I don't know what I would'a done."

"Is that the Mary who was fightin' a man named Gray to get herself free?"

"I b'lieve so, Sam. How you know 'bout her?'

"I heard some folks talkin' 'bout it in town yesterday. They said that Gray fella, he's a bad man. Gets in trouble all the time."

"I wonder if he's the same man what whipped our friend, Pero, a hun-dred lashes all over his body. Cut him all to pieces he did. Pero should'a stayed here with us and he wouldn'a been bused like that."

"He's the same man, Took Pero a long time to get better, I hear. But he could'a got better faster if you had'a been there to doctor him like you did our boy."

"That Gray fella, he never got nothin' for doin' that to Pero."

"Did you 'spect him to, Sarrah?"

"No, but he should'a. It don't sound no better there than it is here. The white folks they still whip us black folks cause they can get away with it. And you still wants to move to Yarmouth?"

"Sarrah, we told our boy we would go with him when he was ready to go, but maybe he should think on that some more."

She never said no more.

33

I is gettin' tired of the white folks who is sayin' they was 'bandoned by the black folk who went to Africa. They wasn't 'bandoned, the way I sees it. They left cause they was tired of bein' 'bused.

If they had'a paid us more money so we could feed our young'uns and our selfs, and gived us good land that we could plant our gardens on, maybe some of them would'a stayed. Now, the white man is complainin' cause he can't get nobody to do his work for him. Do it them selfs, I say. They is just lazy. Long as they got the black folks slavin' for them, they ain't gonna do nothin'.

My Mam, she don't like it when I say this, but I don't like to see nobody hurt real bad, not even the white man. Maybe if he hurt me real bad I might want him to hurt like I is hurtin'. The other blacks, they think I is crazy cause I feel that way, but I tell them that my Mam always told me I ain't s'pposed to hate nobody.

One of them must'a said somethin' to my Mam cause one day we was talkin' and she said, "Sam, boy, how come you don't hate the white man after all he done to you? After all the whippin's you got for nothin' from Henry on Bulloc's farm?"

"Mam, you is forgettin', I got whipped by a black man and I bet Bulloc didn't know 'bout all the times Henry whipped me. B'sides, you always told me, when I was little, that I wasn't s'pposed to hate nobody."

"I did, but that was when you was little. You is a man now and the white man is still hurtin' you. And after all that been done to us, I think it's alright to be hatin' them. They don't care how bad they hurts us. You remember when we didn't have no food and we was almos' starvin? Did they come and give us food for our young'uns? We had to go and beg them for food and most'a the time they runned us off. Then we had to steal so our young'uns wouldn't die or we wouldn't have to steal nobody's animals and cook them like other folks was doin'. You don't have to hate them if you don't want to, but I hates them with everythin' I got in me."

"Mam, you is forgettin' that mos' of the white folks, they didn't have no more'n we did sometimes. People was goin' hungry all over."

"They must'a found food somewhere. They wasn't fallin' down dead in the street like the black folks was."

I never said no more 'bout it cause Mam's hate for the white man was so strong, she don't b'lieve they was hungry as we was sometimes. And maybe they wasn't. I is thinkin' now, maybe Mam is right. They never done nothin' for us. I is gonna have to think on how I feels 'bout them now.

Then things, they got real bad. We had us a real good winter, hardly no snow and it wasn't freezin' like the winter b'fore. Come spring we thought we was gonna plant us a garden and maybe somethin' would grow. But we wasn't gettin' no rain and I heard that the crops the white folks planted started growin', then they up and died cause it didn't rain.

There was a big fire in the woods that went in Shelburne Town and burned almos' fifty houses, and some barns got burned too. I was hopin' there was no animals in them, but I heard after that there was.

The fire it spread in the woods and it was comin' our way. It was burnin' all the trees 'round us. Me and Pap and Prince, and the other folks was watchin', hopin' it wouldn't come close to our huts.

We started runnin' with our buckets to get water to put on the huts that was close to the fire. But the fire it was goin' so fast, we couldn't get 'nough water to put all the fires out.

I seen Miss Jane's hut cetch fire and I was hopin' she wasn't in it. I runned to get her out, but she come runnin' out and I never seen nobody old as her run fast as she was runnin'.

She is ninety years and she said when I got to her, "Sam, boy, I is so used to runnin' away from the whip, when I has to run from somethin' else, it's hard to cetch me." Then she laughed.

I said, "I heard somebody say that Colonel Blucke's house is burnin'. Mam will shore be happy 'bout that."

"A lotta folks will be happy 'bout that, boy. Not many like him. Say he's a crook."

"That's what my Mam says."

We watched the fire and it was goin' the other way from my hut.

I looked to Miss Jane's hut. "Where is you gonna live?" I asked as we watched a wall of her hut fall down. "What you gonna do now?"

"I guess I'll stay with Miss Bridget Cooper, if her hut don't burn down," she said as she looked to where Miss Bridget's hut was.

"Well, I guess I ain't gonna be stayin' with her," she added when the fire started burnin' on Miss Bridget's hut.

A lotta folks' huts caught fire, but they didn't all burn all the way to the ground. It was a good thing, cause some of them folks had young'uns.

Tobias, him and his wife, they had two young'uns that wasn't three years old. Their hut didn't burn to the ground, but they is gonna have a lotta fixin' to do b'fore they can live in it.

There must'a been ten or twelve huts that ain't no more. I don't know what they is gonna do, cause some of them, they got young'uns too.

Mr. Warrington, he said, "I is gonna build my hut back up. I got no choice, Sam. I got me a wife and three young'uns and ain't one of them five years old yet. Mr. Turner, his house be gone and he got his self a wife and three young'uns almos' small as mine. He said he is gonna build his hut back up.'

"Well, me and Pap and Prince, we'll help and you'll be back to livin' in your huts."

I was thinkin' 'bout how lucky we was that our huts didn't burn. Prince's hut caught fire, but we seen it right off and we put the fire out b'fore it burned too bad. It only burned on one side.

Everybody was glad it wasn't worse than it was. We was gonna have a lotta work to do fixin' them huts. I guess the folks who went to Africa, went just in time. They didn't have to watch their huts burn down to the ground.

34

I done some wood cuttin' for Mr. Burton, the baker and he paid me 'nough so I could buy some meat for my fam'ly and he give me a coupl'a loafs of bread b'fore he throwed it out in his garbage bin and it got green.

When I was goin' to Mr. Wood's I was thinkin' bout my friend, James. He been gone for a long time. I heard his master, the Major, he moved his fam'ly and slaves to Yarmouth and that's why I didn't see my friend no more. Yarmouth is the place I is plannin' on goin' soon and I said to Pap a while back that maybe I would meet up with James again.

But I guess that ain't gonna happen, cause when I got to Mr. Wood's butcher shop, the door was open and I heard him and 'nother man talkin' and Mr. Wood he said, "You know that Major Anderson who was here a few years back? I just heard that one of his boys killed his man, James, because James tried to kill the Major with an axe. That boy shot him right in the chest, is what I hear. Killed him stone dead."

"He tried to kill the Major? Why?" said the other man.

"What I heard is that James blamed the Major for his wife's death."

Well, I didn't want to hear no more. I went in the shop and told Mr. Wood I was there to buy a piece of meat cause I just come from cuttin' wood for Mr. Burton. He asked me what meat I was after and I showed him how much money I had. He looked in my hand then he took a piece of meat outta the case and wrapped it up and give it to me.

I told him, "I ain't got 'nough money to pay for that piece of meat."

He looked at me, and at the coins in my hand again, and he said, "You take that meat, Sam, and you go on home now. Be sure you cook it good. You don't want your young'uns to get sick."

I said, "Thank you, Mr. Wood. Thank you."

I runned outta the store and kep' runnin' till I got home to tell Liz all 'bout what happened. Mr. Wood, he's 'nother one who changed how he talks 'bout us. I think it might'a been the riot what changed them.

But happy as I was gettin' that meat for my fam'ly, I was sad cause I losed my friend, James and I ain't gonna see him when we goes to Yar-moth. I wonder what happened to James's Bess. I never heard nothin' 'bout her dyin'. I might not'a heard 'bout James dyin' if I wasn't goin' to the butcher shop.

I wonder if James's other girl is still with the Major. Well, least James and his wife ain't here to know that their Jude was killed by the Major's boys. I wonder if one of them is the one what killed James.

The Major and them boys, they was 'rrested for killin' Jude and they is comin' to court in Shelburne in three days. James, he can't be in the court, so I is goin' for him.

My Pap, he don't understand why I is goin' when I didn't know James's girl. I told him, "Pap, somebody gotta go for James. The Major and his fam'ly they killed all of James's fam'ly cep't his other girl, Diana. Is they gonna kill her, too?"

Pap he said.,"Why does you care 'bout a man you only seen a coupl'a times?"

"Cause he was my friend. If you could'a seen him, you wouldn't be askin'. He was real sad. Slaves is sad almos' all the time, but James, he was sad cause his girl, Jude, was sold away when he was workin' on 'nother farm and he wasn't there to help her. Pap, how would you feel if Master Stoffle sold me or Sis when you wasn't there and when you come back, we was gone?"

"I would'a tried to kill him, even if I got killed. Does you know what James did when his girl was sold?"

"He didn't try to kill his master. He might'a tried, but the nex' day, The Major come to the farm and bought James and his fam'ly what was left."

~

The day comed that the court was gonna start for the Major and his boys and it made no diff'rence what Pap said, I is goin'. For James.

"Pap, is you comin' with me."

"I can't go today, but maybe the nex' time. Sam, you knows how white judges is, they ain't gonna be for the black folks."

I couldn't say nothin' to that cause Pap was right. We is thiefs and li-ars, that's what they thinks 'bout us. But if they want slave labour, I smiled to myself, then they gets us to do their dirty jobs and they pays us almos' nothin' and sometimes nothin'.

I started walkin' to Shelburne and I met up with some other folks goin'.

176

"Where you be goin'?" they asked me.

"I is goin' to the court to hear what that white fam'ly got to say 'bout killin' their slave."

"We is goin' too," they said. "Does you know who that white fam'ly is?"

"They used ta live in Shelburne some time back, but they moved to Yarmouth. The Major, he was in the war in America."

"How you know that?" they asked me.

"I know cause I was friends with their man, James, b'fore they moved to Yarmouth, and he told me. The girl they killed, she was James's girl."

"We was in town the other day and we heard folks talkin'. They was sayin' how the Major's boys they beat her to death for stealin' food. These white follks they was sayin' them boys did the right thing, you gotta keep your slaves in line. She ain't got no right stealin' from the white man. Maybe somebody should'a beat them. We stealed food cause we was starvin and nobody beat us. Maybe she was starvin' too."

"You couldn'a got caught or you would'a been whipped, shore 'nough," I said. "You hear tell 'bout that girl that was gonna get three hundred lashes for stealin' a old dress. After the second whippin' she up and died. She couldn't take no more. I think the judge likes givin' the Negro girls more whippin's than he does the men. I remember Pap tellin' me 'bout the young girl who was gived a hundred and fifty lashes for stealin' two little things, he didn't know what, from a white man's house. We don't know what happened to her, but she prob'ly up and died on the gaoler too."

"I guess that's how it's always gonna be for us black folks," one of them said. "The white man can steal and he ain't whipped, least I ain't seen none whipped, but if it's one a us, they whips us till we falls down or falls down dead. Does you think them white boys is gonna be punished for killin' that slave?"

"Prob'ly not," I said. "But it ain't right."

We walked the rest of the way without sayin' nothin' else.

When we got to the court there was a lot of folks there waitin' to get in. Black folks and white folks. We didn't know if we was gonna get in, there was so many. Folks started pushin' and shovin' soon as the door was opened.

I got myself in and was standin' 'gainst the wall. I could see everythin' that was gonna go on from where I was standin'.

The black and white folks all 'round me started argerrin' and I thought they was gonna fight, but they didn't.

A white man comed up to me and said, "Did you know, Jude?"

I didn't know this man, never seened him b'fore. I looked him in his eyes and said, "Why you wanna know?"

"I was her friend," he said.

I kep' starin' at him. No white man is a friend to a slave woman less he takes her for his woman. A lotta masters, they did that so they could get more babies to sell. I never heard nobody say that Jude had babies.

"Was you her Master?" I asked him, cause I never seen the Major b'fore. It could'a been him.

"No," he said. "I was her friend, that's all. Did you know her?"

"No," I said. "I knew her Papa, James, b'fore they moved to Yarmouth."

He smiled at me and said his name was Israel, then he shook my hand and said he was happy to meet Jude's papa's friend.

The judges, they come in the court and we had to be quiet.

The first day, when the doc said 'bout the beatin' and the cuts that was on her body, I was shocked and I says it again, I is glad that James ain't here to see what been done to his girl.

The last day, Pap comed with me. When the judges said that they wasn't guilty, we thought the black folks was gonna riot. They was mad.

Pap didn't say, "Didn't I tell you the judges wasn't gonna be for the black folks," cause he knew I was mad and if I had'a been close 'nough I would'a hit one of them boys what killed her.

"Let's go home, boy."

We was almos' to the door when the Major was leavin' and a white man runned up to him and punched him in the face. He hollered, "Murderer!"

A white man did it! I was shocked right down to my shoes with the holes in them.

Me and Pap, we left and walked home. We was quiet most'a the way.

Some of the blacks who was there, they had plenty to say. They wasn't talkin' to us, so we just listened.

"Did you hear that Major? He said he can beat his slave if he wants to. And his boys, they is the ones what killed her."

"Does you think they was gonna find them not guilty? If it had'a been a white girl who got killed by a black man, they would'a hanged him. They wouldn'a gived him no trial."

"I guess you is right. Did you see their other slave? They wouldn't let her talk, they read from a paper what she telled the Sheriff. Did you hear the people shoutin', 'Let her speak'? There was almos' a fight b'tween one white man and our Dublin cause the white man said she was a liar. Dublin should'a punched him one, but I guess he didn't wanna get put in the gaol. That slave, she shore looked real sad."

"You'd be sad if you Mamma and Papa and sister be all dead and it be only you left with the ones what killed them. I wonder what's gonna happen to her now."

"I don't know, but I bet they ain't gonna treat her right. Did you see that white man punch the Major in the face? I wish it could'a been me. I bet the Major is gonna have his self one sore face tomorrow."

"And if you did, you would be gettin' the rest of them three hundred lashes that girl never got."

Me and Pap, we fin'lly got home. I told Liz all 'bout it.

"I is sorry it wasn't the way you hoped it would be, Sam," she said. "But you knew they wasn't gonna find the white man guilty.."

"I kinda knew them judges was gonna say they wasn't guilty, but I was hopin'. For James."

35

White folks is always gonna look down on us. We was good 'nough to fight for them, but they don't want us livin' nex' to them. It was time to leave Birchtown, it wasn't a good place to be. We went to town a few days ago, but we couldn't get no work and Mr. Wood and Mr. Burton, they never had no bread or meat they was gonna throw away. I guess things wasn't easy for them either.

We was gettin' low on food so me and Pap, we was gonna go fishin'. Most'a the time I never caught nothin'. Seems like most'a the fish was way out and you had to go on a boat to get them. And like I always said, I ain't goin' on no boat.

Some of the Blacks said if you go fishin' when the tide is comin' in, that's the best time to go, cause some of the fish comes in with the tide. I didn't know how come they knew that, less that's when they went, but I never seen too many of them comin' home with any fish. Well, me and Pap, we was gonna try that.

I wasn't gonna say nothin' 'bout goin' to Yarmouth right off, but I was thinkin' it was time to go. And I was thinkin' maybe Pap changed his mind bout goin'. He ain't never said no more bout it, but I don't think Mam wanted to go and if she don't go, then Pap ain't goin'.

Mam said one time how she was tired of movin' from one place to 'nother. She said, "I is gettin' too old to be doin' all this movin' all the time. When we come here from New Jersey, I thought we was gonna have us a nice piece of farmin' land and a house to live in. That's what we was told, but somebody was shore lyin' cause the farmin' land is only good for farmin' the rocks that are already there. And it seems like it is growin' more rocks every year. It prob'ly ain't gonna be no better in this Yarmouth place. And where is we gonna live? I ain't diggin' no more pits. We got us a hut now, bad as it is, but it's on top of the ground, not under the ground like a grave. Where is we gonna live, you tell me that."

I didn't know where we was gonna live. All I could tell her was, "Mam, there ain't no pits in Yarmouth. I heard a man tellin' Mr. Wood that nobody lives in pits and they wouldn't 'llow nobody to live in pits cause they ain't animals."

Mam never said no more, but I knew she was still sayin' to herself, 'I don't wanna go.' And I knew if she changed her mind 'bout goin', Pap wouldn't go.

Me and Pap, we kep' walkin' to the bay to try to cetch us some fish. I didn't know how we was gonna cetch us any fish with a stick with a string on it, but Pap said we would cause we had us a hook on the string. The hooks Pap made outta a piece of wire that he found. I still didn't know how it was gonna work cause it wasn't very strong. Pap said it would cetch us some small fish, but that's all.

Pap laughed at me b'fore he made the hooks when I told him I ain't never caught no fish and he asked me what I used.

When I showed him my stick and string with no hook on it, he slapped me on the back and he laughed. "Boy, you ain't gonna cetch nothhin' less you got a hook and a worm on the end of that string."

"Where's I gonna get hooks, Pap? Ain't nobody in Birchtown got no hooks."

"Come with me, boy."

We went to Pap's hut. Mam was sittin' at the table mendin' a dress.

"What you men up to today?"

"We was gonna go fishin' wife, but Sam here says he ain't got no hooks."

Mam looked at me. "You can't go fishin' with no hooks. How you gonna cetch the fish?"

"That's what I told him."

Pap went to the shelf on the wall and he took two pieces of wire that he cut from a long piece and he bent it like a hook.

"Where you get that piece of wire, Pap?"

"I found it on the path when I was comin' home from Shelburne the other day. Figgered I might use it for somethin' one day. I guess we need it today."

Well, me and Pap, we had us fishin' poles with hooks on the end of the strings and worms in a can and we was goin' to the bay to cetch us some fish.

I guess Pap knew what he was talkin' 'bout cause we caught us almost ten fish till the hooks come offa our lines.

While we was standin' there waitin' for the fish to bite I said, "Pap, is you still goin' to Yarmouth when I goes? I figger it's time for us to go, cause there ain't nothin' here for us. I ain't sayin' we is goin' tomorrow, cause we has to make plans like we did when we runned away from Master Stoffle's. We has to plan how we is gonna get there and where we is gonna live. I think you and me better go first to see what's there b'fore we take our fam'lies. Prince and Margaret, they already said they ain't goin'. Liz is upset 'bout that, but they is shore they don't want to go."

He never said nothin', just kep' starin' out over the water. I never said no more, cause I figgered when he was ready to tell me what he was gonna do, he'd tell me.

36

After the big fire we had, Miss Jane, she asked me if I was sorry I didn't go with the Blacks from Birchtown who went to Africa.

"Why would I be sorry, Miss Jane? I never come from Africa like you did, and you didn't go back."

"Too old for that, boy. I been away too long. Don't know nobody there no more and I is too old to start all over again."

"Does you remember Pack?"

"I remembers him. He went to that place in Africa a while back, didn't he?"

"He said if he was gonna die, he was gonna die and be buried where he was borned. He don't know nobody there, but he went back cause it was his homeland."

"Well, I ain't Pack. He seen his Mamma die on that ship and get throwed in the water for the shark's dinner. He never forgot what the white man done and he didn't want to stay in the white man's land no more."

"He was sad all the time, didn't seem to bother with nobody. Do you think he's happy now?"

"What's happy, boy? He might not be sad as he was, but he prob'ly ain't happy."

"I is gonna be happy. That Thanksgivin' Day is comin' and we is gonna have us a feast. We never done it b'fore, but we is gonna do it this time."

"What you got to be thankful for, boy? What you got? Prob'ly had more when you was in New Jersey."

"We did, Miss Jane, but we was slaves. We ain't slaves here."

"What feast you gonna have? Where's you gonna get the food?"

"We got some taters that we growed in the summer and I seen some ducks. Maybe I can cetch one or two."

"Did you ever cetch one b'fore? They is cagey buggers, they know how to 'scape."

"No, I never caught none b'fore." I wasn't tellin' her me and Pap and Prince, we tried one time, but they got away.

"If you cetch one, does you know how to clean it and cook it?"

"Does you know how to cook ducks, Miss Jane?"

"I is ninety, I can cook anythin'. You gonna invite me to supper if you cetches one?"

"I shore is."

I better cetch me some ducks. Miss Jane, she can teach our women folk how to cook them.

"Miss Jane, if we don't cetch no ducks, we might have to try to cetch us some of them pigeons that is flyin' 'round. The women folk, they know how to cook them. Will you come to supper anyway, if all we got is pigeons and taters?"

"I shore will, boy. Now, go cetch them ducks," she said, and she slapped me on my back.

I asked her, cause I always wanted to know, "Miss Jane, how did you get them cuts on your cheeks?"

She put her hand to her face and rubbed one cheek with her fingers. "Boy, when we was put in them hell awful ships in Africa and brought to America, we was cut three times on each cheek. That says we was borned in Africa. It was like a brandin', but they didn't use no hot brandin' iron, they used a sharp knife."

"Didn't it hurt?" I asked.

"Now, that be a stupid question, boy. Course it hurt. Give me a knife and I'll cut your face and you can tell me if it hurts. I was only a little girl, must'a been ten or eleven, not shore, so it hurt like heck."

"Where was your Mamma, did they cut her, too?"

"Yes, they cut her, too, but after we got to the castle, some men come and taked her and I ain't seen her no more."

"I'm sorry, Miss Jane."

"Why is you sorry? You didn't take my Mamma. Don't you feel sorry for me. I is here, ain't I, and I is gonna be here for a while to come."

Miss Jane, she walked towards her cabin. She started laughin' long and loud.

I heard her laughin' and thought, "I wonder what she's laughin' at."

When I got back to our shack, I told wife, "Liz, that Thanksgivin' Day is comin' up and we is gonna celebrate like the white folks does. We is gonna have us a feast."

"Is you crazy, Sam? Where is we gonna get the food?"

"We got us some taters and me and Pap and Prince, we is gonna cetch us some of them ducks that is always in the bay." I didn't tell her that I ain't told Pap and Prince yet.

"Ducks? Seems to me you men tried to cetch them ducks b'fore and all you got was wet from head to toe. So, how is you gonna cetch them now? And I ain't never cooked no duck b'fore."

"That's okay, Liz, cause, Miss Jane, she said she knows how to cook anythin' and she'll show you how to do it. She's comin' to supper."

I went back out to find Pap and Prince. They is gonna think I is crazy too, cause of the last time we tried to cetch some. Pap was outside pilin' wood, but I didn't see Prince nowheres.

"Pap, where's Prince?"

"He's gone in the woods lookin' for firewood. What you want him for?"

Might as well just say it. "We gotta cetch us some ducks."

"What you say? Never heard you."

"You heard me, Pap. We gotta cetch us some ducks."

"You wants to get wet again, does you?"

"We ain't gonna get wet this time. I got me a plan on how we is gonna cetch them." I don't have no plan, but maybe Pap and Prince does.

"And if you got a plan," I went on, "that's better, ain't it?"

"You ain't got no plan, does you?"

"I can figger out how to cetch them. If we cetch some, Miss Jane, she'll show our women how to cook them. I already asked her to come to supper."

"Okay, boy. We'll try to cetch them ducks again."

The next day we went to the bay. Miss Jane, she watched us when we walked past her hut. She was leanin' 'gainst the door with her arms crossed over her breasts.

She hollered to us., "I seen some ducks in the bay this mornin' and they is still there."

Miss Jane went inside her hut, laughin' so hard as she closed her door, we thought the ducks would hear her.

Maybe they heard her and maybe they didn't, but we didn't cetch even a feather.

As we struggled back up from the water, Pap said, "Boy, I told you we wasn't gonna cetch no ducks. All we is gonna cetch is a cold cause that water was cold. We is gonna have to try to cetch us some pigeons."

"Pap, we could'a caught them if you and Prince didn't make all that noise."

"Me and Prince? And what was you doin'? Runnin' to the water like the devil was chasin' you. You was makin' noise the same as we was."

"Here comes Miss Jane." I said.

She stopped in front of us lookin' at the water runnin' down our faces. "Boys," she said. She always called grown men boys, 'less they was old as her. "Didn't cetch no ducks, I see."

"No, Miss Jane," said Prince.

She took her hands out from b'hind her back and dropped three ducks on the ground in front of us. And they was already plucked and cleaned.

"I will be to your hut tomorrow to show your women folk how to cook them. Then we will have us a feast," she said.

We just stared at her and she put her hands in the pockets of her baggy men's britches and walked away whistlin'. We stared at the ducks layin' on the ground.

"Where she get them?" I asked Pap and Prince.

Pap had a big smile on his face. "That woman, she caught them ducks and she plucked and cleaned them. Is we stupid? A ninety-year-old wo-man caught our supper and all we caught was wet."

We all started laughin'. Then we picked up the ducks and went home. We shore wasn't gonna tell the women folk that we caught them cause they would'a knew we didn't . So, we told them that Miss Jane caught them.

Mam said. "Figgered. Miss Jane can cetch anythin'. I seen her go down to the bay with a sharp stick and she poked it in the water. When she pulled it out there was a fish on it. I bet she knows how to do things that nobody can do. She been 'round a long time and she had to survive the best she knew how."

"She is gonna come for supper tomorrow and show you all how to cook them ducks, cause you never cooked none b'fore."

"That's good, cause we want them cooked right. If Miss Jane is gonna show us how to cook them ducks, we'll have us a feast tomorrow," said Mam.

Miss Jane, she come knockin' on our door in the afternoon. When I opened it she was standin' there with a bag. She come in and dropped it on the table.

"Some carrots for our supper," she said.

"Where you get them, Miss Jane?" I asked.

"I growed them, that's where I got them."

"How can you grow anythin' without somebody stealin' them right outta the ground?"

"When you gets to be my age, boy," she said, "ain't nobody gonna steal from you. I guess they figger if I can live to be ninety, I gotta be a strong woman, so they leaves me and what's mine 'lone. B'sides, a coupl'a the younger men and women helps me with my garden and I gives them some vegetables. Nobody steals from me cause my helpers, they watch over my vegetable patch."

"I guess we gotta be ninety b'fore nobody steals from us cause they is always raidin' our garden."

"Boy, get them to help with the garden and share some of the crop and they won't steal none and they'll help to pertect it."

"Me and Pap and Prince, we grows our gardens tagether, but they still steals from us."

"Boy, boy, boy," she said, shakin' her head. "They is fam'ly and fam'ly ain't gonna steal from you. It's the others what does the stealin'."

I never said no more, but I was gonna talk to Pap and Prince when they gets here and tell them what Miss Jane said. I don't know if it will work for us, cause we ain't old as Miss Jane. Pap didn't know how old he was, but when they put his name in that book that all the Negroes was in when they left New York, he told them he was fifty. I figger he must be seventy now or close on it. Maybe the younger folks will think he is old and help us like they did Miss Jane.

"Okay," said Miss Jane. "Where's them ducks, Elizabeth?"

"Miss Jane, you can call me Liz, like everybody else does."

"Is your name Liz or Elizabeth?"

"It's Elizabeth."

"Then that's what I'll call you. Don't like them short names, myself. Not 'spectful, I say."

She looked at me. "Boy, you make shore we have us plenty of wood for the fire. It has to be hot to cook them ducks good."

"Yes, Miss Jane, there is plenty wood outside. You tell me when you wants more."

I has to laugh at Miss Jane. She always calls me boy 'stead of my name. Maybe she don't know my name. I'll have to tell her one time.

She nodded and went back to jabberin' with Liz, Mam and Margaret. They was all 'round the table, doin' what Miss Jane was tellin' them to do.

"I cleaned them good," she said. "But it be good if you puts more water to the inside again to make shore all the blood is gone. Don't want no blood left in them. It'll make you real sick."

Mam, she scrubbed them ducks inside and out. I was sittin' at the table watchin'. I wanted to know how to do it too.

I never did that to the pigeons we caught and ate. We must'a been lucky that we didn't get sick, cause we killed them and cleaned them, and then we cooked them and ate them right off. We didn't clean them good as the ducks was gettin' cleaned. I won't do that no more.

Pap and Prince come in the cabin. When them ducks started cookin' they shore smelled good.

Pap kep' sayin', "Is they done yet?"

The last time he said it, Mam said, "They ain't gonna be done for a time yet. You men go on outside, you is in the way. Git."

There was a lotta us in that little hut. We was big men and the women was kinda big, 'specially my Liz. After she had them four babies, she didn't lose no weight. If she heard me say that, she would slap me one good. But it's true. Then there was the four young'uns.

We went outside and sat in the sun. It was high in the sky and it was still warm. Course, we knew that wasn't gonna last, cause winter was soon comin'. We had us some rickety stools that we was sittin' on that reminded me of my friend Joseph's old three-legged stool that me and George kep' waitin' for him to fall offa. But he never did.

We was talkin' away and we could smell them ducks cookin' right through the door.

Pap said, "They better hurry up and get done. I is hungry."

I opened the door and put my head in. "Is them ducks almos' done? We is hungry."

"They be done purty soon," said Liz. I'll tell you when you can come in."

B'fore I closed the door, I took one big smell. Boy, was them ducks gonna taste good. I heard Liz chucklin' when she closed the door right in my face.

The food was fin'lly cooked and Liz opened the door and told us to 'Come on in.'

We runned through that door b'fore she closed us out again.

There wasn't 'nough room for everybody to sit 'round the table, but Mam found a board somewhere and made a bench for the young'uns to eat on and we brought in our stools and all us grown-ups sat 'round the table. We was sittin' so close our arms was touchin', but when we started eatin' nobody noticed cause that food was shore good. There was taters and carrots and so much duck.

I said to Miss Jane, "Miss Jane, you is gonna have to show us how to cetch them ducks."

"Be happy to Boy," she said as she filled her mouth full of taters.

I seen she didn't eat no duck and I said, "Miss Jane, how come you ain't eatin' no duck?"

"I don't eat no meat most'a the time, it don't sit in my belly good. I mostly eats fish."

"You should'a told us, we could'a caught you a fish so you wasn't only eatin' taters and carrots. It don't seem right."

"That's okay, boy. I is injoyin' what I is eatin' just as much as you is injoyin' what you is eatin'."

I looked over at my Liz and she was lookin' at me. She shook her head cause she didn't want me to say no more.

But I didn't think that was what it was. I think Miss Jane, she wanted us to have all the ducks for our selfs. I did see her cetchin' fish a lotta times, but I ain't never seen her cetch meat. She caught them ducks and we never seen her and we is outside most'a the time. I wonder if she caught them after it was dark.

I guess it don't matter. I figger she got to be ninety by not 'splainin' nothin' to nobody. And it ain't nobody's bis'ness anyway, I say.

We had us our feast and we all laughed 'bout us men fallin' in the bay tryin' to cetch them ducks.

And we was thankful.

37

Seemed like winter was always comin'. We could feel it in the air. We didn't get us no four feet of snow and we didn't have us a lotta storms, but it was cold. Me and Pap and Prince, we made shore we had plenty of wood cut and piled.

When spring come, it come early and we was hopin' we was gonna be able to plant us a little garden this year and get some veg'tables.

In the summer, Miss Jane, she showed us how to cetch them ducks. It took us a while to learn, cause we is so feet heavy we didn't know how to sneak up on them. Miss Jane, she showed us what berries to put down for them. They don't eat all kinds, cause some is poison to the birds, but she said they like blueberries, so when we picked some for our self, we picked extra when we wanted to cetch ducks.

We had us a lotta laughs tryin' to cetch them ducks. Miss Jane, she shook her head every time the ducks got away. She was patient with us, I don't know why. I didn't have no patience and that's prob'ly why I never caught no ducks, she said.

Pap and Prince, they caught three and they laughed at me cause I didn't cetch none.

I could see Miss Jane was gettin' firstrated with me, but she kep' right on tryin' to show me how to cetch them. Ventu'lly I caught me one and she laughed like a little girl and clapped her hands tagether. She was proud of me.

"Boy, you fin'lly cetched your self a duck. You did good. You think you can do it again."

I had a big smile on my face.

"I caught me a duck, Miss Jane, I caught me a duck. I know what I has to do now and I can do it again. Took me a long time, didn't it, Miss Jane?"

"It shore did, boy. It shore did."

~

It seemed like summer just come and now we is waitin' on winter again. It ain't set in full yet. We had us a coupl'a days when there was a bit of snow, but it didn't stay on the ground. Got warm a few days, but some days the wind was blowin' so cold, I kind'a wished we was still livin' in the pit, cause the wind didn't blow through the dirt.

I told Pap, "Pap, I gotta put some sod on the outside of our hut cause sometimes the wind blows right through the logs."

"Didn't I tell you that, boy? Why you think I put some on mine? You says you gotta do it. Well, let's get to it b'fore it gets too cold and you can't get it done."

Pap was right, as he always is. I guess cause he is older, he knows more.

One day I was sittin' at my table and thinkin' 'bout the Thanksgivin' we had last year. We had us a real nice time. The other day when I was to Mr. Wood's butcher shop I heard a woman tell him to save her a ham for Christmas.

Christmas? We ain't never had us no Christmas, no place that we was. Slaves ain't 'llowed much of anythin', let 'lone a Christmas.

But I was a thinkin'. 'Stead of us havin' a Thanksgivin' again, why can't we have us a Christmas? I don't know what you had to do to have a Christmas, but I bet Liz knows. She works for the white folks and I bet they talk 'bout it come this time of year.

Liz was gettin' supper one day and I said to her, "Liz, we had us a real nice Thanksgivin' last year, didn't we?"

"We shore did, Sam. We shore did," she said, smilin'.

"Does you think we can have us a Christmas this year 'stead of 'nother Thanksgivin'?"

She stared at me for a minute, not sayin' nothin', then she smiled again and her eyes they light up. "Yes, Sam, I think we can have us a Christmas. We ain't never had none b'fore, but I seen how they does it in the white folk's houses. We can't have the dec'rations like they does, but, Sam, does you want a tree?"

I was gettin' excited. "What kind'a tree?"

"I can show you if you wants one. You'll have to cut it down and it can't be no big one cause our hut is only small. I got some rags we can tie on it and we can get us some pine cones to put on it, too."

She got quiet again. I knew she was gonna say somethin' then she stopped.

"What is it, Liz? What was you gonna say?"

"When I was at Mr. Burton's house last year when they was havin' their Christmas, there was presents under the tree for everybody, 'specially the young'uns. Where is we gonna get us presents for our young'uns?"

"We still got us a little time, I'll think of somethin'. Me and Pap and Prince, we can make somethin' if we can find some wood. We'll go to the lumber place in Shelbune tomorrow to see if we can get us some pieces of wood that they ain't gonna use."

I stopped talkin' cause I was thinkin' on it. I smiled at her. "I'll find presents for our young'uns."

"Sam, we shore is gonna have us a nice Christmas. We know how to cook them ducks now, Miss Jane don't have to show us, but I want you to tell her to come to our house cause we is gonna have us a Christmas."

"I is gonna go see her today and tell her 'bout it. And, Liz, I is gonna make her somethin' outta wood if I can get 'nough. Maybe a little stool like the ones we got."

"That would be wonderful."

Me and Liz, we planned our Christmas that day and we was gonna make shore it was as grand as our Thanksgivin' was.

I went over to Pap's. Him and Prince was outside, cuttin' and pilin' wood. Seems like they was always cuttin' and pilin' wood.

"Snow's comin', boy, we gotta make shore we got us 'nough wood cut and piled."

"I'll help. I piled mine this mornin'. I'll have to get more b'fore the snow comes hard, but I is okay for now."

"You is always waitin' to finish gettin' your wood. You always gotta get more'n you think you is gonna need. Remember that winter when we had snow to our waist and we couldn't get us no wood? We was cold that winter. I ain't gonna be with no wood no more. Me and Prince, we is gonna pile wood all 'round our huts and you better do the same. When we is finished here we'll come tomorrow and help you, cause you never know when the snow is comin'," Pap said, lookin' at all the wood they piled.

Pap was right as us'ull. And all that wood piled 'round the cabin will make it warmer inside, cause the wind won't get in as much.

While we was pilin' their wood I was tellin' them 'bout me and Liz's plans for us havin' a Christmas feast and 'bout makin' presents for the young'uns.

"What you think, Pap? You and Prince wanna help? We is gonna have Miss Jane over and she won't have to show nobody how to cook this time. She can sit there by the stove and keep warm and wait for supper to be done."

"You know we'll help, boy."

"We is gonna have us a tree and Liz, she said in the white man's house, for Christmas, they got presents under the tree for their young'uns. Where is we gonna get presents for my young'uns? And I wanna make Miss Jane a stool like we got. Pap, can we do that? Make Miss Jane a stool and find somethin' to put under the tree for our young'uns?"

Prince was standin' there quiet like. He's not much for talkin', but when he does, sometimes he don't want to stop. I guess it has to be what he's talkin' 'bout that makes him want to say somethin'.

"I say we can do it," he said. "I'll make Miss Jane's stool. I was sittin' on the ones you and your Pap made and they is kinda wobbly. Miss Jane will be sittin' on her ass on the ground more'n she'll sittin' on her stool."

"What you talkin' 'bout? You didn't fall offa them," I said.

"That's cause I is a big heavy man and it won't go nowheres while my ass is sittin' on it. Miss Jane, she's like a bird, she got no weight to her. The wind can blow her away."

Well, he was right 'bout that. Miss Jane is just a little thing and it seems like she's gettin' smaller and smaller every day.

I looked at Prince. "Does you think Miss Jane is alright?"

"What you mean?"

"It seems like she's losin' weight all the time. I hope she ain't sick."

"She's old, boy and old people they don't eat a lot, maybe that's all it is. But we'll watch out for her. Do whatever she needs done."

"Okay, Prince, I feel better 'bout that. If you wants to make her stool that's okay. Pap, does you know what we can make?"

"Let me think on it. We still got us some time."

"Pap, that Mr. John Johnson, ain't he a carpenter? Maybe he can help us. Prince, maybe he can help you make Miss Jane's stool."

"Don't need no help," said Prince.

Mr. Johnson, he's a carpenter. You ain't."

"Don't need no help," he said and he walked outta the hut.

"Boy, you ain't got a lick'a sense. I think you made him mad. He might be mad 'nough that he don't wanna make the stool."

Pap was right. I ain't got a lick'a sense. If Prince don't make Miss Jane's stool, where is we gonna get us one?

The next day me and Pap was sittin' at Pap's table, talkin' 'bout what we was gonna make. We ain't never made no toys b'fore and we was gonna have us a hard time.

"Pap, how is we gonna make toys when we don't know how?"

"I don't know, boy."

The door opened and in come, Prince. He just looked at me then he went right back out again.

"Where's he goin', Pap?"

"I don't know, boy."

The door opened again and Prince come in carryin' a stool.

"You made that?" me and Pap said.

Pap picked it up and was lookin' it over. "This is beautiful, Prince," I said. "We didn't know you could do carpenter work."

"There's a lot 'bout me you don't know, Sam, cause I don't tell nobody what I can do. I just does it. And I told you I don't need no help. If I needs help, I'll ask for it. You fellas know what you is gonna make yet?"

"We don't know, and even if me and Pap knew what we was gonna make, we ain't got no toy makin' tools. So we can't make nothin' anyway."

"I know somethin' we can make that the young'uns'll have fun with. Has you ever hear tell of a wood whistle?"

"I seen them whistles b'fore," said Pap. "They gotta have a hole down the middle, don't they? How is we gonna cut that? And where is we gonna get the wood for to make them? '

"We got what we need right outside," Prince said. "You know them branches that is on some of them blocks of wood? That's what we need. We just has to make shore they is big 'nough 'round, and dry. The wood gotta be dry. Mr. Johnson, he might have somethin' to cut out the middle, cause carpenters, they need all kinds a tools. Let's go cut us some of them branches then go have a sit down with Mr. Johnson and see if he can help us."

Wood whistles. Me and Pap, we would'a never thought 'bout that. The young'uns is gonna have a first good Christmas and they is prob'ly gonna make us crazy blowin' them whistles all the time. 'Specially if they is in-side all the time cause there is too much snow outside.

I thought we was gonna have us a early winter. We waked up one mornin' and there was snow on the ground. It wasn't a lot, but we figgered this was gonna be the start of a long and hard winter like we had a coupl'a years past, but it was gone the nex' day cause it got warm again. I was shore hopin' we wouldn't get no snow b'fore we had us our Christmas.

We got us our whistles made. Mr. Johnson, he had a tool that cut the middle almos' out. He said you couldn't cut it all the way out cause the whistle wouldn't blow if you did.

Liz, she found some ribbon to tie on Miss Jane's new stool.

"Where'd you get that pretty red ribbon, Liz?"

"When I was in Shelburne, workin' at Mr. Burton's house, he give me some stuff to throw away and there was a piece of ribbon mongst it. I asked him if I could have it and he told me take whatever I want. So, I took the ribbon and there was some pieces of cloth. See?" she said, holdin' it up. "Some of the pieces is only small, but I figger we can put them on the tree with the other pieces I got."

She tied that ribbon 'round the leg of Miss Jane's stool and it was the prettiest present we ever did see. Considerin' we ain't never seen no presents b'fore.

Everybody come to supper. There was me and Liz and our young'uns, Pap and Mam, and Prince and Margaret and Miss Jane.

Margaret, she is a lot like Prince. She don't talk much either, less it's somethin' she wants to talk 'bout. Liz said her Mamma was always like that. Even when she got somethin' to say, she says it and that's all. But Liz said sometimes it can take a long time for her say what she wants to say.

When we gived Miss Jane her stool, she looked at it a minute then she said, "Is that for me? Nobody ever gived me nothin' b'fore. Thank you."

She sat her ass right on it like a queen sittin' on her throne, makin' us laugh.

We ate the ducks we caught all by our selfs and we had us some veg'tables and taters. The vegetables was gived to us by Mr. Burton after Liz told him we was gonna have us a Christmas.

Mr. Burton, he wasn't always good to us. Remember me tellin' you 'bout the time I had to go and beg for some food cause we never had none for almos' a week and I went in his bak'ry and he throwed a loaf of green bread at me and called me a black beggar and told me to get outta his store? I ain't never forgot and I ain't never gonna forget. He used to call us names too when he was talkin' to other folks. Like "Those Niggers is gonna have a school?" Like that. Them was the times when nobody had hardly nothin', not even the white folks. Some of them was almos' bad off as we was.

I don't know what made him change his mind 'bout the black folks, but he must'a. Maybe it was the riot.

We had us our Christmas and it was grand as our Thanksgivin'. We is gonna do it again nex' year.

The snow didn't start comin' hard till almos' the end of the year. It snowed hard for two days and we had us almos' two feet of snow. Seemed like I was always cleanin' snow from our door. Couldn't wait till it got done snowin' cause we might not a got outta the house.

We kep' a watch on Miss Jane and done what needed doin'. She didn't have to get no wood in or snow to melt to have water cause we did it for her.

The first time we went to her hut to help her she said,"I ain't no cripple. I can get my wood and water myself. You think I is too old to do what needs to be done?"

"No, Miss Jane, but there's a lotta snow on the ground and we was here shovelin' and it only took a minute to get you some wood, and snow for water. If we come and do it for you, you won't have to go out in the cold. Didn't you tell me your old bones was gettin' cold?"

"Shouldn'a telled you nothin'," she said, but she had a little smile on her face when she said it. "Well, if you is gonna do that for me all winter, I is gonna sit here and stay warm."

She sat down on her stool, straight as a tree ,and watched us lug in wood and snow.

"Is you gonna let me melt my own snow?"

"Yes, Miss Jane, we thinks you can do that your self."

She slapped me upside my head and said, "Get outta here and go home and look after your young'uns."

When we closed her door we could hear her laughin'.

But I was still worried 'bout her.

38

Winter was fin'lly over amd spring was springin' up, like Mam always said. We had us a coupl'a bad storms and a lotta snow, but not like the winter we had so much snow it was up to our waist.

Miss Jane, she passed on just as spring was comin. She told me one time, "Boy, if you comes here and I is gone to the other side, just put me in the box and bury me deep. I don't want no fuss. I is almos' ninety-one and it's time for me to go."

"Don't say that, Miss Jane," I said. "You is gonna be here for a long time yet."

Now, boy," she said, takin' my hand in her bony fingers. "You know, some folks they pass on and they is younger than me. I might'a been a slave all my life, but I had a good life, good as it could be bein' a slave. But you gotta do what you gotta do to make your life better'n it was. Now, you do as I say. I want no fuss."

"Alright, Miss Jane. We'll do what you want."

We buried Miss Jane on the hill b'hind her hut. She said when it rained the water would run down the hill and it won't go in her buryin' box. She didn't care if other folks didn't like her bein' buried on that hill, that's where she wanted to be. And I say, if anybody can live long as Miss Jane, they can shorely have what they want.

I miss Miss Jane.

It wasn't long b'fore somebody moved in Miss Jane's hut. It was a fam'ly and they had three young'uns. I was mad, cause that was Miss Jane's and ain't nobody else should be livin' in it.

Pap said, "Boy, Miss Jane is gone and somebody gotta live in it. She wouldn't want it to sit empty. That fam'ly, they was livin' in a pit. You know what that's like and you didn't like it cause it almos' made Liz sick in the mind. I hear that the woman movin' in Miss Jane's was gettin' sick like Peggy. You remember how she up and walked in the bay one night cause she couldn't live in the pit no more? Maybe gettin' outta the pit will make this woman better. Them folks needs that hut, boy."

"You is right, Pap, but all I can see is Miss Jane sittin' outside her door in the summer on her stool. But now that the fam'ly is in a hut 'stead of a pit, I hope his missus is gonna be okay."

~

It was between spring and summer and we had to get us a garden planted. We still had to walk ten miles to get to the land that was give to us for plantin'. We is still pullin' rocks the frost pushes up outta the ground in the spring, but we can still do our plantin'.

We did what Miss Jane said. We got us 'nother man and his missus to plant with us and watch the garden so nobody would steal our vegetables b'fore they growed. Come fall we had us almos' 'nough vegetables for the winter.

I don't like talkin' 'bout the nex' winter, cause Mam, she took sick b'fore winter set in and she was sick all the winter. We had to tend to her almos' every day and do everythin' for Pap that we did for Miss Jane, cause he wasn't gonna leave Mam 'lone, not for a minute. We had to cut and pile his wood, and when the snow come, we had to shovel and fetch 'nough snow so they would have some water.

Pap, he said, "I ain't goin' outta the hut and leavn' my Sarrah 'lone. If I goes out and she calls for me, I ain't gonna be here. Boy, you is gonna help me, ain't you?"

"You is my Pap and Mam. What you needs done, I'll do. Me and Prince, we is gonna make shore you has plenty of wood cut and piled b'fore winter and we'll bring some in by the hearth when you needs some. Sis will take care of Mam's bathin'. You won't have nothin' to do but be with Mam."

"You is a good boy, Sam. You is a good boy."

Pap still calls me a boy when I is a growed man. I guess I'll always be his boy.

With all the bad we had in two winters, I forgot to tell you that my sister, Sarrah, she got her self married to Charlie Wilson and now she got her self a baby on the way. When she gets close to havin' her baby, my Liz, she said she would help Mam with her bathin'.

Liz, she got her self a lot to do with our own four young'uns to tend to, but she said. "Don't you worry 'bout that, Sam. How come you still calls them young'uns? Jenny she's almost twenty-two she is, and she got herself a fella. And John, he's gonna be twenty nex' winter. Prince Edward and Polly, they'll be goin' on their own soon and Polly, she got her eye on a young fella on the other side of Birchtown. They shorely ain't young'uns no more. Jenny and Polly can help me with Mam, and John and Prince Edward, they can help you and Papa gettin' the wood cut and piled."

"You is a strong woman, Liz. I don't know what I would'a done if you wasn't here to help."

I asked Liz why she called our boy Prince Edward and she said cause that was her Papa's name. I didn't know that. I is learnin' somethin' new 'bout Liz's Papa, seems like, every day. Like he said to me and Pap, there's a lot 'bout him we don't know.

The doc, he come out from Shelbune three times to see Mam after me and Liz's papa went in and begged him. He didn't want to come in the winter cause he might get him self caught in a snow storm, but after he come the first time he come two more times.

He said to Pap. "I am sorry, Sam. There is nothing I can do to help her. She has a bad infection in her lungs and a lot of folks are getting it and they don't survive it. I am sorry."

"There gotta be somethin' you can do, Doc. My Sarrah, she can't die."

"I'm sorry, Sam, I really am," he said, rubbin' Pap on the back.

Mam, she passed on just as spring was springin'.

I went over to their hut to see what Pap needed, and he was sittin' there holdin' Mam's hand and cryin', "She's gone, boy. Mam is gone."

"When, Pap? When?"

"Last night," was all he said.

"Why didn't you come and get me, Pap? You shouldn'a been here all by your self."

He didn't say nothin'.

I went out to get Liz, Prince and Margaret. The women folk would get Mam ready for buryin'. Me and Prince made her buryin' box.

Mam, the same as Miss Jane, wanted to be buried on the hill.

"My boy, Sam," she said. "When I is gone, you bury me on the hill nex' to Miss Jane so the rain will run down the hill and it won't come in my buryin' box. And, Sam, you take care of you Pap. You hear me? You take care of you Pap. Me and Miss Jane, we'll be watchin'."

That's what I did.

I miss my Mam.

39

Mam's been gone a year now and Pap is still havin' a hard time 'ceptin' it. We all is. She was always the strong one in our fam'ly, but I know she wouldn'a wanted us to grieve forever. We gots to get on with our lifes.

Pap moved outta their hut to 'nother one.

I told him, "Pap, you gotta stay in your hut. Don't you want to be 'round all the memries you made there? What would Mam say if she knew you wasn't stayin' in the hut you made together? She worked hard as you buildin' it and you ain't livin' in it."

"I can't stay there, boy. There is too many memries and it hurts me to think 'bout them. Mam would do the same as I is doin'."

"No, she wouldn't, Pap. She would get on with her life cause there is nothin' she could do to bring you back. Don't you remember what she said to you when she was dyin'? She said, 'Don't you mourn me, Sam. I had a good life with you and my young'uns, even if we was slaves. We was always together, 'cept when we runned away. And now we is back ta-gether again. You live your life, Sam, you hear. If you don't, I is gonna come back and smack you one good. And don't forget. You listen to everythin' that's bein' said.'"

Pap sighed. "I remember, but I can't get on with it like she said. I tried, but I can't."

"When did you try, Pap? I don't remember seein' you tryin' anythin'. Pap, maybe if we move to Yarmouth like we talked 'bout. What does you think?"

"I don't know, boy. I don't know. Maybe we should. Maybe it's time."

"I'll talk to Liz, but if she ain't ready, then we has to wait a while longer. It's gotta be when she's ready, cause Prince and Margaret, they already said they ain't movin' nowhere. And Liz, she might not want to go cause her Papa and Mamma ain't goin'. Pap, me and you we still has to go to Yarmouth our selfs first to see if we is gonna get us work and a place to live. We can't go if we got no place to live."

"How we gonna get there, boy? It's too far to walk."

"Let me think on it, Pap."

Pap, thought on what I said and he moved back in his hut. The folks what moved in when he moved out, went to the one he moved in after Mam died. He didn't think they was gonna let him have his hut back, but I talked to them and they did. He's not happy, but he's better bein' in the hut where him and Mam lived.

I talked to Liz while I was thinkin' on how we was gonna get to Yarmouth. "Liz, does you think you is ready to move to Yarmouth? I is havin' it hard findin' work in Shelburne and I think Pap has to go to some place that ain't here. Since Mam died, he ain't his self. He don't want to do nothin' and go nowheres. I asked him if he was ready to move, but all he said was maybe it's time."

"Sam, I know you want to go to Yarmouth, but all we know is what's here. There must be work you can get somewhere. Maybe you could get some work in Yarmouth and we could still live here."

"How is I gonna get to Yarmouth everyday and get back home? I can't walk cause it's too far. We is gonna have to move, if I wants to find work."

Liz , she just looked at me for a minute. "Well, I ain't ready to go nowheres yet, Sam."

"You think on it. Me and Pap, we still has to go our selfs to see if there is gonna be work for us and to find us a place to live. I is gonna have to see if somebody from Shelburne is goin' so's we can get us a ride there and back home. We might have to stay a coupl'a days."

"You do that, Sam, then we can talk some more on it."

I been thinkin' on how we was gonna get to Yarmouth, and I ain't got no answer. There was a coupl'a people who had wagons and would'a took us, but they wasn't comin' back the same day. They said it was too far to get back b'fore dark. Mr. Burton, he was goin', but he was stayin' five days. I can't stay that long, but we could'a stayed two days if we had to.

Well, we didn't get us to Yarmouth for almos' four years. Our Jenny, she took up with a fella from Shelbunne and got with child. We couldn't go nowhere. But I was still plannin' on goin' whether Pap went with me or not.

Mam's been gone almos' them four years and Pap, he's still havin' it hard. He took it in his head that he had to go talk to Mam sometimes.

I asked him, "Does she talk to you, Pap?"

"Is you makin' fun of me, boy? You know she can't talk to me. You thinks I is crazy, doesn't you?"

"No, Pap, I ain't makin' fun of you and I don't think you is crazy, but you goes there a lot."

"I ain't hurtin' nobody boy, I'll go when I wants."

And he never said no more.

One day I went to Shelbune to cut some wood for Mr. Wood. He always paid me money and he give me a loaf of bread that his missus made. I was tellin' him 'bout me and Pap wantin' to go to Yarmouth to see if we can get us some work and a place to live. He told me he was goin' to Yarmouth, but he wasn't comin' back the same day. He was gonna be there for two days.

"We can stay two days," I said.

"I am going at the end of the week and I will be leaving before daylight. Where were you planning to sleep at night?"

"We never give it a thought, Mr. Wood. We'll have to think on that."

I guess I been doin' a lotta thinkin' on things lately. Mr. Wood he looked at me.

"Well," he said. "You can sleep in the wagon. If you have any warm clothes, you better bring them because it still gets chilly at night. Can you be ready to go when I go?"

"Yes, Sir, Mr. Wood. Thank you," I said.

I runned outta his shop with my bread under one arm and my money jinglin' in my pocket. My pocket used ta have a hole in it and I lost my money one day, but Liz, she fixed the hole so I don't lose no more money. The day I lost my money I runned all the way back to Shelbune lookin' on the ground all over, but I never found it. I think somebody found it and was spendin' it right away.

We didn't have to walk all the way to Shelbune. Mr. Wood, he picked me and Pap up right outside Pap's hut. We wasn't s'pectin' that, but we shore was glad.

Liz, she packed us some food in a sack so we would have somethin' to eat later. We was gonna be gone for two days and she put extra in there even though we didn't have us much in the hut. We climbed in the wagon and I waved to Liz as we got outta sight.

Mr. Wood was takin' the old road to Yarmouth that folks started buildin' years ago, but they never finished it. I don't know why. It was real bumpy and we was bouncin' all over the place. Mr. Wood said a man name of James Hamilton lived on this road a ways up.

"How can anybody live in here?" I asked. "Does he travel to get work?"

"No." he said. He has a very large house that he uses as an inn and tavern. He seems to be doing quite well, from what I hear, because people who travel this god-awful road stay there instead of making the long trip all the way to Shelburne in one day."

Me and Pap, we never said nothin'. We was lookin' for that house that Mr. Wood told us 'bout when he said, "Keep a sharp eye out for bears."

"Bears!" Me and Pap said tagether. We turned our heads 'round so fast it's a wonder we didn't snap our necks right off.

We kep' lookin' this way and that way. We didn't see no bears, but the wagon almos' got stuck in a hole.

Before we seen the hole, Mr. Wood he said, "Men, if the wagon gets stuck in a hole you will have to push it out. I don't know why they didn't finish this road. How do they expect folks to get from one place to another?"

"We can shore push it out if we has to. We can do that. Don't you worry."

But we was thinkin', if the wagon gets stuck in a hole, it can break the wheel off purty quick. We was hopin' it didn't get in no hole.

We was lucky cause we didn't get stuck. When we come to the end of the road, we come out to a place called Tusket. It shore looked diff'rent than Shelburne and Birchtown. There was no pits and huts here. Didn't that man tell Mr. Wood last year, b'fore Mam died, that there wasn't none? I heard him with my own ears, didn't I? There shore was some big houses.

"This is as far as I'm going, Sam," Mr. Wood said. "Do you know where you are going?"

"No, sir," I said. "But we'll just wander 'round and ask folks if they know where we can get us some work and a place to live if we moves here."

"Don't forget, I'll be leaving day after tomorrow. I'll be staying here for those two days and my wagon will be right here. Just climb in whenever you want. I'll make sure it is known that you are with me so you won't be bothered."

"Thank you, Mr. Wood."

I was wonderin' how I was gonna get down outta the wagon. I was sittin' so long and been bounced 'round so much, my bad leg was painin' somethin' fierce.

Pap must'a seen me rubbin' it cause he said, "Boy, your leg botherin' you?"

"Some, Pap. Some."

"Can you get down to the ground?"

"Yes, Pap. I'll just stretch my leg a bit b'fore I climbs down."

Mr. Wood, he seen me rubbin' my leg and heard what me and Pap was sayin'. "Sam, what's the matter with your leg? Did you hurt it?"

I told him what them men did to me durin' the riot some years back and that my leg is still givin' me trouble now and again.

"That riot was something we all want to forget, but I didn't know you got hurt. I'm sorry about that, Sam. How are you going to walk around if your leg is paining you?"

"I'll be alright, Mr. Wood. Once I is walkin' a bit, it ain't too bad. It's cause I was sittin' for a long time and gettin' bounced 'round on that bumpy road."

"You take care of that leg. Don't forget, be back here when I'm ready to leave before first light day after tomorrow."

"We'll be back. Thank you again for bringin' us."

Mr. Wood, he tipped his hat then went to the door of the house his wagon was in front of. It was a big house, too. I shore would like to have me a house big as that. If I did, then Pap could live with me and Liz and he wouldn't be 'lone all the time.

I turned to Pap. "Mr. Wood said we wasn't in Yarmouth Town, but a ways out. How is we gonna get there, Pap? And if we can get there, how is we gonna get back? The folks here don't know us and they shore ain't gonna give no ride to strange black men. Prob'ly scared to death of us."

"Let me think on it, boy."

Seems like Pap is thinkin' on it like I is always thinkin' on somethin'.

Pap was quiet seemed like a long time, then he said, "Boy, if we can hitch us a ride first daylight, we might have us the time to go work huntin', but we won't have no time to hunt for a house for us to live in right off. And how is we gonna pay for it if we does find us one?"

"We can't go to town tonight, cause it's too late, but we can see what this Tusket place has here. Maybe we can find us some work here and we won't have to go to Yarmouth."

I looked 'round and seen a black woman comin' our way. "I'll ask that woman, she might know."

Pap looked to where I was lookin'. "If she's a slave, she ain't gonna tell us nothin'."

"Missus," I said when she got close. When she looked at me straight on, I knew she wasn't no slave, cause all the slaves I use ta know, they wouldn'a looked you in the eye, they was always lookin' round to see if somebody was watchin' them.

"Well, if it ain't Sam," She said.

"You knows me?" I asked.

"Course I knows you and you Pap. Don't know me no more, does you?"

I stared in her eyes. "Missus Abigail, is that you? I thought you was gone back to Africa with all the other folks."

"Now, why would I go there? I wasn't borned in Africa, I was borned in America. What you men doin' here?" she said, lookin' from me to Pap.

Pap, he wasn't sayin' nothin' and I think that was cause I knew Missus Abigail better than he did. Me and her George, we went fishin' in the bay sometimes. Never caught nothin', but it wasn't cause we didn't try.

"Does you live 'round here now?" she asked.

"No, we is still in Birchtown. We come with Mr. Wood to see if we can get us some work so we can move here. There ain't hardly no jobs left in Shelburne and we figgered it was time to leave."

"You have to go to Yarmouth Town to find work. Not much work for men in Tusket, less you wants to go fishin'."

"Fishin'? On a boat?"

"How else you gonna go fishin' and make money? You plan on usin' a stick and string with a hook?" She laughed at that.

"Does you live in Town?" I asked her.

"No, I lives down the road a ways. You see that big house there on that hill, that's my house. My George built it for me b'fore he passed on." She sighed. "I miss my George. I shore does."

"I sorry, Missus Abigail. What he die from?"

"Don't rightly know. We went to bed one night and when I waked in the mornin', he was dead cold b'side me."

Me and Pap, we looked at her house. "George was a good man,." I said. "Me and him, we had a lotta laughs when we went fishin'. He was a hard worker and he took care of his fam'ly good."

I looked at her house again. "It must'a cost a lotta money to build your house."

"My George, he walked to town every day and did whatever jobs he could get so's he could build a nice house for me and our boy, Joseph. A grand house, he called it."

"If we move here, does you think we can get us some land?"

"You shore can. You might have to wait a long time. cause I had to wait nigh on two years for mine. Does you know Anthony Miers? He is waitin' on his grant and he is gonna get it too."

"I don't know him. Where's he from?"

"I think he comed here from Birchtown, b'fore me and my George, but I ain't shore."

"I don't know everybody who was in Birchtown. There was a lotta people there."

"There shore was. Sam, is Captain Snowball and his Violet still in Birchtown? Me and Violet, we was good friends b'fore me and my George left."

"I ain't seen them. I don't know where they is. They might'a went to Africa with the other folks."

"I don't know where he got the name of Snowball. He's black as night," she said and she started laughin'. She was laughin' so hard me and Pap, we had to laugh.

"I best be goin'," she said. "Gotta go to the white folks' houses to clean their dirt for them. Had me four to do today, only one more, then I is goin' home. Lazy people, they mus' think I is still a slave, what with the little bit of money they pays me. While it still be in my brain, cause stuff don't stay there for long, if you gets to town tomorrow, there is some bad black fellas what is always gettin' in trouble. Mind you stay clear of them or you'll feel the whip cuttin' in your back."

"W'll stay clear, Missus Abigail. I had 'nough of that in New Jersey. And it was a black man what give me the whippins," I said.

"Black man? He should'a been shot." She was quiet for a minute then she said, "Where is you stayin' tanight?"

"We come with Mr. Wood and we is gonna be here for two nights. He said we can sleep in his wagon. We has us some warm clothes cause he said it gets chilly at night."

"You can stay with me," she said, lookin' up at the sky.

I looked too and it didn't look too good. There was some black clouds rollin' in.

"Gonna rain," she said.

"Can we, Missus Abigail? We has to tell Mr. Wood where we is gonna be so he don't think we got our self lost."

"You go tell him and I'll be back this way in two hours. You can wait by my house so I'll know where you is. Gotta go."

She turned and walked away sayin', "Snowball? Black as night he is." She was laughin' so hard some folks who was walkin' by looked at her like she was loony and they was almos' runnin' to get past her.

Me and Pap, we started laughin' too and them folks, they almos' runned past us. They prob'ly think all black folks is crazy. That made me and Pap laugh harder. It was good to hear Pap laugh again.

"We better tell Mr. Wood where we is gonna be, Pap."

We knocked on the door to the house Mr. Wood went in.

The man who opened the door was s'prised to see two black men standin' on his step. "What do you want?" he shouted. "Get away from my house, you bloody beggars."

"We would like to see Mr. Wood, please, sir. He bringed us with him from Birchtown."

"A likely story," he said.

Mr. Wood, he come to the door when he heard the man shoutin'. "Sam, is everything alright?"

"Yes, sir. I just wanted to tell you that we is stayin' with a friend of ours from Birchtown till you leaves. Missus Abigail, her house is that big one on the hill over there."

He looked to where I was pointin'. "Okay, Sam. I will pick you up there. We'll be leaving at first light day after tomorrow, don't forget."

"No, sir, we won't forget. Thank you, sir. Missus Abigail, she said it's gonna rain tonight."

He looked up at the sky. "I believe she is right. Don't forget to take your things out of the wagon."

I heard that other man say to Mr. Wood when he closed the door, right in our face, "You brought them niggers with you?"

And I heard Mr. Wood say, "No, I brought two men with me."

Me and Pap, we looked at each other when he said that, cause one time he was callin' us that name too. Least we hasn't heard him say that name in a long time.

That was when he owned the slaves and Jude was one of them. Maybe if he hadn'a sold her, she would still be 'live today. But James, he wouldn'a met up with his girl again. Must'a been meant to be that way, I guess.

I looked at Pap. "Pap, let's see if we can find somebody who is goin' to town tomorrow and will give us a ride back, too."

We started walkin' off down the road.

40

We got us to town and back. A Mr. Lent, he was goin' and said we could go only cause we was with his friend, Mr. Wood. That was okay with us cause it meaned we didn't have to walk. He said if we was at Mr. Shipley's store when he was ready to come back to Tusket, we could come with him. We didn't know where that was, but we would shore find it.

We told him, "We'll be there Mr. Lent. Thank you."

We was all over town and we didn't find no jobs that we could do that day. I think there was some, but some of the folks looked at us like we was gonna steal from them. I guess cause we is strangers to them and they don't trust no black strangers. Maybe some of the black folks who lives in Yarmouth steals from them, but that ain't us.

We was where Mr. Lent told us to be. It wasn't hard to find cause all we had to do was ask somebody and after they looked at us strange for a bit, they told us how to get there.

Now we is back in Tusket and it ain't no point thinkin' what those white folks in town thinks cause it's most all white folks what thinks bad things 'bout us anyway.

That's what Missus Abigail told us b'fore we went to town: "You be back b'fore ten o'clock tonight or you ain't gettin' in my house. Can't trust nobody after it gets dark."

"Missus Abigail, we don't know how to tell time."

"Well, you better learn quick if you is gonna move up here and get jobs. You gotta know to be there on time. If you is late, you ain't gonna have no jobs. They'll send you runnin' in a hurry."

"We'll ask somebody what the time is 'til we learns."

We is back and it's after ten. It wasn't our fault cause Mr. Lent, he was late leavin'.

It was rainin' a little and when we got to Missus Abigail's the sky it opened up and the rain come down soakin' us to the skin.

We pounded on her door and she yelled through it, "Who's there?"

"It's me and Pap, Missus Abigail. Can we come in? It's rainin' awful hard."

"Didn't I tell you if you was past ten you wasn't gettin' in? How do I know it's you and you Pap?"

"Missus Abigail, you know it's us. Don't you know what we sounds like?"

She was quiet for a minute, then she opened the door 'nough to peek one eye out. She started laughin', then she opened the door wide to let us in. "You looks like somebody throwed you in the river. Get your selfs in here and don't you drop no water on my clean floors. If you do, you'll clean it up. I ain't your slave. And don't call me Missus, makes me feel old."

She laughed harder when we went in and closed the door. "Did you find any jobs?"

"There is some, but we would have to do all kinds of jobs to make us some money so we can move here. I think we can do it, but I has to talk to my Liz. Abigail, the white folks, they seemed to be 'fraid of strange black folks."

"They don't trust strangers. You get used to it. I just ignores them."

She looked at Pap. "You is awful quiet. Doesn't you wanna move? Maybe your Sarrah, she won't wanna move way up here."

Pap looked at Abigail and I knew she could see the sad that was always in his eyes. "My Sarrah, she passed on four years ago," was all he said.

"I is sorry to hear that," she said, pattin' Pap on the shoulder. "She was a real lady, even when she was cussin' almos' much as some of the men in Birchtown."

Then she laughed. "I liked that 'bout her. A lady one day and hard as rock the nex'."

Pap laughed, too. "That was my Sarrah. But I shore do miss her, Abigail."

"I is shore you do, Sam. I is shore you do. I miss my George too, as ornery as he was at times. But we has to go on, Sam, they wouldn't want it no other way. You gotta live, Sam. You gotta live."

We was all quiet for a bit, then she said, "Well, I is goin' to bed. Got me two houses I gotta clean in the mornin'. When is you leavin'?"

"Mr. Wood, he said he would pick us up first light. I shore hope it ain't rainin', if it is, he might not go."

"If he don't you can stay here till he goes. Won't see no black folks out on the road, less they means me harm."

"That shore ain't us, Abigail."

"But the sun, it's gonna be shinin' bright in the mornin'. My bones is tellin' me the rain is almos' done."

She went to bed. I shore hoped she was right.

Me and Pap, we laid on our cots. Pap, he went to sleep right off, but I laid there a long time listenin' to the rain hittin' the roof, soundin' like rocks hittin' it, that's how hard it was rainin'.

I fin'lly went to sleep and when I waked up the sun was shinin' through the window. I was shore glad of that.

Abigail, she was up b'fore us and she had a big pot of coffee on the stove and there was some bread and eggs on the table. Eggs. It been a long time since we had us some eggs. Abigail, she cooked them and boy was they good.

We ate that food like we ain't had nothin' to eat in a long time. But when you ain't had some foods, like them eggs, for a long time, almos' never, you forget what it's like havin' good food sometimes.

Abigail, she put some eggs in her mouth and she was talkin' 'round them. "Is that crook, Blucke, still in Birchtown? Is he still stealin' from people? Don't know what his Margaret seed in him."

"Everybody says he's a crook, but if he been stealin', he ain't been caught. His Margaret, she up and left him when he was takin' up with that young girl they brought with them from New York."

"You don't say. Best thing Margaret ever done and I knew somethin' was goin' on with him and that girl, Isabella. Always lookin' at her, he was."

"Well, now she's with child."

"You don't say. Hmmm."

We was waitin' for her to say somethin' else, but she went back to eatin' her eggs.

Mr. Wood, he come when he said he was comin. We thanked Abigail again and when we was goin' out the door she gived us a bag with some bread with butter on it to take with us.

We had butter on the bread she give us when we got up and when I asked her where she got it, she said, "Ain't you never had butter before?"

"No, we hasn't. Does it cost a lot of money?"

"Boy, you make it your self. Ask your Liz, she might know how. If she don't, somebody will know. All you need is milk."

"Well, I guess we ain't gonna have us no butter, cause we ain't got no money to buy us no milk."

We thanked Abigail again and I give her a big hug.

"Get offa me, you crazy man," she said, but she was laughin'. "If you come back this way, I'll be here, if God is willin' to spare me a few more years."

"God don't want you just yet, you is too ornery," I said, laughin'.

"Get," she said and she closed the door on us.

Me and Pap we went outside where Mr. Wood was waitin' and we could hear her laughin' till we was away from her house.

Mister Wood, he asked us, "Did you men find any jobs you could do?"

"We was told that sometimes they needs men to unload the boats and other folks needs wood cut, but that ain't all the time. We is lookin' for jobs where we is workin' every day. And we didn't see no houses empty where we could live. Abigail, she told us that if we wanted to live in a house we would have to pay cause all the houses is owned by other folks and some of them don't want no black folks livin' in their houses."

That ain't 'xactly what she said. She said they don't want no Niggers livin' in their houses, but I wasn't tellin' that to Mister Wood, cause he used to call folks that name. How some folks can change. I don't know what made him change, but it was a good thing he did.

It was almos' dark when we got home. It took us a long time to get there, cause that old road that we come on to get us to Tusket was so soft after the rain the wagon got stuck in the mud three times. We didn't think we was gonna get it out and after every time we was so full of mud, if we had'a been white, you wouldn'a knew it.

Mr. Wood, he got some mud on his self too, but not much as me and Pap. We did most'a the pushin' anyway. And we was lucky a wheel didn't break off cause we hit one of them holes real hard.

When we got home and I opened the door to my hut, they all come runnin'.

Our Jenny's Sarrah and Sadie, they is almos' four. Twins they is, but they shore don't look nothin' like each other. Them two was runnin' 'round all the time.

Jenny, she had a hard time birthin' them babies. It was a good thing Liz and Mam was there to help Miss Hannah. There was shouts for joy when them two babies popped out, cause that's how Liz said they come out. Liz got her hands full when Jenny was workin' and wasn't there to help.

Polly, she left when Prince Edward did. She changed her mind 'bout the fella in Birchtown she had her eye on. Said he was a lazy no-good-for-nothin'. They went with John and they was in Sissiboo. That's where they said they was goin'.

When Charlotte and Nancy come home they helped their Mamma with the young'uns. Our fam'ly was shore growin'.

"Pap, Pap," said Sadie, "we didn't think you was comin' back. How come you was so long?"

Them young'uns shore can talk. They is gonna be smart ones, I can tell.

They called me Pap cause I is their grandpap. That no-good man Jenny had, left her when she was carryin' them and runned off with 'nother girl. If he comes back this way, I'll show him what for, for doin' that to our Jenny. When I told her what I was gonna do, Jenny smiled at me and said.

"Papa, it ain't gonna happen again. I is done with him."

"I hope this time you means it, girl, cause you had a real shine for him and when you feels 'bout a man like you did 'bout that no-good-for-nothin', it's hard to let go sometimes."

"I means it this time, Papa. If he comes back I'll punch him in the face and tell him to get."

When I smiled at her she said, "I means it, Papa. I do."

I never said no more cause she would'a got mad. We should'a had all boys then we wouldn'a had to worry 'bout no girls gettin' their hearts broke by no-good-for-nothin's.

My grandbabies took me outta what I was thinkin'. They was pullin' on my arm.

"Okay, Sarrah and Sadie, let your grandpap come in and sit down for a minute," said Liz.

I give Liz a big hug. "I missed you."

"You is only been gone two days. I was hopin' you was only stayin' one."

I looked 'round. "Where's Jenny?"

"Jenny is workin' in Shelburne. She'll be home soon. Did you find if there is gonna be work for you and your Pap? And is there gonna be somewhere for us to live?"

"There's all kinds of jobs, but we is gonna have to do more'n one, cause nobody wants somebody to work for them all the time. There is houses, too, but you has pay to live in them. That's why I would have to work more'n one job. I can't make no money just doin' one job."

All she heard was that we gotta pay to live in a house.

"You gotta pay to live in them? We don't pay nothin' here. How come we has to pay there?"

"We don't pay nothin' here, Liz, cause we built our hut with our own two hands, but in Yarmouth the houses is owned by other folks."

"Well, I don't know if I wanna go there and live if we has to pay to live in a house."

"We won't be goin' yet, so we got plenty time to think on it."

We might not be movin' to Yarmouth less Liz can get it outta her head that we has to pay to live in a house. Maybe I better talk 'bout somethin' else.

"Liz, does you remember George Price and his Missus, Abigail?"

"I shore do, Sam. She was a nice lady. Hard sometimes. I liked her. Why?"

"George, he passed on a few years back and Abigail, she owns a big house that George built for her. That's where we stayed, 'stead of havin' to stay in Mister Wood's wagon."

"Sam," Liz said all excited. "If George built them a house, can we build ours so we don't have to pay nobody to live in one?"

"Where is we gonna get the money to buy the boards? Abigail lives in a place called Tusket, a ways from the town, and she said her George walked to town every day and did all kinds of jobs and saved his money. B'fore George built his house, he had to pay somebody to live in a house. And we would have to pay somebody too, 'til I could save 'nough money."

She never said no more, but I could tell she was thinkin'.

41

Me and Pap, we is in Yarmouth livin'. Liz ain't with me and I is sad and mad 'bout that.

She looked me square in the eyes and said.

"I ain't goin', Sam."

"What you mean you ain't goin'? You gotta go."

She put her hands on her hips and she said, "I ain't gotta go nowhere I don't wanna go. You and your Pap, you go and you build me a house like George made for Abigail, then you send word for me and I'll come."

"Liz, George was a long time buildin' that house. He had to work every day doin' all the jobs he could do to make 'nough money to get it built. And Abigail, she was workin' too, cleanin' people's houses. She went with him, Liz. She didn't stay here till he had her a house built. You gotta go with me. A wife has to go wherever her man goes."

Why did I say it that way?

"No such thing, Sam. I ain't gotta go nowhere I don't wanna go. And I ain't Abigail."

"But, Liz!"

"Don't you, 'but, Liz,' me. I ain't goin'. You build me my house and I'll come. You hear me, Sam?"

She never said no more.

B'fore we left for Yamouth, Pap said he had to visit somebody. I knew he was goin' to visit Mam's grave.

He was gone almos' a hour and when he come back he was awful quiet. I thought he was gonna say, 'I ain't goin', boy. I ain't leavin' your Mam.'

But he s'prised me when he said, "Let's go, boy. Time to start fresh."

We packed what we had and it was still dark when we started out walkin', hopin' somebody would stop and give us a ride. A couple wagons passed by, but they never stopped to ask where we was goin' or if we wanted a ride.

When we was halfway down that road, a man we never seen b'fore stopped and asked where we was goin'.

"We is goin' to Yarmouth to find us some work."

"Hop in," he said. "That's where I'm heading. I don't bite," he added when we just stood there.

Pap looked at me and nodded. We got up in the wagon and off we went.

He told us his name was David. He didn't give us no other name, I guess he figgered we didn't need to know it cause we prob'ly wasn't gonna see him no more anyway.

So, me and Pap we is here now. We is workin' on the dock, unloadin' ships that comes in, and we is cuttin' wood for some of the white folks. We ain't makin' a lotta money and I can't save much cause we has to pay for where we is and we has to eat.

We can't really call where we is livin' a house, cause it's a barn. There ain't no animals in it now, but you can still smell somethin'. I guess it was better'n us livin' in the fields. I is gonna save all the money I don't need so I can build my Liz her house.

Pap he said, "I'll help you boy. What does I need money for?"

Me and Pap, we got our selfs settled in. I had to keep a eye on Pap cause I seen that he was gettin' tired quick like. He was gettin' on in years and I shouldn'a 'spected him to work hard as I can even with my leg botherin' me some.

I never told the people I was workin' for, cause I was 'fraid they would send me away cause they thought I was a cripple and couldn't do the work.

One house I was to cuttin' wood, the Missus come out and seen me limpin' and she asked me, "Sam, did you hurt your leg?"

"It hurts a bit, that's all."

"What did you do to it?"

I didn't want to tell her what happened, but she seemed like a nice lady and she brought me and Pap some tea and biscuits out one day when we was cuttin' wood. So I told her 'bout the riot in Shelburne and what them soldiers done to me.

"Those bastards," she said. "You go on home now, Sam, and you rest your leg. You can finish cutting that wood tomorrow if you feel up to it."

"But Missus..."

"Don't you, 'but Missus' me, Sam. You do what I say."

I start to laugh.

"What are you laughing at?"

"My wife, she says that to me. 'Don't you Liz me, Sam.'"

Missus, she start laughin' too. "I guess all us women say the same thing to our husbands. Now, go on home, Sam, and rest that leg."

"Thank you, Missus."

I went home and did what she told me. It felt some better the next day, but I wouldn'a had to go to no jobs that day other than finishin' cuttin' her wood, so I stayed home and rested some more. B'sides, me and Pap, we cut 'nough the day b'fore and she wouldn'a runned outta wood to burn.

Me and Pap we never got in no trouble when we was in Birchtown or Shelburne. We was in Yarmouth almos' six months when we met some men who was livin' outside of the town. They come to town to work too.

One of them, Manuel Jarvis, but most folks called him Manny, he was the slave of Doc Bond. Me and Manny, we was talkin' one day after I finished on the dock.

I asked him, "Manny, how come there is no black fam'lies livin' in town? Least I ain't seen none."

"I lives in town with Doc Bond, but me and my Kate, we ain't got us a house of our own. Slaves don't got no property here. I is s'prised you is 'llowed to live in the town cause they don't like black folks 'round here. They think we is all thiefs."

"Doc Bond, he 'llows you to work for somebody else?"

Manny, he said, "Doc Bond, sometimes he says I can go to work only for one day and make my self some money and he bought me my Kate so I wouldn'a been 'lone all the time."

I never said nothin'. But I thought to myself, *He bought him his Kate, like they is animals they buys and sells*. Then I thought, *I been free for so long, I forgets my fam'ly was bought and sold like animals b'fore we come to Birchtown*.

Manny, he was quiet for a time and he looked sad.

"What's the matter, Manny?"

He just looked at me, then I could see he was gettin' mad and I thought he was gettin' mad at me. "Like I said, Doc Bond and his Missus, they was always good to us and treated us good. Till my Kate had us our first baby. A girl it was."

"What they do, Manny, sell her?"

"No, they didn't sell her, they gived her to their girl and she named our baby Hester. We wasn't 'llowed to give her a name. I asked him, 'Doc, why you give our baby to your girl?' You know what he said? 'Manny, she wanted the baby cause she ain't got none.'

"I got mad and I said. 'Doc, my Kate ain't havin' no babies for nobody else. They is ours. Let your girl get herself a man and she can have all the babies she wants.' He never said nothin', I don't think he s'pected me to talk back to him."

"Did you and Kate have more babies?"

"Yup, but he never taked no more from us. I guess cause I got mad at him and he never seen me mad b'fore."

"I is sorry they took your baby, Manny. They shouldn'a done that, but when you is their slave, they can do what they want."

I was s'prised that Doc Bond did that cause he was the Doc what said them boys murdered Jude. Maybe he changed his thinkin' 'bout slaves after the boys got away with murder. Cause why would he take Kate's baby and give it to his girl? I guess there's no 'splainin' how the white man thinks.

42

Them fellas that Manny was hangin' with sometimes, they was nothin' but trouble.

I remember what Abigail said to us when we told her we was gonna move to Yarmouth. "Some of the black men what comes to town, they is bad company. They is always gettin' them selfs in trouble and if you keeps company with them, you is gonna get your self in trouble just like them. And when you gets in trouble, you will be goin' home with lashes on your backs. Stay away from them."

Well, we wasn't 'bout to get mixed up with them. Manny said they was his friends, but I wouldn't call them no friends, cause friends doesn't do things to get you in trouble. But Manny should'a knew better. He didn't have to do what they was doin'.

I don't know how come Doc Bond 'llowed him to go 'round with them. He must'a knew 'bout them and that they was trouble. Maybe he shouldn'a 'llowed Manny to be on his own much as he did. I ain't never knew no slaves who could come and go as they wanted, but I guess Manny was doin' it. Manny and his friend, James, who shore wasn't like my friend James, was stealin' all kinds of things.

Me and Pap we tried to talk to Manny. "Manny," I said, "I thought you said that Doc Bond gived you all you need? Why is you stealin'?"

"So what?" he said. "He taked my baby girl, didn't he?"

You is stealin' cause he took your baby girl? What 'bout your other young'uns? If you is in gaol, who is gonna look after them? Is you gonna let your Kate do it all? Maybe Doc Bond shouldn'a let you run free all the time and maybe he'll sell your young'uns if you ain't there."

"He tries to sell my young'uns, I'll kill him."

"Now you is talkin' crazy."

Me and Pap we couldn't talk no sense in him. He wasn't gonna stop stealin'. We tried to tell him he was travelin' with the wrong fellas. The likes of Jack Fell, James Landers and 'nother fella named Isaac Jordan. I don't know how come they wasn't in gaol all the time, cause all they did was steal.

My Mam, God rest her soul, used ta say, "Men has to be boys some-times."

So I guess that's what me and Pap was. It was over a whole year that Manny and his friends was stealin' and they dragged me and Pap right in over our heads like Miss Dolly went over her head in the bay. But I guess we can't blame them, cause me and Pap, we is grown men, we ain't little boys who don't know no better.

I said to Pap one day, "Pap, maybe we shouldn't be stealin' from those folks. We ain't stealin' cause we needs anythin'."

"No, boy, we don't. But gettin' free stuff is better'n havin' to pay for it, ain't it? And that rum shore tasted good, didn't it?"

"Pap, you never used to drink, and if Mam was here, she'd give you what for."

"Well, she ain't here is she?" Pap snapped.

He was quiet for a time.

"Boy, I miss my Sarrah. We was tagether a long time. How come God he took her from us? She wasn't s'pposed to go b'fore me. She was always doin' things when I wanted to sit and do nothin' most'a the time. Why did God take her, boy?" he said again.

"I don't know, Pap. I miss her too."

Those fellas, they was stealin' a long time and me and Pap right 'long with them b'fore we got our selfs caught. That Jack Fell, he made the mis-take of givin' some of the stuff he stole to a woman he thought wouldn'a told on him. He should'a knew she wasn't gonna go to gaol for havin' that stolen stuff in her house.

She told on him right quick. She might'a even went to the p'lice b'fore they come lookin' for her. Nobody knows for shore.

He should'a knew cause she never used the same name all the time. One time it was Dinah Ackerman, 'nother time it was Dinah Smith, and then it was Dinah Jordan. Nobody knew what her real name was and she prob'ly didn't know either.

She told the p'lice that Jack brought her a blanket, some beef and some other food that he said he took from Mr. Shipley's store. That was a long time ago. I never heard the p'lice told her she had to give it back. I bet she ate all that food and put the blanket on her cot. Jack shouldn'a trusted her.

All them fellas, when they was caught and was in court, they said they wasn't guilty. I think the p'lice, they knew they was guilty alright and they was prob'ly laughin' at them when they said not guilty.

Me and Pap, we knew we was guilty and we said so. We stole rum and James, he brought some more for Pap to hide for him. He give me some, too, but I wasn't hidin' it.

When we come up to court the judge, he looked at me and Pap, and I remember them words like they was said yesterday: "Shall receive publikly twelve lashes on the bare back."

And I had to pay Mr. Marshall twenty shillin's. He's the man the rum was stole from. Where was I gonna get twenty shillin's?

Pap, he was to be gived the same 'mount of lashes and he had to pay thirty shillin's. I guess cause he tried to hide the rum. I don't know why that was cause we had the same 'mount of rum.

I is sorry my Pap had to be hurt. He said he got us in trouble cause he already knew how to steal and he told me it was easy and he would show me how. But it wasn't Pap's fault. I shouldn'a told Pap what them fellas was doin'.

He said, "I should'a told you no, boy, should'a tried to stop you. I is you Pap and Pap's is s'pposed to pertect their young'uns."

"Pap, I ain't no young'un no more, I is a grown man and I know right from wrong. I wouldn'a stopped, cause I didn't want to. Now you is in trouble too. I think James might'a telled on you cause you wasn't with us when we got caught. If he did, I is gonna give him what for."

"You is in 'nough trouble, boy, don't go addin' fightin' to it ."

The day come when we was to get the whippin's. I asked the gaoler, "Please don't whip my Pap. He's a old man and he ain't never had a whip put to him b'fore. Whip me 'stead. Please, Sir."

He never paid me no mind. He pushed me down and tied Pap's arms to the post. I run to my Pap and the gaoler pushed me down again.

"You get outta the way," he said. "Or I'll give him his twelve and I'll give you another twelve for being in the way."

Pap looked over at me and said, "Stay there, boy. I is gonna be alright."

That gaoler, he brought that whip down on my Pap's back, one, two, three, four. I counted the lashes till it got to twelve.

The gaoler stopped, but if he hadn'a, I would'a 'ttacked him and hit him with the whip. I wouldn'a cared how many lashes he gived me.

My Pap, he is a strong man. He never made a cry or a holler when the whip was cuttin' in his back.

When he fell to the ground I runned over and picked him up. The gaoler, he told me to get back where I was.

I yelled at him, "I ain't goin' nowhere, I is takin' care of my Pap. If you wants to whip me more'n twelve lashes, there ain't nothin' I can do 'bout it, but I is lookin' after my Pap."

He never said nothin', he just watched me pick up my Pap and move him away from the whippin' post. I knew when my whippin's come, I wasn't gonna make no cry or holler either. I was gonna be strong like my Pap.

Me and Pap, we went home with our backs stingin' and bleedin'. Pap s'prised me when he took some medicine outta one of his sacks he kep' in the corner of our house.

"Where you get that, Pap? That looks like what Mam use to make to tend to our cuts."

"Mam made this b'fore she died. I kep' it case I needed some. Well, I guess we need it, boy."

We doctored our backs tagether. He put some on mine and I put some on his.

"Pap, if Mam could see us, she would smack us but good."

"More'n once, boy. More'n once."

43

I knew Pap was gettin' sadder and sadder after we got them whippin's. He never had no whippin' b'fore, not even on Master Bulloc's farm where that damn Henry, he liked takin' the whip to the slaves. I got me plenty till we was sold to Master Stoffle.

One day, me and Pap was sittin' to our table and he was starin' down in his cup of coffee, not sayin' nothin'. He was gettin' quieter and quieter every day.

"What's the matter, Pap? You is awful quiet. I is sorry you had to get whipped, cause you ain't never been whipped b'fore."

He looked at me and I didn't think he was gonna say nothin'.

"No, boy, I ain't never been whipped b'fore, but the whippin' ain't as bad as what happened to my friend, Ace, when we tried to run away from where we was at. That was b'fore I met your Mam and I never told her 'bout it either. Since my Sarrah died. I thinks 'bout him a lot, more'n I did b'fore. Him and me, we was real good friends and I seen him die a horr'ble death. Somethin' I hopes you never sees or knows. Whippin's ain't nothin'."

"You tried to run away before? What happened?" I asked.

"Me and Ace, we was young and foolish and full of ideas of what we was gonna do and where we was gonna go when we was free. Slaves was always wishin' they was free, but we never s'pected to be free. But we was shore gonna try. We made our plans and one day off we went."

Pap stopped talkin' for a few minutes. He got awful quiet and he was starin' at the wall. I was thinkin' he might'a forgot what he was gonna say. I was hopin' he wasn't gettin' sick in the mind like folks was gettin' who was livin' in them pits.

Losin' Mam changed my Pap. He didn't hardly laugh no more and he didn't want to do nothin'. If it was gonna make him sad to talk 'bout his friend, then he don't have to.

"Pap, you don't have to tell me if you don't want to."

222

"I ain't told nobody b'fore and sometimes I think 'bout it and I can see it all in my mind like it was yesterday. Maybe if I tells somebody, I won't think 'bout it so much."

"Okay, Pap, you tell me."

"We started runnin' to the woods. We didn't get far when we heard the overseer, Willie, a big man with muscles like a horse, yellin' for us to stop. We didn't see him when we started runnin', but he must'a seen us. Willie was a vilent man and he injoyed causin' pain on the other slaves. He was a slave his self, but he didn't care who he hurt, long as master give him anythin' he wanted. Master didn't know that Willie was trainin' his dogs to kill and one time one of master's dogs 'ttacked 'nother of his dogs and killed it. Master loved his dogs and didn't know why one of them went wild like it did. Master had to do away with it. If master knew Willie was trainin' his dogs to hunt and kill, he prob'ly would'a sold Willie, or killed him 'stead of his dog cause Master, he wouldn'a set the dogs loose on a man. He would'a told Willie to 'whip the bastard till he can't stand up.' but he wouldn'a told him to set the dogs loose. He figgered a good whip-pin' was all that was needed to bring his slaves in line.

"Willie set the dogs on us that day, and when we heard the dogs b'hind us we was 'termined they wasn't gonna cetch us, We runned faster. We runned through bushes and under tree branches. We figgered if we stayed in the woods, Willie and the dogs might not find us so easy. We should'a took the old dirt path from the start, but dumb as we was, we thought that goin' through the woods was gonna be better.

"We was runnin' so fast we was outta breath and we wanted to stop and rest, but we couldn't, cause long as we could hear the dogs barkin' we had to keep runnin'. We wasn't gonna let them cetch us. If they caught us and if they didn't kill us, we was gonna wish we was dead.

"The muscles in my legs and back was burnin' and my lungs felt like they was on fire. We could hear the dogs gettin' closer and closer. I kep' lookin' back to see if Ace was keepin' up and two times he falled down cause he tripped over roots that was stickin' outta the ground. He got back up, but I seen a cut on his hand and his feet was all scratched and bleedin' cause he didn't have no shoes on. He didn't have no shoes. I knew soon as the dogs got the smell of Ace's blood in their noses we was gonna be dead, shore as I is sittin' here tellin' you this story.

"When I turned to check on Ace, I seen two of the dogs jump on his back and drag him to the ground. They was closer than we thought. There was no point to me runnin' no more, they would'a caught me for shore. I falled down on the ground and curled up in a ball with my hands over my head, waitin' for the other one to jump on me, but Willie called him off. I know that folks nearby could hear Ace screamin' when them dogs tore at him till he was dead. I peeked up at Willie and he was standin' to one side, watchin' them dogs rip pieces offa Ace.

"Then he called them off. I got sick in the grass and Willie looked at me and said. 'Next time it will be you layin' there dead.'"

"Oh, Pap," I said. "How come you never told Mam? She prob'ly could'a helped you get it outta your mind some. She was good at doin' that."

"You knew that Mam was 'ttacked by a dog? Every time I see the scars on her leg left by that dog, I sees Ace and what the dogs done to him. I wasn't tellin' my Sarrah 'bout that."

"She could'a helped you, Pap. I know she could'a."

"Maybe when I go home to Birchtown, I'll tell her 'bout it and tell her I is sorry I didn't tell her b'fore."

I didn't say nothin' to that. I shore wasn't gonna say, 'Pap, Mam is dead. She can't hear you tellin' her nothin'.' If it is gonna make him feel better to talk to Mam, he can talk to her all he wants.

"I is goin' home permanent to Birchtown, boy," he said, lookin' in my eyes. "I shouldn'a come here. I is goin' home and I is gonna tell my Sarrah what I done and what was done to me. I know you think I is crazy sayin' I is gonna tell your Mam things, but, boy, your Mam will always be there. I might not be able to see her, but she's there. I wish she had'a smacked me upside my head when we first talked 'bout movin' to Yarmouth b'efore she passed. We might never got us in no trouble and I wouldn't have these scars on my back."

I didn't say nothin' for a bit. Maybe Pap goin' home to Birchtown is what he needs to do. He shore ain't happy here. I asked him, "When is you goin'?"

In a coupl'a days. I still has to cut some wood for a coupl'a folks then I is gonna see if somebody is goin' to Shelburne. You come with me, boy. What you think your Liz is gonna say when she hears you been whipped?"

"She ain't gotta hear less you tells her."

"She's gonna wanna know why I come back and I ain't gonna lie to her."

Pap got up from the table. "I is gonna get my things tagether then I is gonna see if somebody is gonna be goin' to Shelburne, so I don't have to walk."

Pap's mind was made up and I couldn't change it. And I don't know if I wanted to. Maybe he'll be more his self if he's back to where Mam is.

44

Pap's been gone 'bout four days and I had to do my work and his too, cause we always worked together. I got home from work and I was tired. We was unloadin' boats most'a the mornin', then I had to go and cut wood for four folks.

I didn't mind cause I can save the extra money for buildin' Liz a house. But I always wondered who cut their wood b'fore us black folk come 'long.

I was gettin' myself somethin' to eat when the door opened and there stood my Liz. She never said nothin', she come in and closed the door. She looked mad, but was I glad to see her.

"Liz," I said, runnin' to her. "What is you doin' here?"

She just stared at me a minute, then she said, "Take off your shirt, Sam. I wanna see your back."

"Why you wanna to see my back?" I knew right off that Pap told her 'bout the whippin's.

"Take off your shirt," she said again.

I figgered I better do like she said. I took my shirt off and I was slow to turn 'round. When I did, I heard her take a deep breath.

She said, "Oh, Sam." And she rubbed her fingers over the scars.

I turned 'round and put my shirt back on so she couldn't see them no more. When I looked at her she was cryin'. The last time I seen her cry was when we lost two of our young'uns to the fever when they was babies.

"Don't cry, Liz. It don't hurt no more," I said, puttin' my arms 'round her.

"I should'a come with you when you moved here. I should'a come. You wouldn'a got your self in no trouble."

"It ain't your fault. Me and Pap, we is grown men and we was stupid. We knew better, but we did it anyway."

I never got to say no more. The door banged open and Jack Fell was standin' there with the sun settin' b'hind him.

"You son of a dog, Sam. You is a sly one. You got your self a woman. I told you all you needs is a woman. If your woman don't want to come with you, you find 'nother."

"I told you I don't need no woman cause I got my Liz."

"But your Liz ain't here."

"Ain't I?" said Liz, her voice got hard as the rocks outside.

I thought Jack's eyes was gonna come right outta his head.

Liz, she was gettin' madder and madder. I seen her reach for the broom. I didn't know what she was gonna do with it, but I didn't like the look in her eyes. I figgered I better take it from her. I wasn't fast 'nough.

She swung that broom and hit Jack on the arm so hard, I thought she might'a broke his arm.

"You get outta our house. And don't you come back," she yelled.

She swung again and Jack, holdin' on his arm, runned outta the door so fast I thought he was gonna fall right down. I heard him say when he was runnin' down the road, "Damn crazy woman."

"Liz, what was you doin?"

"I was sweepin' the dirt outta our house, that's what I was doin'."

I start to laugh. "You is somethin'. Chasin' a grown man with a broom outta my house."

"Our house, Sam. I is just cleanin' our house now that I is here."

"You is stayin?"

"I is."

I picked her up and swinged her 'round. We was laughin' and laughin'.

After I put her down I asked her, "How you get here?"

"Mr. Wood, he was comin' to Tusket and he said I could come with him if I want. I packed all my stuff and when he seen what I had, he brought me right to your door. He had to ask somebody if they knew where you lived cause he didn't know. My stuff is outside, we best get it in b'fore somebody steals it."

My Liz is here and we is tagether again.

45

I never got in no more trouble and them fellas me and Pap got mixed up with, they don't come 'round me no more since my Liz sent Jack runnin'.

He must'a told his friends, "Don't go 'round Sam's. That woman of his is a crazy woman. She chased me with a broom and she hit me on the arm and damn near broke it."

I bet they laughed at him for lettin' a woman chase him with a broom. Every time I thinks 'bout it I laugh at how fast he was runnin' down the road.

I guess Liz, she didn't mind livin' in a barn. Least it had a wood floor cause Mr. Lewis, he put one down when me and Pap was livin' here.

She was walkin' 'round the barn and she said, "What's that smell I been smellin'? Smells like animals."

I was kind'a 'barrassed to tell her, but she would'a figgered it out her self anyway. "This used to be a animal barn, but there ain't been none in it for long time. Mr. Lewis in that house over there," I said, pointin' out the window, "he owns it and he rented it to me and Pap so we would'a had us a place to live."

She was still walkin' 'round lookin' at everythin'.

"What you lookin' at, Liz? There ain't nothin' here but a stove, two cots and a table and two chairs."

She looked over at me. "Do you think this Mr. Lewis will sell it to us?"

"Sell it? To us? You wanna buy a barn?"

"Sam, look 'round. This is a big barn and the roof is way up there," she said, pointin' up. "If we can buy it, we can make us a house. Does you know somebody who can help us do that when we got us 'nough money to buy the boards to make the rooms? Sam we could have us our own room," she said, she was so excited ' bout what she was seein'.

I never really paid no 'ttention how big it was b'fore. "Maybe we could, Liz. But what 'bout the smell? How is we gonna get that outta here?"

"I'll get rid of the smell. Sam, you is gonna have to go see the folks what owns this barn and see if they wants to sell it to us. If it ain't too much money. You do that first thing in the mornin'."

I was scratchin' my head as I looked 'round. I guess I could see what she was seein'. I always knew my Liz was smart.

She kep' walkin' round, pointin' here and there and talkin' to her self. I heard her say, "The steps can go there so Charlotte and Nancy can go up to their own room. They only need one for both a them. I'll get a diff'rent stove and put it over there cause that one ain't big 'nough and I'll have me a table and chairs over there. Maybe I'll bring what furniture I got in Birchtown. No, I can't do that, I give it to Pap."

"Liz, what is you mumblin' 'bout?"

"I ain't mumblin', I is plannin' our house."

"What if Mr. Lewis, he won't sell it to us? What we gonna do then?"

"He's gonna sell it. He's gotta. Just you wait and see."

The nex' mornin' I went to see Mr. Lewis. I didn't see nobody 'round, but I was hopin' he was home.

I didn't say nothin to Liz, but I heard he was gonna tear the barn down cause he wasn't gonna use it for nothin'. I don't know where I was gonna live if he done that. I guess me and Pap was lucky he let us live in it b'fore it got tore down, but I shore hope he'll sell it to me and Liz. Maybe he don't want nobody livin' nex' to him, 'specially a criminal, and that's why he's gonna tear it down.

I knocked on the door two times, but nobody come to open it. I was gonna go back home when the door opened and Mr. Lewis was standin' there.

"Morning, Sam. What can I do for you today?"

Then he just stared at me. I guess he must'a heard 'bout the whippin's. Maybe he won't want to sell me the barn.

"Mr. Lewis," I said. "Mornin', Sir."

I wasn't shore how to ask what I wanted, but I couldn't just stare at him.

"Well, Sam, I don't need any work done today."

"No, Sir. I ain't lookin' for work today and I wasn't shore if you wants me workin' for you no more cause of the trouble I was in."

"Are you going to steal from me, Sam?"

"No, Sir, Mr. Lewis, I ain't gonna steal from nobody no more. My Pap, he went home to Birchtown and my Liz, she come to be with me yester-day."

"Your Liz is here, that is good. So what can I do for you today?"

He never said no more 'bout my trouble, so I figgered it was gonna be okay for me to ask him what I come here for.

"I is here cause I hear tell you is gonna tear down that barn I is livin' in."

"You heard correctly."

"Well, I was wonderin' if you would sell it to me and my Liz so we can make us a house outta it. I can pay you a little bit every time I works and Liz, she's gonna try to find some houses to clean. I know it's gonna take a lot of money and work, but we is willin' to do a little bit now and again till it gets done."

There, I said what I had to say, and my heart, it was beatin' so fast I thought it was gonna pop right outta my chest.

Mr. Lewis, he stared at me for a few minutes b'fore he said, "Well, Sam, if you are sure you really want it, I will give it to you. It will cost quite a bit to make it into a house, but I know you can do it."

"Yes, Sir. Me and my Liz, we is hard workers and we needs a house so we can bring our fam'ly here to live with us. They still got some growin' to do b'fore they can be on their own." I kind'a smiled at him.

"My Liz, she is over there now, plannin' how she wants it done. I told her she better not do no plannin' cause you might not want to sell it to us."

"I am not selling it to you, Sam. I am giving it to you. Let's just call it a present."

"A present. Nobody never give me a present b'fore. Thank you, Sir, Mr. Lewis. Thank you. I best go back and tell my Liz what you said."

I turned and runned home. I runned in the house and I could hardly talk.

"What is it, Sam? Is somebody chasin' you?" she said, and she runned to the window to see if there was somebody out there.

"No, Liz, nobody is chasin' me. I just come from Mr. Lewis's house. You ain't gonna b'lieve it! You ain't gonna b'lieve it!"

"Ain't gonna b'lieve what? What is you so excited 'bout?"

"Mr. Lewis, he give us the barn. He don't want no money cause he was gonna tear it down. If we wants it, we can have it. I told him we wants to make us a house outta it. Liz, he give us the barn! He give it to us!"

Liz was b'side her self. She couldn't say nothin' for a minute, then she shouted right out and I bet Mr. Lewis could hear her all the way to his house.

"We is gonna have us a house," she said. "And we ain't gonna have to pay to live in it. It will be ours."

~

Me and Liz, we was both workin'. Cause I didn't have to pay Mr. Lewis no more for livin' in the barn, we could save that money for the house.

Liz said the first thing we need is a outhouse. Well, she was right 'bout that. Me and Pap, all we had was a bucket. Mr. Lewis, he told us we needs us a outhouse, but we never got 'round to makin' one and we didn't have no boards anyway, so we digged a hole the next day and buried what we done. Now we won't have to cause we can go and we can empty it in the outhouse cause there is a hole already there.

I laughs 'bout that sometimes.

We was startin' to work inside the barn. We got a little bit of boards sometimes when they had some broken ones at the sawmill in Brooklyn, and they give them to me if I could find a way to get them to my house.

Brooklyn was a little walk away from town, but it wasn't far as Tusket. Us'ully somebody was comin' back to town and they would bring me and my boards right to my house. There was some nice people in Yarmouth and there was some name-callin' ones too.

Mr. Lewis, he told me, "Sam, don't you pay any attention to them. They are ignorant and should know better, but they don't."

Somebody told me one time that Mr. Lewis, he called black folks them bad names, but he never called them to me, that I heard anyway. And I ain't heard him call them names to nobody else. So maybe he didn't.

We got 'nough done in our house that our Charlotte and Nancy is livin' with us now. They was stayin' with Jenny till we could get them here.

We goes to Birchtown when we can get a ride there to see Pap and Jenny and her young'uns. Pap wasn't home the last time we was there and I asked Jenny, "Is Pap okay, Jenny? Does he still go talk to Mam?"

"Sometimes he does, Papa, but Pap, he is doin' fine. He's still workin' cause he said he gotta have money to eat and it keeps him busy. Papa," she said, kinda laughin'. "There's this woman, I think you knows her, Miss Betsy, she was married, but her man, Daniel, passed on a few years back. Well, she got her eyes on Pap, but he ain't done no lookin' on her yet."

"Miss Betsy, yes, I know her. She's a nice woman. I hope Pap starts lookin' her way cause Mam wouldn't want him to be 'lone."

46

We been in Yarmouth almos' three years and now there is 'nother war comin'. Some American ships is always waitin' in the waters just outside of town hopin' to capture the ships that was leavin'. Sometimes a war ship had to take them out so they wouldn't be captured.

Me and Liz, was gettin' scared cause if they is American ships maybe they is lookin' for runaway slaves to take back to America and sell back to their master.

Mr. Lewis, he said, "They aren't here to capture the coloured people, Sam. They are privateers and they want the cargoes that the ships leaving Yarmouth are carrying. You don't have to worry."

How does he know they ain't after us black folk? They ain't gonna say, "We want your niggers, we is takin' them back to their masters."

Well, we is stayin' right here close to our house. We is only gonna go out when we has to work. We has to keep our eyes and ears open cause we gotta know what's goin' on all the time, and what we been hearin' was makin' us 'fraid.

We was sittin' home one night and we thought we heard shootin'. If them Americans was gettin' close 'nough to do some shootin' I shore ain't goin' out, cause if they seen my black face, they shorely would'a tried to capture me.

Mr. Lewis, he said again that ain't what they was here for, but when you is a runaway always hidin' so you don't get sent back to your master, you don't trust no Americans.

Liz, asked me, "Is the war ever gonna be done, Sam?"

"I hope so, Liz. I hope so. We just has to watch close every time we is out. Don't trust nobody you don't know. If somebody strange comes at you, you run fast as you can to home."

"You only has to tell me one time, Sam."

~

It was two years b'fore the war was over. Seemed like we was always hidin'. Now we didn't have to keep lookin' to see if somebody was lookin' for us.

Our girls, Charlotte and Nancy, they growed up to be fine lookin' women. They looked just like their Mamma. It's a good thing, cause they shore wouldn't wanna have my ugly face.

"Sam, our girls is soon gonna wanna go on their own."

"I know, Liz, you don't have to rimind me. I don't want to lose my young'uns."

"They ain't young'uns no more and they is gonna wanna have fellas."

"Young'uns grows up too quick," I mumbled. "And they is only white fellas here, where they gonna find them any?"

Liz laughed. "They is goin' back to Birchtown, that's what they told me today when you was to work. There will only be me and you here, Sam. Is that so bad?"

"Long as we is together, Liz, that ain't bad."

Me and my Liz, we had us a passel of young'uns. Almos' one every year. When I started countin' them, it was eleven. Our Charlotte was the last one we had before we moved to Yarmouth.

My Pap and Mam and Liz's Papa and Mamma, they told us we had to stop havin' babies cause we couldn't feed what we got sometimes.

Pap told me, "Boy, you gotta put your horse in the barn and leave him there four or five years."

"What you talkin' 'bout, Pap? I ain't got no horse. Where is I gonna get a horse?"

Pap, he just looked at me and shook his head. He said, "Boy, you is dumb sometimes."

Well, I ain't got no horse. If I did, we prob'ly would'a ate it when we didn't have no food for a time. Pap can say some funny things sometimes.

I told Liz what Pap said, and she put her hand over her mouth so she wouldn't laugh. "Your Pap is right. Maybe you should, Sam."

I was gettin' mad. "We ain't got no damn horse. You see a horse 'round here, Liz? You is talkin' crazy as Pap."

"Sam, what does you make babies with?"

"What does I make babies with?' I thought about that. Then I started laughin'. Me and Liz we laughed and laughed. "I guess I is dumb," I said.

Pap was right when he said we couldn't feed what we got sometimes. When we was in Birchtown, me and Liz, we didn't eat a lot and sometimes we didn't eat nothin', but we made shore our young'uns had somethin', even if was only a little bit, when we could get it. They was hungry sometimes and they cried when they was, but none of our young'uns died cause they was starvin' to death like some of the other folks in Birchtown.

It shore was quiet in our house now. They is all grown and gone on their own. We sees some of them sometimes, but most'a the time we don't. We know most'a the girls stayed in Birchtown, but the boys, well, they said they wasn't stayin' no where special.

Me and Liz, we was talkin' one night 'bout the kinda life we had, "Liz, we had us a good life, didn't we? We had us some bad times, but we come through them okay."

"Yes, we did, and look at all the young'uns we got us. I'd say them was good times, but we don't want to think on the bad times no more."

"Sometimes you can't forget the bad times. Pap was always tellin' me I had to put the past b'hind me cause it was no good thinkin' on what's already been done cause you can't do nothin' 'bout it."

"He's right, Sam. But maybe sometimes you has to talk 'bout some of the bad times cause it might make you feel better'n not talkin' 'bout it."

"Can we talk 'bout some of the bad times we had?"

"If it will make you feel better, Sam." My Liz, she knew what to do all the time and I think my Mam teached her how to help folks by talkin' to them, like my Mam did durin' the times when folks was tryin' to hurt them selfs. Some she could help and some she couldn't.

"Liz, remember the day I bringed home that meat and it had worms on it? You cleaned it all off and cooked it so's we could eat it. Nobody got sick 'cept for John and I thought it was cause I bringed home that rotten meat."

"I remember, but I told you it wasn't your fault that John got sick. He got himself a weak belly, is all. If it was cause the meat was bad, we would'a all got sick. Is you still worryin' 'bout that?"

"I thinks 'bout it a lot cause I don't know what I would'a done if my boy had'a died."

"Sam, them was the times when nobody had hardly nothin' to eat and they had to eat whatever they could find. Some ate their animals, remember? I couldn'a done that, I don't think. I was glad we didn't have no animals."

"But a coupl'a times when we couldn't get food for our young'uns for a coupl'a days and they was cryin' cause they was hungry," I said, "I wished we did have us a animal. Seemed like even the ducks and pigeons was stayin' away cause they knew we was gonna cetch them and eat them."

"If you was cetchin' them like the first time you tried, they wouldn'a had to worry 'bout bein' caught," she said, laughin'.

I was laughin' too. "All I caught was a whole lot of water in my shoes and britches, till Miss Jane showed us how to do it. We had us a better life than some of the other folks had, some died right on the road cause they was hungry. Liz, I was 'fraid it was gonna be me one day."

"You never told me that. When did you think that?"

"When nobody could get no food and even the white folks didn't have much. I come back from town one day and I told you I had some green bread that I found, but it was only a little piece and I didn't want to bring it home cause it wasn't 'nough for everybody. It was hardly 'nough for one of the little young'uns. I ate it. I felt bad cause I should'a bringed it home.' Nother time I told you I had berries or somethin' so you wouldn't know I didn't have nothin'."

"Oh, Sam. You should'a told me. What would we a done if you wasn't there?"

I couldn't say nothin' to that.

We sat there quiet, thinkin'. I feeled some better talkin' 'bout it. But we still don't talk 'bout the two young'uns what died.

47

I realized I ain't seen Pap in some time, so I went to find Liz.

"Liz, does you have any work to do for a few days?"

"No, Sam. Why?"

"I wanna go visit Pap and you ain't seen your Mamma and Papa in a long time. Mrs. Poole don't need no wood cut b'fore the end of the week and I got no other jobs to do."

"You find us a way to get to Birchtown and we'll go. We can see Jenny and the girls, too. How long you wanna stay?"

"We can stay three days, if we can find us a way back home b'fore I has to go to Mrs. Poole's. I'll ask 'round to see if somebody is goin' and comin' back."

We got us there and back. Folks 'round here was good. Seems like every time I wanted a ride somewheres, somebody would take me and bring me home.

When we got to Pap's we got us a good surprise. Pap was keepin' company with Miss Betsy. I was so happy to see a smile on his wrinkled face. His hair was so grey, I almos' didn't recanize him.

I think he was happy to see me, but he had a funny look on his face. He prob'ly thought I was gonna be mad cause he got himself a woman. But I wasn't and I shore was gonna let him know.

"Miss Betsy, I is happy to see you. It's been a long time. How is the fam'ly?"

"It's been a long time, Sam. My boys is all grown and gone on their own. How is your fam'ly?"

"They is grown and gone too." I looked over at Pap.

"What is you doin' here, boy? I didn't know you was comin'."

"How was I gonna let you know, Pap? I is here cause I missed seein' your ugly face. Where you get all the grey hair from? I almost didn't recanize you."

Miss Betsy put her hand on Pap's arm and said to him, "Sam, I is goin' over to visit Margaret."

She looked at me. "Sam, is Liz with you?"

"She's over to her Mamma's. You'll see her when you goes there. Pap, Liz will come by in a little while."

"I'll be back, Sam," she said, lookin' at Pap. "You have a nice visit with your boy."

After Miss Betsy left I looked at Pap. I never said nothin' bout Miss Betsy bein' there, He can tell me all 'bout it if he wants.

"Pap, you know that barn me and you was livin' in? Well, it ain't no barn no more. I went to see Mr. Lewis and asked him if he would sell it to me cause he was gonna tear it down and he give it to me. Me and Liz, we saved our money and we made us a house outta it. And that animal smell that was there, Liz cleaned it all out. We even got us a outhouse. We don't have to take the bucket out and dig a hole to bury it like me and you did."

"Boy, you mus' be rich to do all that. But I is glad you and Liz got your selfs a house."

"Maybe sometime you and Miss Betsy will come visit. We got us four rooms and you can have one of your own to stay in while you is there."

"Boy, 'bout Miss Betsy," Pap said, scratchin' his head. "Is you okay with me havin' 'nother woman?"

"Pap, I is happy you found your self a woman and if you is happy, I is happy. Mam would want you to be happy. Didn't she tell you when she was dyin', you had to go on livin'? You got a good woman in Miss Betsy, Pap."

We was talkin' bout all the folks 'round Birchtown that me and Liz hadn't seen for a time. "Pap," I said. "We seen our Jenny and her girls b'fore I come to visit with you. Boy, them girls shore has growed. We met Jenny's man, too. Seems like a right nice fella and, from what we can tell, he treats her good. Does you know if he does?"

"He does, boy. And he comes and helps me when me and Miss Betsy needs wood cut and carried in. He's a good man. I is keepin' a eye on him. If he hurts her, I'll hurt him. You don't have to worry 'bout your girl."

"You is a good grandpap, Pap." I remembered something I wanted to tell him. "Pap, somebody said that Mr. Samuel Marshall died the other day."

"Too bad he didn't die b'fore he had us whipped for stealin' his rum."

"Pap!"

"Nothin' wrong with what I said, boy. I bet you feels the same way, but you don't wanna say. And what 'bout that young girl, Harriet, he had whipped for stealin' a piece a ribbon? It was prob'ly throwed out in the garbage box. I ain't sorry I said it and I ain't sorry he's dead."

"I is sorry 'bout Harriet, but, Pap, we did steal his rum."

"If a white man had'a stole it, you think he would'a been whipped like we was? He might'a been put in the gaol for a few days or maybe he would'a had to pay him for the rum, but he wouldn'a been whipped. We was whipped and we had to give him money cause we is black."

I didn't have no answer to that cause Pap was right. That's the way it's always been.

"Boy, I guess you wouldn'a heard, livin' in Yarmouth. Mam was right, Blucke, he was a crook. He got 'cused of stealin' money that didn't b'long to him and now he's gone. Ain't nobody knows where he went to. They ain't seen no sign of him nowhere. Somebody said his clothes was found all tore to pieces and they think maybe a wild animal got at him. I wonder what's gonna happen to that girl of his."

"I guess she'll be on her own, 'less she takes up with 'nother fella. She's only young, some man will want her. If Mam was here, she'd be shoutin' for joy 'bout Blucke. She always said he was a crook. She wouldn'a wished him dead if a animal did get him, she would'a wanted him throwed in the gaol."

~

I got to go to Shelburne one day to visit with Mr. Wood.

"Good to see you, Sam. What are you doing down this way?"

"I come to visit my Pap and Liz her Mamma and Papa."

After we talked a bit, he give me a piece of meat to take back to Pap. Good meat that he didn't throw in his garbage box.

"Thank you for the meat, Mr. Wood," I said when I went out the door.

Them three days shore did go by fast. Seems like we just got there and it was time to go home. We had us a nice visit and Pap and Miss Betsy said they would come visit us nex' time.

Least it wasn't rainin' and the sun was shinin' when we headed to home. We got back home b'fore it got dark. I was glad 'bout that. We was tired too.

~

Time shore does go by fast. We been livin' in our house a while now. Mr. Lewis passed on a few years back and b'fore he died he told me that my fam'ly was the only coloured people livin' in Yarmouth Town and we owns our own house. Ain't that somethin'?

When I told that to Liz, she said, "I knew that, Sam. Has you ever seen other coloured folks? I ain't talkin' 'bout those men who got you and Pap in trouble."

"Now, Liz, they didn't get me and Pap in trouble, we got our selfs in trouble. We is men, we knew what we was doin'."

"I guess I shouldn'a blamed them for you gettin' in trouble. But they don't live in town, so we is the only coloured folks what does."

"Ain't that somethin', Liz?"

"It shore is."

We was the only ones livin' in the town for a coupl'a more years, then my sister, Sarrah and her man Charlie Wilson moved down the road from us. They built them selfs a house. All her young'uns is grown and gone on their own, just like mine is.

When her last two boys was gettin' ready to go on they own, I told Sarrah, "They is too young to be on their own."

"Sam, my Peter, he's the same age as your Prince and he's been on his own for almos' five years. He's doin' alright ain't he? You can't pertect my boys like you was always tryin' to pertect me."

"You is right, Sarrah. I keep fergettin' how old they is, but they is like my own boys. Where is that man of yours today?"

"Charlie's gone to work with Mr. Halloren on his fish truck. He don't like goin' out on the fishin' boats, he said he might fall off or the boat might sink. He said the pay is good, but money ain't no good to you if you is dead."

"He's a smart man, your Charlie. That's why I ain't goin' on no boat. Once you is dead, you is dead."

48

Me and Liz, we is gettin' older and Liz she wasn't feelin' good for some time. She always says it's the weather, but I think it ain't that. My Mam always said it was the weather and she ain't here no more.

One day we was sittin' there and Liz, she said she had to go lay down.

"What's the matter, Liz? Is you alright?"

"I ain't feelin' good, Sam. My belly it hurts and I is feelin' sick and I is bleedin'."

"Why didn't you tell me you was ailin' b'fore? I is goin' get the doc. You lay there and I is gonna come right back. Don't you move."

I runned outta the house down the road fast as I could. Doc lived a long ways away, I had to go down my road and up 'nother. I didn't think I was ever gonna get there.

I pounded on Doc's door and I was shore hopin' he was home. He opened the door right away. I didn't know what I would'a done if he wasn't home. I was breathin' so hard I couldn't say nothin' for a minute.

"What is it, Sam? What's wrong?"

"It's my Liz. She is sick and she didn't tell me. Can you come and help her?"

"What's wrong with her?"

"She said she's got pain in her belly and she said she is bleedin'. Hurry, Doc."

"You go hook up the horse to the wagon. She said she was bleeding?"

"Yes, Sir. That's what she said."

Doc had a funny look on his face when I said she was bleedin' and I was gettin' scared. How come she was bleedin'?

I runned outta Doc's and got the horse and wagon and when Doc come outta his house we was to his door.

"Move over, Sam." Doc said as he got up and took hold of the ropes and made the horse take to runnin'. We was home in almos' a minute, it seemed like.

"She's in here, Doc," I said when I runned in my house. Doc was right b'hind me. I showed him where she was.

He went over to her and put his hand on her head. "Well, Liz, what seems to be the matter? You have pain? Show me where?"

I was standin' nex' to the bed watchin' everythin'. Liz put her hand b'low her belly.

"And the blood, where is that comin' from?"

I could tell she didn't want to tell him. I took her hand and I said, "Liz, you tell Doc what he wants to know and don't you leave nothin' out. He can't help you if he don't know where you is ailin'."

She looked over at Doc. "It's comin' from where it ain't s'pposed to come from no more."

"Are you bleeding all the time?" asked Doc.

"No, not all the time."

He was askin' her all kinds of questions and he was pressin' in her belly. "Does it hurt here?"

"No."

"Here?"

"A little bit."

"Have you thown up, Liz?"

"No, but I feels like I wants to a lotta time."

I was standin' there listenin' to everythin' what was bein' said. She was tellin' Doc all kinds of things she never told me. Me and Liz, we is gonna have us a talk when Doc fixes her up and she's better.

He said , "Liz, I am going to have to examine you. Is that alright?"

She looked over at me. "Sam, you go in the kitchen till Doc gets done."

"I ain't goin' outta this room. Why does I gotta go?"

Doc came over to me and he whispered in my ear, "Sam, she will feel better if you aren't here when I examine her lower body. Do you under-stand what I am saying?"

I looked over at Liz. "Alright, I is goin', but I don't like it. I'll be right on the other side of that door, Liz. You holler if you needs me."

I went in the kitchen and closed the door to our room. It seemed like Doc was in there a long time. What was he doin'?

When he come out I didn't like the way he looked at me.

"What's wrong with my Liz, Doc? Is she gonna be alright?"

"Sit down, Sam."

"I ain't sittin' down. What's wrong with my Liz?" I almos' yelled at him cause I was really gettin' scared.

Doc looked at me for a minute then he said, "Sam, Liz has a cancer up inside of her and it's bad. There is nothin' I can do for her other than give her something for the pain. The cancer will grow and the pain will get worse. I have to tell you that so you will know."

"What is a cancer, Doc? Can't you cut it outta her? Ain't that what you does?"

"A cancer is like a big sore, but it keeps growing. The cancer inside of Liz has been there for some time and it has grown too much and it isn't done growing. Sam, some of what I do is operating on people, but I'm sorry, there is nothing I can do for Liz. I gave her some medicine to help with the pain and it will make her sleepy. She is almost asleep now."

Me and Doc, we was still in the kitchen so I could talk to him without Liz hearin' what I was sayin'.

"Where is I gonna get the money to get her the medicine? I is only workin' 'nough so we can have food and wood."

"Don't you worry about that, Sam. I will give you medicine when Liz needs it."

"Doc, is my Liz gonna die?"

"Some patients with this kind of cancer can live a long time and some go quickly. I can keep her comfortable with this medicine, but she has to take it easy. She can't go outside and cut wood and I don't want her doing any outside work. I know she cleans houses, but she can't do that any-more. I want her to rest as much as she can."

"She'll do what I tells her, Doc, or I'll tie her to the bed. Then she can't do nothin'."

Doc laughed. "You don't have to do that, and I think she'll do what she is told. I'll come back tomorrow afternoon, then I'll check on her three times a week. Take good care of her."

After Doc left I went to my Liz and sat on a chair b'side the bed till she woke up. It seemed like a long, long time. Must'a been hours. A coupl'a times I leaned close to make shore she was still breathin', but I guess it was the medicine that was makin' her sleep so long.

She fin'ly waked up and looked over at me. She had the big smile on her face she always has for me.

I took her hand. "Liz, does you want somethin' to eat? We still got some soup left from what you made for supper last night. It's still good, I smelled it."

"I don't want nothin' right now. Maybe in a bit. Sit down," she said, pat-tin' the bed b'side her. "Sam, I is sorry I didn't tell you how bad I was feelin'. I didn't want you to worry 'bout me."

"I is s'pposed to worry 'bout you. Was you ever gonna tell me how bad you was feelin'? Doc said you got a cancer inside and it's bad. Did he tell you that?"

"Yes, he told me. Sit with me, Sam. I think I is gonna go back to sleep for a little while. That medicine shore makes me sleepy."

"I ain't goin' nowheres. I be right here."

My Liz is gonna die. What is I gonna do without my Liz? I gotta tell Pap and he can tell our young'uns who is in Shelburne and Birchtown. How is I gonna get a message to them way down there? Maybe somebody might be goin' that way and they can tell Pap for me. Liz she is gonna say they don't have to know, but they does.

There was nobody goin' to Shelburne, but Mr. Burton what owned the bak'ry, he come to Yarmouth to get some supplies for his store that he couldn't get in Shelburne. I seen him when I went to Mr. Shipley's store to get me some bread.

"Sam, how are you? It's been awhile since I've seen you. When you came to visit your Pap, one time I think. How is Liz? I suppose all of your children have children of their own now."

"Mr. Burton, yes they does. But, my Liz, she ain't doin' good. She got a cancer inside her and Doc said there ain't nothin' he can do."

"I am so sorry to hear that. Is there anything I can do?"

"Yes, Sir. When you goes home, if you would tell my Pap cause I got no way to tell him."

"I will do that. I won't be going home until tomorrow, but I will tell him."

"Thank you, Mr. Burton."

49

I told my Liz that Mr. Burton was gonna tell Pap and Pap will tell our young'uns what is in Birchtown and Shelburne. Liz, she said what I knew she was gonna say, "They don't has to know, Sam. They is only gonna be sad."

"You think they ain't gonna be sad if they hears their Mamma is gone and they didn't know she was sick? They does have to know, Liz."

"How you gonna tell all of them?. The boys, John and Prince Edward, we don't even know where they is now. They said they was goin' to Sissiboo, but we don't know nobody up that way 'cept our Margaret and we got no way to get word to her either."

"If we can't get word to all a them, we can't, but some of them will know their Mamma is sick and maybe they know how to find the others and tell them."

"Well, I ain't talkin' 'bout that no more. I is scared when I talks 'bout it, Sam. I know I is gonna die and I is scared."

"I is scared too, Liz, but if we is talkin' 'bout it—"

"I ain't talkin' 'bout it."

"Alright, Liz."

"Let's talk 'bout some nice things what happened. Sam, does you remember when our Margaret married that nice fella, David Rubert, from Sissiboo? And they got married right here in the church we goes to, the Holy Trinity Church."

"I shore does. That was a grand time, wasn't it, seein' our girl get herself married. And we had us a party and nobody said we can't and we didn't get throwed in gaol cause we did. Your Papa and Mamma, they came and Pap and Miss Betsy and our Jenny and her girls and Charlotte and Nancy. We shore had us a houseful that time."

"It was beautiful. Margaret, she gotta have young'uns now and I wish we could see them. I bet they is all growed and gone on their own. I bet she knows where John and Prince Edward is, if they is still in Sissiboo."

"Maybe, Liz, but we still don't know nobody goin' that way who can get word to them. Been more'n twenty years and Margaret's young'uns prob'ly got young'uns of their own. We is prob'ly great-grandpaps and Mams."

"I wish I could see my grandbabies."

~

I was sittin' in the kitchen one day while Liz was sleepin'. I didn't want to make no noise cause Doc said she needed to sleep much as she can.

I heard a wagon outside and figgered it was somebody goin' by. It stopped by my door so I opened it and looked out.

Outta the wagon climbed Pap, Miss Betsy and three of my girls, Jenny, Charlotte and Nancy. I was s'prised to see everybody.

"What you all doin' here?" I asked them.

My Jenny, she said, "We come to see our Mamma and help you and we is stayin' till you don't need us no more."

I didn't know what to say, but I was shore glad they was here.

After my fam'ly come from Birchtown, Doc must'a told folks they was to my house, cause some of them bringed us all kinds of food. My girls, they cooked that food and they cleaned and did everythin' for their Mamma.

I said to them one day, "You all gotta go back home to your fam'lies. You can't stay here all the time."

"We told our men we would come back when our Mamma and you don't need us no more. And that's that," said Jenny. "They said to us, 'You all stay long as you needs to. Your Mamma and Papa taked care of you, you gotta take care of them.'"

"So, that's what we is doin'," said Charlotte and Nancy.

I was shamed, cause I thought our young'uns forgot 'bout us when we wasn't there no more.

Pap and Miss Betsy, they stayed three days, cause Pap, he borrowed the wagon and he had to get it back to Shelburne. He told me, "You get word to me when to come back. I can borrow the wagon anytime I needs it."

My Liz, she wasn't doin' good. We stayed nex' to the bed all the time, just like Pap did when Mam was ailin'. We wasn't leavin' her for nothin'. Doc he was comin' almos' every day now and givin' her medicine for the pain.

When she was awake sometimes, me and our girls, we all sit with her and talked 'bout when they was young'uns and some a the things what they done and Liz would laugh. It was good to hear her laugh, but it wasn't strong like b'fore.

She told Jenny, "Jenny, you take care of you Papa. He's a old man, you know."

"Who is you callin' a old man?" I said, makin' her laugh.

But she was tired again, I could see so I told her, "Liz, you go back to sleep now. You needs your rest."

"Okay, Sam."

And she closed her eyes and went to sleep.

~

It was almos' the middle of summer when my Liz closed her eyes and didn't wake up no more.

Doc was with us and he looked at us and said, "I'm sorry, Sam, Liz is gone."

"Is you shore, Doc?" I said, starin' at my Liz.

Yes, I'm sure."

Me and our girls, we cried for their Mamma and my Liz.

Our girls, they got their Mamma ready. They put her best dress on her and we buried her in the Holy Trinity Cemetery. I put a wooden cross to mark where she was and me and our girls we cried again.

I sent word to Pap, but he couldn't come back till after she was in the ground.

I miss my Liz. I know why Pap went to visit Mam after she died. I is doin' the same.

I is walkin' kinda slow these days. My leg is painin' almos' every day, and sometimes I need me a walkin' stick, but ain't nothin' gonna keep me from goin' to my Liz.

And ain't nobody sayin, "Why is you goin' there all the time, she can't hear what you is sayin'."

But I wants to b'lieve she can.

I was goin' down the road to my Liz again one day and Mrs. Poole, she come outta her house. She had a big bunch of flowers in her arms.

"Sam, you going to the cemetery again?"

"Yes, Mrs. Poole, I is."

She looked at me kinda sad like. "Here, you take these flowers and you put them on your Liz's grave."

I took the flowers. "Thank you, Mrs. Poole."

I walked down the road with the flowers for my Liz in my arms.

~

Elizabeth (Liz) Van Nostrant passed away November 19, 1837.

Her husband, Samuel (Sam) Van Nostrant, passed away June 25, 1839.

Author's notes

When the American Revolution began in 1775, John Murray, Earl of Dunmore and Governor of the colony of Virginia, promised freedom to all Negroes who fought with the British. Slaves sought refuge with the British by the thousands.

Among those who chose to escape their bondage were Sam VanNostrant Sr. and his family. It wasn't until 1777 that this family decided to run. For some unknown reason, Sam Jr. did not go with them.

After escaping from their owner, Christophe (Stoffle) Van Nostrant, Sam Sr., his wife, Sarrah, and their daughter, Sarrah, joined the elite group of guerrilla fighters known as the Black Brigade, commanded by Colonel Tye (Titus), himself a runaway slave. Sam and his family remained members of that Brigade until the end of the war. Included in Sam Sr's story are some of the battles he may have fought in and other duties the Black Brigade was told to perform.

Fiction plays a large part in Sam Sr's stories, as there is no account of exactly what he and his family did during the war.

On November 30, 1783 they boarded the ship *L'Abondance* and set sail for Nova Scotia. Their *Book of Negroes* entry states that they were going to Port Mouton. It also states that Sam Sr., his wife and daughter were formerly the slaves of C. Van Nostrant of Acquackenack, New Jersey.

In 1779, Sam Jr. finally made his escape. It is not known where he went, and he is not included in the names in the *Book of Negroes* who were members of the Black Brigade. It can be assumed that he made it safely behind the British lines because he arrives in New York in 1783 with a wife, Elizabeth (surname Princes), and a small child. There, Elizabeth was reunited with her parents and brother.

Sam Jr's entry in the *Book of Negroes* states that he and his family were indentured to John Moore and that Sam was formerly the property of Stoffle Van Nostrant. In the spring of 1783, Sam, Elizabeth, and their child boarded the ship *Baker and Atlee*, bound for Port Roseway (later renamed Shelburne), Nova Scotia.

What had been promised the Negroes who fought for the British, land and shelter, were not there. The free Black Loyalists were sent to a small community that had been plotted out for them, called Birchtown. With no shelters, the people had to find a way to protect themselves from the elements. Some built sod houses and others dug what were appropriately called pit houses, holes in the ground with a roof over them. For some those pit houses probably became their graves.

Their lives were a living hell. With no decent shelters and no workable farmland, famine that affected both blacks and whites, extreme racism, race riots, forest fires, disease, and the physical and emotional turmoil took their toll on everyone. How would they survive? Some did and some did not.

A head count showed that there were numerous artisans living in Birchtown: carpenters, sawyers, coopers, sailors, ship carpenters, ropemakers, caulkers, bakers, cooks, barbers, shoemakers, tailors, chimney sweeps, and a doctor. Where would they have the opportunity to ply their trades? Certainly, the white men, who could do the same jobs, were not going to hire the black man.

In 1792, John Clarkson convinced more than one thousand Blacks to emigrate to Africa to form a new colony in Sierra Leone. That reduced the population of Birchtown considerably, but it did not make the hardships any the less challenging for those who remained.

Those who left for Sierra Leone were gone before the devastating forest fire in Shelburne County in June, 1792. Many of the poorest Blacks were most impacted by the fire.

Below are the names of the Black Loyalists who were used in *Two Sams*. Their particular stories in this novel are fiction drawn from many facts, but it is the mention of their names that is important.

Sam Van Nostrant Sr.: Sarrah, his wife; Sarrah, their daughter. No causes or dates of death are available for them. We do not know if Sam Sr. remained in Yarmouth or returned to Birchtown.

Sam Van Nostrant Jr., Elizabeth Princes, his wife; daughters Jenny, Charlotte, Nancy, Polly, and Margaret; sons John, and Prince Edward.

Elizabeth passed away November 19, 1837, cause of death unknown. She was buried in the Holy Trinity Anglican Cemetery in Yarmouth. Sam passed away June 25, 1839 and was buried in the same cemetery.

After a time some of that land was expropriated and used to put in a rail line. The graves that were in that section were removed to Yarmouth Mountain Cemetery.

Prince Princes; Margaret, his wife; Nicholas, their son. As far as can be determined, this family remained in Birchtown.

George Price, labourer; Abigail, his wife; and a son. Abigail was living in Tusket, Yarmouth County and owned a large house that is still there to this day. She also received a land grant.

Moses Wilkinson, preacher, a blind man.

Moses Halstead, shoemaker; Molly his wife; and one child.

John Brown, doctor; Peggy, his wife; and three children.

Colonel Stephen Blucke' Margaret, his wife; Isabella Gibbons, adopted daughter. Colonel Blucke was head of the Black Brigade. Margaret left him and returned to New York. He began a relationship with their adopted daughter, Isabella. He was accused of stealing money and disappeared. People believed that he was killed by a wild animal because of his torn clothing that was found. He lost his home during the Shelburne forest fires.

Daniel (Arche), sailor; Betsy, his wife; and two children.

Dublin (Miller), seaman.

Dolly (Gilfillan).

Jacob Howard; Peggy, his wife; and two babies.

Captain Nathaniel Snowball, ship carpenter; Violet, his wife; and four children.

Boston King, carpenter; Violet his wife.

David George, farmer/preacher; Phillis, his wife; and three children.

Jane Thompson lost her home during the forest fires.

Bridget Cooper lost her home during the forest fires.

Mr. Warrington (Joseph), lost his home during the forest fires. He had a wife, and three children under the age of five.

Mr. Turner (Robert), lost his home during the forest fires. He had a wife, and three children under the age of six.

Mr. John Johnson, carpenter; Judith, his wife; and two children.

Pero Davis – it is not known if Pero was residing in Birchtown, but it is possible. He was abused by Jesse Gray while Gray was living in Argyle, which was part of Shelburne County at that time.

Mary Postal and Flora and Nell, her daughters. Owned and sold by Jesse Gray despite her claims of being free.

Lydia Jackson was illiterate and was tricked into signing a thirty-nine year indenture, then was brutally abused until she ran away. She was kicked while she was lying on the ground and it is not known if she lost the baby she was carrying at the time of the abuse.

Others who lost their homes in Birchtown during the forest fires of 1792, but are not mentioned in the story:

> Peter Harding, a wife, four children under the age of twelve.
> Tobias Johnson, a wife, two children under the age of three.
> London Jackson, a wife and a child under the age of eleven.
> Peter Pharo, a wife and three children under the age of nine.
> Samuel Dixon and a wife;
> James Thompson, a wife, two children under the age of seven.
> Moses Kelly, a wife, three children under the age of seventeen.
> Joseph Raven and a wife
> George Wise, a wife, two children under the age of seven.
> Samuel Whitten, a wife, five children under the age of ten.
> Thomas Cooper, a wife, two children under the age of seven.
> Samuel Bolton, a wife, three children under the age of ten.

Why is it important to remember these names? These people suffered through hell and some, but not all, came out stronger on the other side. They helped to shape the lives of Nova Scotia's Blacks and the Blacks who migrated to other areas.

Never forget them!

Sharon Robart-Johnson
February, 2024

Sources

Birch, General Samuel, *Book of Negroes*, NY, 1783.

Clarkson, John, *Clarkson's Mission to America*, 1791-1792, Halifax: Public Archives of Nova Scotia.

Farish, James C., MD, articles written in 1821 and published in August, 1892 in the *Yarmouth* (NS) *Herald*.

Hill, Richard "Dick", Nova Scotia Archives and Records Management (NSARM), RG60 Shelburne Court of Sessions Records, 1783-1842. File #25.3, October 16, 1787.

Hodges, Graham Russell, 'Black Revolt in New York City and the Neutral Zone: 1775-83', in Gilje, Paul A. and William Pencak, *New York in the Age of Constitution 1775-1800,* Teaneck, NJ: Fairleigh Dickenson University Press, 1992.

_____, *The Black Loyalist Directory: African Americans in exile after the American Revolution,* NY: Garland Publishing, Inc. in association with the New England Historic Genealogical Society, 1996.

_____, *Root and Branch: African Americans in New York and East Jersey 1613-1863,* Chapel Hill, NC: University of North Carolina Press, 1999.

Kimber, Stephen, *Loyalists and Layabouts: the rapid rise and faster fall of Shelburne, Nova Scotia 1783-1792*, Toronto: Doubleday Canada, 2008.

London, T. L., "Yankee Doodle or the Negroes Farewell to America", London: Charles and Samuel Thompson, not later than 1776.

Marble, Allan Everett, C.G. (C), *Deaths, Burials, and Probate of Nova Scotians, 1800-1850, from Primary Sources,* Volume 4 (P-Z), Halifax: Genealogical Association of Nova Scotia.

New Jersey State Archives, R. Group: Court of Oye and Terminer/Circuit Court. Series: Minutes, 1730-1820.

Nova Scotia Archives and Records Management

Raddall, Thomas H., 'Tarleton's Legion', in *Collections of the Nova Scotia Historical Society*, Volume 28, p. 28.

Robertson, Marion, *King's Bounty: a history of early Shelburne*, Halifax: Nova Scotia Museum, 1983.

_____, *The Chestnut Pipe: folklore of Shelburne County*, Halifax: Nimbus, 1991.

Whitfield, Harvey Amani, 'American background of Loyalist slaves' in *Left History* 14:1, 2009.

About the author

Sharon Robart-Johnson has a rich cultural background comprised of both African and European ancestry. Her European roots reach beyond the Expulsion of the Acadians in 1755, to the arrival of the Black Loyalists in Shelburne in 1783, and to a slave who was brought to Digby County, Nova Scotia in 1798.

Born in the South End of Yarmouth, she is a thirteenth-generation Nova Scotian. Her passion for researching Black history began in 1993 and has continued.

In 2009 her first book, *Africa's Children A History of Blacks in Yarmouth, Nova Scotia,* was published; and in 2022 she published *Jude and Diana,* an historical novel which won Robbie Robertson Dartmouth Book Award for fiction.

Sharon is a past member at large of the Board of Directors of the Yarmouth County Historical Society, which owns and operates the Yarmouth County Museum and Archives, and she has five years of archival experience.